# THE KOOL KOLORED KIDZ

*Paving the Way for the "New Normal" - A Novel*

*Henry Vanderbilt Johnson Ph.D.*

ISBN: 1495291146
ISBN 13: 9781495291142
Library of Congress Control Number: 2014903626
CreateSpace Independent Publishing Platform
North Charleston, South Carolina

# TABLE OF CONTENTS

# CHAPTER 1
# COUNTDOWN BEFORE THE KLAN RALLY

***This is our home and this is our country. Beneath its soil lie the bones of our fathers; for it some of them fought, bled, and died.***

***—Paul Robeson***

The apartheid tradition in Hyde County appeared to be unshakable and rigid in the mid to late 1960s. Tension continued to escalate between the black and white community after Erskine and the guys elected to do away with the black- back- door patron policy at Mr. Ben's cafe. Two weeks after Erskine and the guys descended upon Mr. Ben's café a major Ku Klux Klan rally was advertised to take place in MiddleTown, a small rural community. The Kool Kolored Kidz was not formally organized at this point; so, the Ridge Rovers elected to intervene to curtail future Klan activity in the Engelhard black community. We met at Sammie's house immediately after school to discuss our plan. Ben Junior,

Sammie, Byron, Joseph, Raymond, Larry, and I met promptly at 4:00 p.m. Martin, Miguel, and Leroy were extremely late so we elected to go on with the meeting. Ben Junior decided to chair the meeting. However, for the most part, meeting was conducted very informally. He opened with a very thought-provoking question. The question was, "What are we going to do about the planned Klan rally on Saturday? Shall we simply ignore it, or should we bring an end to this stupid activity for good?"

Sammie stated, "I don't know about you guys but I think we should rid the county of Klan activity for good. I think we should take a stand and let the Klan know that they don't scare anyone around here. Our parents won't do anything; so, we have to take the lead!"

Larry responded to Sammie's suggestion by asking, "Are you suggesting that we should put some heat on the Klan to let them know we mean business?"

Joseph interrupted Sammie's response by stating, "Wow! Man that sounds good. Let's ambush them when they pass the Ridge Store en route to the rally. We can hide in the corn field and as they slow down in front of the Ridge Store, we can give them a serious surprise!"

Byron stated, "We all have BB guns and sling slots. Man! We can really give them a surprise attack. It'll be just like on television. I can't wait!"

Ben Junior asked, "How about you, Henry? Since you don't really live on the Ridge, are you with us? I would hate for those Klan boys to catch you alone as you walk home one evening and try to make an example out of you. If you don't want to be a part of this, we all understand. It's really dangerous for you to even walk to Scrouge Town each evening like you do. However, since none of us have telephones, we simply look for you on the school bus each day. Again, we all understand if you elect to sit this one out."

I told the guys that I was with them. Yes, it did get a little scary walking home some evenings, especially when it was dark. There were times when the white guys would slow down in their pretty cars and give me the middle finger. They even called me ugly names like koon and Jungle Boy. However, I would keep on walking home and if I sensed that it is necessary to run, I would run full speed. I was not too proud to run. My Mom always said a good run is better than a bad stay. There are days when I just could not stand the name-calling. So, I called them names right back and I gave them the middle finger in response. I knew name-calling was stupid; however, it felt good to feel stupid at sometimes.

I told the guys, "Even though I don't live on the Ridge, in my heart, I live right next door to each of you. So, yes, I am with you 100 percent."

Ben Junior smiled at me and said, "For some reason, I sensed that you would be with us. Tell me, is your BB gun still jamming?"

I reluctantly responded, however, I said, "My BB gun only jams when I try to load it real fast. When I place a little oil in the chamber, it works quite well."

Ben Junior nodded and said, "You need to handle that before the planned attack. The only thing that we want to do is scare the Klan and let them know that they cannot disrespect the black community anymore. We want to send the message that we will not tolerate the Klan throwing fliers and other hate mail in our yards and church grounds. We simply want to send the message that enough is enough. It is time for the Klan to leave us alone."

Joseph responded to Ben by saying, "Suppose we make it real interesting! Do you remember when we put water in balloons last week and had a water fight? Let's pee in balloons and throw them on the cars when they slow down for the right turn to go to Middle Town for the rally. You know every car has to come almost to a complete stop when they turn to go to Middle Town. We can hide in the ditch near the highway and shower them down with some good day-old black pee. We can pretend the balloons are hand grenades. In fact, let's make sure the pee is at least two days old. There's nothing like the smell of two-day pee. Once the pee hits them, they'll have second thoughts about parading in the black community. I know they will be seriously upset."

The guys loved Joseph's suggestion. And we all agreed to save our urine and place it in the balloons for the great Klan rally. Sammy raised his hand and adamantly stated, "Look, I ain't handling nobody else's pee. I don't even want to deal with my own. My pee can get rather strong. It's almost like acid at times."

We simply smiled at Sammie and continued with the meeting. The fliers that were thrown in our yards and on the church grounds indicated that the Grand Wizard, leader of the Knights of the Ku Klux Klan, and the Grand Dragon would serve as grand marshals for the rally. We didn't care about the Grand Wizard or the Grand Dragon; we were primarily concerned about curtailing the fear factor within the black community. Our ultimate goal was to convince the Klan to stay out of the black community. We were not interested in injuring or maiming anyone. We simply wanted to make a statement. . . Stay out of the black community! Our defense arsenal was essentially BB guns, slingshots, a few rocks, and oyster shells. The balloons filled with urine would essentially serve as a means to infuriate the Klan. We were young and stupid and we didn't even know it. Little did we know, the Klan carried automatic weapons and were protected by the Sheriff's Department. They had constitutional rights and the Hyde County Sheriff's Department maintained a presence to protect those rights. The Klan was accorded the freedom to assemble just like any other group or organization.

Raymond and Joseph explained to the group that they only had their BB guns and four slingshots. Ben Junior told them to bring what they had and maybe by Saturday they could make a few bows and arrows. Seemingly, our entire arsenal was makeshift and antiquated. The meeting adjourned and we left the meeting feeling excited and enthusiastic about our plan.

It was not dark so we began playing basketball in Sammie's yard. We played until it got so dark that we could not see the goal. Our games were very competitive and truly fun-filled. It was always additional fun and more competitive when we had an audience. When guys in the neighborhood like Goose, Dallas, Claudie James, Ben Howard, and Erskine watched us play, we really showed off so we could get a complimentary statement from them at the end of the game. A simple pat on the back and a statement like "Good Game" did wonders for our self-esteem. Claudie James and Goose were consummate legends on the basketball court and they were our idols.

These guys were like giants; nothing less than legends to us and we truly idolized their status on our mud and dirt basketball courts. There were numerous stories told about Claudie James and Goose's extraordinary basketball skills. Goose was known for his swift passing, fancy dribbling, and hook shot. Claudie James was known for his fantastic scoring under pressure and his unbelievable leaping ability. He was also a masterful shot-blocker. Ben Howard said most guys jump as high as they can; however, Claudie jumped simply high enough to get the job done. Ben Howard declared that Goose and Claudie James could dunk the basketball while standing right under the rim with absolute ease. He described Goose and Claudie James as being comparable to Michael Jordan and Scottie Pippen and stories about their legendary basketball skills and triumphs never became boring. We would sit near Ben Howard and hang on to every syllable and word to exit his mouth. When we played basketball, we always welcomed feedback from our self-proclaimed legends. Claudie James had a ready smile and Goose was a real jokester.

A statement like, "Wow! Young Blood, you got a real nice game!" meant a great deal to us. We wanted our icons and legends to be proud of us.

Dallas would customarily say, "Gee, Prez! You got some sweet moves. You looked like Earl the Pearl Monroe out there."

I would simply smile to myself and walk away trying to look tall. It was amazing how much a simple positive statement meant from someone that you idolized. I slowly and exhaustedly walked home after an afternoon of strategic planning and an evening of exhilarating basketball. My day felt complete and purposeful. My heart was not heavy in hatred nor did I reflect on the potential Klan confrontation with any semblance of malice. After having walked about half way home, Donnie, son of wealthy white-American farmer, and Marshal, a white southern-Baptist preacher's son, passed by and gave me the middle finger. I immediately reciprocated by giving them two very pronounced middle fingers. Donnie slammed his brakes so hard that his tires began to squeal. He and his friend jumped out of his car to confront me about my response to them. My heart began to pound uncontrollably; however, I was determined to camouflage my true state of being.

I didn't want Donnie and Marshall to sense that I was even remotely scared. However, they were older and much bigger, and I was alone. I didn't have Joseph, Raymond, or Ben Junior to help me deal with these guys. Donnie stood in front of me and Marshall stood directly behind of me. They were too close to me for comfort. Regardless, I knew that I wasn't going to run anywhere. I could feel Marshall breathing heavily on the back of my neck. Donnie stood so close to me that I could smell the terrible stench of his cigarette smoking and cheap cologne. His clothes and his hair smelled as if he had spent the entire day at the Engelhard Town Tavern. I didn't know whether Marshall was going to stab me in my back or simply slice me on the back of my neck. However, I was looking directly at Donnie and I could see the fear in his eyes. He was at best a Hyde County racist form of Barney Fife and I knew that I could give him a terrible beat-down with little effort.

Marshall was more intimidating than Donnie because he was more muscular and he didn't appear to be afraid at all. He manifested an air of confidence about him that was undeniable. Nevertheless, I was actually trembling in my dirty, ragged Converse All-stars. However, I was determined to man-up and handle the situation like a proud black man. I wasn't going to run, even if they elected to stab me in my stomach or cut me across the back of my neck. I was determined to hold my ground with relentless courage. Never the less, at heart I hoped that Ben Junior, Joseph, or Raymond would somehow magically appear. I knew I could handle Donnie; I sensed that he was just as scared as I.

Donnie was timid and essentially a "bad boy" wannabe. He was so skinny and so mouthy that it was easy to conclude that he was at best a "pushover." He stood basically nose to nose with me when all of a sudden Marshall bent down and Donnie pushed me over his back. I immediately hit the asphalt road, and my left hand slammed against the pavement and shattered the face of my watch. Uncle Randolph had given me the watch for Christmas and I absolutely cherished it. I tried to jump to my feet immediately; however, Marshall pushed me back down and Donnie stood over me yelling, "Look boy, don't you ever give us the middle finger again! The next time it happens, we'll break your arm instead of your little cheap-ass watch. You colored boys think you're tough; but, we got something for your black asses."

## CHAPTER 2

# MY HEAD IS BLOODY, BUT UNBOWED

***The test of a first-rate intelligence is the ability to hold two opposed ideas in the mind at the same time, and still retain the ability to function.***

***—F. Scot Fitzgerald***

I tried to get up but Marshall pushed me down again with a violent force. They turned around laughing and slowly walked to their car as I sat on the pavement and looked at my prized possession watch. I looked at my watch and cried because my favorite uncle had given it to me. My left wrist ached terribly; however, I was ultimately concerned about my watch. Donnie and Marshall hopped into their beautiful blue and white Ford Fairlane 500 and sped off squealing tires. I slowly walked home; crying each and every step. I felt alone and I felt detached. Nevertheless, I knew I had to clear my eyes before entering the living room where my sisters and my parents sat. I had crafted a macho persona with my siblings and I knew that I could not allow them to see me with tears in my eyes.

The next day as I prepared for school, my baby sister, Vanessa asked me why I wasn't wearing my watch. She was very perceptive and she knew how much value I placed on it. Vanessa looked at me and asked, "Junior, did you lose your watch? Mama told you to leave that watch at home. Did you take it to school and let someone steal it?"

I replied with, "Yes. That's right! Somebody stole it and you don't have to rub it in my face. It's no skin off your back; so, why are you worrying about it?"

I walked out of the house and stood near the road until the school bus arrived. My wrist was swollen and it ached terribly. However, I knew Mom didn't have any extra money to take me to see Dr. Liverman. As I sat on the school bus, we passed by Donnie's house. He was standing in his front yard wiping off his car. Ervin, our school bus driver, blew his horn as Donnie religiously wiped his car. When Donnie noted that it was a bus load of black students, he immediately gave us the middle finger. Ervin gave him the middle finger as well and continued out trek to Davis School.

During recess, Ben Junior, Sammie, Larry, Raymond, Joseph, Byron, and I met behind the gym to discuss our plans for the Klan rally. We all agreed to meet at the Ridge Store at 2:00 p.m. on Saturday. Everyone had saved their urine but me. It was difficult for me to save my urine because my younger sisters, Jackie and Vanessa were always in my bedroom. They were always meddling into my affairs. Ben Junior gave each of us five huge balloons. He told us to pour the urine into a Pepsi bottle and then stretch the balloon over the mouth of the bottle. He said the mouth of a Pepsi bottle was a perfect fit for the balloons.

Byron raised his right hand and asked, "What about the bows and arrows? Did you and Sammie make each of us one?"

Ben Junior looked around at each of us and adamantly stated, "Sammie and I talked about the bows and arrows and concluded that we really did not want to hurt anyone; we simply wanted to deliver the message that the KKK was not welcome in the Engelhard black community. We concluded that the BB guns, sling shots, a few rocks, and the balloons filled with pee would convey our message."

Sammie encouraged us to be sure to be at his house by 2:00 p.m., sharp. The bell rang for our next class and we all went to our respective classes. I went home that afternoon and oiled my BB gun really well and tested the strength of my two sling shots several times. After oiling my BB gun and making sure my sling shots were functional, I took the shortcut through the woods and went to Sammie's house to play basketball. We played until it was too dark to see the goal. I wouldn't take the shortcut through the woods to go home because the snakes often lingered in the walking path. It was relatively easy to see the snakes during the day; however, at night it simply was not safe.

As I walked home, I readily noticed that traffic was inordinately heavy. I concluded that there were probably a lot of people coming to Engelhard for the massive "Klan Rally" in MiddleTown. I was tired; very tired, but I walked with a fast pace to get home because I was terribly thirsty. I had to walk pass Donnie's house to get home and I prayed that he and Marshall would not see me as I walked passed his house. A door slammed just as I was about to pass Donnie's house. My heart began to pound and I began to sweat like an escaped slave. Donnie's dad, Mr. Cecil, had guest for the evening and they were leaving. I heard Mr. Cecil say, "It's really good to see you boys. Thank you for the information. Donnie and I will be in MiddleTown by no later than 3:30 p.m. I agree with you, we got to keep the coloreds in their place. This will be a real wake-up call for a lot of white people."

I continued my walk to get home. Just as I was about to enter my road, I noticed a station wagon that was heavily clouded with smoke. Three young white males sat in the car laughing and joking. They were drinking Budweiser and smoking a funny looking and funny smelling cigarette. The guy driving the station wagon, got out of his car and asked, “Bud, aren’t you taking a big chance by walking the roads alone in the evening like this? Don’t you know a big ‘Klan rally’ is scheduled to take place in MiddleTown tomorrow? A lot of white folks around here don’t really like your kind; so, you better be careful. As for me and my friends, we don’t have any problems with the coloreds. In fact, Wilt Chamberlain and Bill Russell are two of our favorite basketball players. And we really love Bill Cosby and Sidney Poitier; they are hilarious. Flip Wilson is really one of our favorites as well.”

Then one of the white guys sitting in the backseat said, “Ask him if he would like a cold Budweiser. We have plenty beer in the trunk. Give him a cold beer. He looks rather thirsty. He’s either scared as hell, or thirsty. Regardless, give him a cold beer.”

The guy driving the station wagon put his pointer finger up and said, “Wait a damn minute. I’m so high that this boy looks like he is shining like new money. Damn, he is awfully black.”

The guy sitting in the middle of the backseat said, “Come on now! Give the boy a cold beer. We got plenty.”

I turned toward the guy who was driving the station wagon and noticed that he was standing on the side of the road urinating. He smiled and said that he had drunk one, just one Budweiser too many. He looked at me and asked, “Can I see your penis? I heard that black guys have really large penises and I just want to know if this is indeed a fact. Look, I’m not gay; I love women. I just want to know if this is a myth or if it is indeed, true. I want to see for myself. I have heard a host of stories about black guys and how heavily endowed they are. Can I see your penis, please?”

I responded with, "No! You can't look at my penis! That's disgusting! Black people just don't pull out their body parts and put them on display. That's not right!"

Then he began to vomit relentlessly. He held his stomach and cried. "Oh! My God! Please help me; God, please help me."

He looked at me and wiped his mouth. Then he said, "Bud, you don't have to worry about anything. We aren't going to harm you. We are journalism students from North Carolina State University. We came here to cover the Klan rally that's supposed to take place tomorrow. In fact, we drove down from Raleigh on Thursday and decided to go to Nags Head to have a little fun. We've been drinking and smoking for the last two days. Would you like a cold beer?"

I said, "No. I don't drink. I am thirsty but I don't drink beer. Do you have a Coke or Pepsi?"

He yelled to someone in the backseat, "Jamie, do we have any Cokes left? If so, pass me one. This guy looks like he could use something cold to drink."

Jamie reached his hand through the back window and said, "What's up man? Here take this cold Coke. It's all yours. We got some chips and some cookies, would you like some?"

I accepted the cold Coke and thanked him. Then Jamie asked, "Look Soul Brother, we got some powerful weed back here, would you like a smoke. This stuff is powerful, Brother. It'll make you cry like a little baby."

I didn't want to offend anyone, so I said, "No, thanks anyway. I have asthma and it affects my breathing."

After I said no to the invitation to smoke some weed, I turned to the guys and asked, "Why do white people refer to most black males as "Bud", my name is Henry? In fact, my name is Henry Vanderbilt Johnson, Jr. My name is not "Bud." The guy sitting in the far left got out of the station wagon and said, "My name is Paul Stevenson and it is a pleasure to meet you. I am from Iowa and I have never met a black person before. You know, you don't talk like the black people on the *Amos 'n' Andy Show.* You talk like we do and you use Standard English. I can't wait to tell my parents that I met a black person."

The guy sitting in the middle of the back seat stepped out of the station wagon and extended his hand and said, "My name is Keifer and it is indeed a pleasure to meet you. I am from Buffalo, New York and this is the first time that I actually met a black person. Tell me, I don't want to offend you and I really want to be politically correct. Do you people prefer to be called black, colored, Afro-American, African-American, Negro, niggra, or person of color? I really don't know what to call you people."

I looked at each of the guys and adamantly stated, "Truthfully speaking, I can't speak for all black people. As for me, I prefer to be called Henry. Now, as a people collectively, I refer to black people as black Americans. Then again, there are black people who prefer to be called African-American or Afro-American. However, "colored people" or "niggard" is never socially acceptable and is quite offensive. Terms like niggard and colored people are terribly demeaning. In fact, depending on the time and place, these words bring out the worse in black people."

Jamie interrupted and asked, "Bud, I mean Henry, I thought it was an insult to call a colored, excuse me, I mean a "black American" black. I was taught in my high school that to refer to "black people" as "black" was a major insult. I am really confused. Even in my diversity class at North Carolina State, we were told to never refer to coloreds, I mean "black Americans" as black. Supposedly "black" is right up there with the N-word. Are you sure 'black' is socially acceptable for coloreds. Excuse me, I apologize; I mean black people."

# CHAPTER 3
# WHAT SHALL WE CALL YOU PEOPLE?

***Drag your thoughts away from your troubles—by the ears, by the heels, or any other way you can manage it. It's the healthiest thing a body can do.***

***—Mark Twain***

I scratched my head and said, "Like I said, I cannot speak for all 'black people.' However, I can speak for myself, and I prefer to be called Henry. I call 'black people', black Americans. I am not insulted with the term black. Nevertheless, there are other black Americans who find the term insulting and very demeaning. You see the term 'black' is often associated with something negative. For instance, black eye, black list, black mail, black market, black sheep, and black widow are all viewed in a negative sense. Therefore, the term *black* is a very controversial term. Again, I have no problem with being called a black American."

Just as I was about to give another perspective on *black* and 'black American', Donnie and Marshall drove up in their beautiful Ford Fairlane. Donnie stopped immediately and rushed out of the car to ask, "Did this boy give you all the middle finger too? He tries to be a smart niggra. Let's take this little koon down this dark road and teach him a lesson or two. We will probably get a brownie point or two with the Grand Dragon tomorrow at the Klan rally. My dad would be so proud of me if I taught this little koon a real good lesson. We don't have to hang him; but, we can stretch his little boney neck a little."

Jamie, Paul, and Keifer listened to Donnie and then shook their head. Jamie looked directly at Donnie with a stern and stoic demeanor. He said, "His name is Henry. In fact, his name is Henry Vanderbilt Johnson, Jr. We don't like the terms koon and niggra. Those terms are not part of our vocabulary and shouldn't be a part of yours either. You see, unlike you, we're students at North Carolina State University and we don't have time for this country hillbilly nonsense. You farms boys really need to get a real life. In fact, why don't you and Joe Bob go shoot some rats or something? You are getting on my last nerve."

Donnie tried to interrupt but Jamie but he continued his diatribe with "If you stopped here to insult Henry, I suggest that you hop into your pretty little car and keep going where you were headed. Quite honestly, I can't stand people like you. You are at best, a disgrace to all white people and I have a personal low tolerance for people like you. Now move on before I lose my temper. Just for the record, I studied and practiced Ju Jitsu and Karate for ten years. If you don't believe me, try me! I would love to break your arm and a couple fingers. Please! Please! Try me; simply take one swing at me!"

Marshall became irritated and walked to Jamie and asked, "Gosh! Why are you taking up for this little koon? You don't even know him like we do. He disrespects us every time we see him. And don't let him get with the other koons; he'll really show his little black ass then. I can't believe this; you are going to side with this 'boy' over your own people. Gosh! This world is really becoming sicker and sicker by the minute. It seems to me that everybody is taking up for the coloreds, except for the coloreds themselves. They don't have to do a single thing for themselves because of white people like you. Really, that's why the coloreds are so lazy and shiftless. That's why most of them are on the welfare system and using up our tax dollars. And that's why I can't stand their black asses. A hardworking white man just doesn't get any respect at all anymore. The white man's rights are totally disregarded. It is white people like you who confuse the niggras. They think they are equal to us and they think they can sit and eat anywhere they choose. They even want to drink from public water fountains and ride in the front of buses where we sit. Can you imagine that?"

Keifer took off his shirt to showcase his muscles. He turned toward Marshall and angrily stated, "Look, I've heard enough. I wrestled in high school for four years and I am on the wrestling team at North Carolina State. I suggest you get in your pretty little car, right now! And I mean, right now!"

Donnie and Marshall hurried to their car. They took off spinning tires and kicking rocks and oyster shells on us. Dirt and dust flew up like a light tornado. Jamie looked at Paul and said, "Man, I am so glad that's over. For a minute there, I thought I was going to have to get down a little bit. Those guys were wrong, 100% wrong. Regardless, it's over now."

Paul asked, "What are we going to do about gas? The car won't even start. I don't want to run the battery down trying to get it started."

Jamie turned toward me and asked, "Do you know where we can find some gas. We just need enough to make it to Engelhard. Once we get there, we'll fill up and be on our way."

I thought for a minute and said, "Mom just bought five gallons of gasoline for me to use in the lawn mower. I am sure she will give you a few gallons to get to Engelhard. If you don't mind walking for about a half mile, I'll ask Mama if it is okay to let you have the gas."

Jamie gave me a very serious look and then told Keifer and Paul to lock the doors of the car because they had no other option. Keifer called to Jamie and said, "Hold up. If I'm going to walk a half mile, I'm going to get a whiff of this powerful weed again. I just can't see walking a half mile without at least a little buzz. Man, I've got to get my smoke on to deal with these backwoods folks."

Paul responded with, "That sounds good to me. My buzz is almost gone and we haven't even made it to the Klan rally. After meeting Donnie and Marshall, I need something to cope with all the dynamics. Southern hospitality can be a real trip."

I watched as Paul took out a small plastic bag filled with a leafy substance. He then went into his back pocket and produced a small packet that contained very small slips of paper. Paul took a very small portion of the green leafy product and placed it in the center of the small slips of paper. He rolled the paper together and licked it. The paper appeared almost saturated with saliva. Then he went to his front coat pocket and found a cigarette lighter and fired up the strange looking cigarette. It smelled terrible; however, Jamie and Keifer stood around in anxious anticipation. They were like two small children anxious to be breastfed. I watched in amazement and disgust as I witnessed three adult men voluntarily place their lips on a spit-wet strange looking cigarette. The whole scene was absolutely nasty.

After about twenty minutes, we began to walk up my road to get the gas. For some unknown reason, Paul and Jamie began to laugh uncontrollably. They began to look at me strangely and laugh like I had said or done something hilarious. I began to feel a little uncomfortable. Keifer sensed that I had begun to feel a bit uncomfortable when he said, "Look Henry, Paul and Jamie have a serious buzz right now. The thing about weed is that it has the capacity to make you hallucinate and everything becomes funny. You don't have to worry about anything. Those two guys are totally harmless. They're simply on a serious high."

We continued our trek to my house. Before getting to my house, we had to pass Mrs. Vick's house and Mr. Preston's house. Everything was quiet at Mrs. Vick's house because they didn't own a television. However, they did own a radio and typically had it turned to gospel stations. My friends Nancy, Elmira, and Linda had apparently gone to bed because there was no movement in the house. As we continued to walk, I noticed Sam and Johnny Boy sneaking a cigarette smoke near the wood pile. I didn't say anything; I simply kept walking and peripherally watching Paul and Jamie. They continued their laughing and giggling with each step.

Just as we were approaching Mr. Preston's house, Cousin Janie, his wife, opened the front door and threw out some dishwater. She looked up and saw me with Jamie, Paul, and Keifer and yelled, "Preston get the shotgun. The Klan has caught Junior and they're walking him down the road to lynch him. Get your shot gun! Get it now! Hurry up! Preston move! Hurry! Hurry!"

Mr. Preston pushed the front door open and sternly said, "Let him go. Let him go right now! Let the boy go! Don't let me have to say it again!"

When Mr. Preston burst out of the front door with his shot gun, Keifer and Jamie fell on the ground laughing uncontrollably. They were so high that they didn't even know that their lives were in danger. I watched them as they rolled around on the ground; get up; fall down again, and then high-five each other as if they were watching a comedy program on television. The weed that the guys smoked had altered their sense of reality and they appeared to be on another planet. I watched attentively as the guys turned several shades of red as they laughed uncontrollably. They were so happy and filled with joy that their laughter became contagious. For some unknown reason, I began to laugh as well. It was strange, very strange.

## CHAPTER 4

# THE UNFORGETTABLE FEAST

***Without faith it is impossible to please God, for he that cometh to God must believe that He is.***

***—Hebrews 11:6***

Mr. Preston was in the process of shaving; therefore, shaving cream was still on his face. He was somewhat tall and muscular and very, very, dark. Keifer and Jamie looked at him and went berserk with laughter. The weed that they had smoked finally kicked-in and seeing Mr. Preston with a thick lather of shaving cream on his face and his tall extra dark frame made their marijuana-high surreal. The guys responded to Mr. Preston as if he were an alien from the *Twilight Zone.* I raised my hand in response to Mr. Preston and said, "Mr. Preston, I am fine. These guys are okay; they're not trying to harm me. They gave out of gas near the stop sign as I was walking from the Ridge Store. I am trying to help them out. Mama bought five gallons of gas on Saturday and I am going to see if she will let them have enough to make it to Engelhard.

Cousin Janie stood in the doorway holding a tight grip on a major league baseball bat. Her grandson, Nathaniel, had received the bat for Christmas; however, she kept it within close proximity for personal protection. She had a stern and no-nonsense look on her face as she maintained eye contact with each of the guys. After I explained to Mr. Preston that I was fine, he looked at me and said, "Let me know something! Janie thought the Klan had finally gotten you and they were marching you to the old oak at the end of the road for an old fashion lynching. You know the Klan is supposed to be here tomorrow and a lot black folks in this here community have been a little nervous. We just ain't taking no chances. It's better to be safe than sorry."

Paul turned toward me and asked, "Man, what's that smelling so good? After getting my smoke on, I've got the munchies. My stomach is growling like a German shepherd. I don't know what it is; however, it smells mighty good. Gosh! I am so, so, hungry!"

Mr. Preston responded immediately. He said, "Janie has on a pot of collard greens seasoned with smoked ham. She has freshly dug new potatoes and the best cornbread dumplings east of the Atlantic Ocean. Janie's crispy-fried streak-of-lean and streak-of-fat is the best in the county. We have some potato salad left from Sunday and she is slow-roasting a yard hen. She even has some angel eggs because we don't eat devil eggs in this house. There is no room for the devil around here. Right now, we are simply waiting for the homemade biscuits to brown. I might be a little prejudiced because she is my wife. However, she can really workout in the kitchen."

Keifer looked at Paul and said, "I am hungry as well. I feel like I could eat an elephant. My buzz is essentially gone and I am about to starve. If I don't eat something real soon, I am going to faint. I have never eaten collard greens before. Nevertheless, I would gladly try some tonight. They really smell good! Do you have enough dinner to share a little with us?"

Mr. Preston responded with, "My mom told me to never turn away a hungry man. She always preached to us about being neighborly. If you boys are hungry, I'll have Janie to place extra chairs at the table."

Cousin Janie heard Mr. Preston's remark and adamantly asked, "What do you mean, Janie will place extra chairs at the table? There is absolutely nothing wrong with your hands. I work every day just like you do. If I cook the meal, you can at least place the extra chairs at the table. I am not your servant; in fact, I am not anyone's servant. Don't try to show off around these here boys. You know I will put you in your place. Don't try to get brand new on me, Preston."

Mr. Preston irritatingly looked at Cousin Janie and said, "Janie, don't you start. I ain't in for your mouth this evening. You need to be quiet; we have guest tonight. I don't feel like hearing your nagging again this evening, especially in front of our guests. Do you understand where I'm coming from? You need to be quiet!"

Cousin Janie wiped her hands on her apron and angrily asked, "What do you mean by I need to be quiet? I'm a grown woman; in fact, I am sixty-eight years old. Nobody tells me when I can speak or when I need to be quiet. I am married to you; but, I am not your servant and I will use that bat on you, just like I will use it on the Klan. So, let's not get too pushy around here, okay?"

Mr. Preston was smart enough to know when to be quiet and when to move to another subject. He never responded to Cousin Janie; however, he embarrassingly looked at us and said, "Boys, simply bear with me for a few minutes and we will break bread together. Janie and I would be honored if you would have dinner with us. We seldom have guests for dinner during mid-week. It would be wonderful to have the company. It gets kinda lonesome around here at times since all the kids are married and moved away. Really, you know, we've never had white people have dinner with us. This is a first for us; can you imagine that? Janie talks a little too much; but she is an excellent cook. I love her with all my heart. She talks a little rough; but, she is soft around the edges. Janie is good people."

All of the guys appeared to be fixated on Mr. Preston's every word. They appeared to be mesmerized with him and his way with words. Even though a little tobacco juice trickled down the corners of his mouth and his hands trembled with age, he was a master storyteller. I was really hungry just like the guys and I had heard about Cousin Janie's masterful culinary skills. Cousin Janie saw me as I turned around to go home. She authoritatively said, "Junior, you just as well sit right on down with these here boys. You haven't had dinner, right?"

She told us to wash our hands and to take a seat at the table. I noticed that Paul, Keifer, and Jamie stood up and began to look around. Jamie asked, "Where is the bathroom? We need to wash our hands."

I stood up and told the guys to follow me. I went straight to the pump in the front yard. As I approached the pump, the three guys stood there as if they were absolutely dumbfounded. Then Keifer asked, "What kind of contraption is this? It looks like some type of antique. In fact, it looks like something from the *Twilight Zone*."

I said, "Gentlemen, this is a pump. Mr. Preston and Cousin Janie don't have inside plumbing; this is where and how they get their water. It may be a bit primitive; however, the water is probably the best that you will ever drink. Mostly, all of the black people around here have outside pumps and outside toilets. The black community is poor; very poor. Basically, this is how we live."

Jamie asked, "How does it work?"

I demonstrated by pouring water in the spout and lifting the handle of the pump. As I pulled down on the pump's handle, the guys appeared amazed. Water began to rush out of the pump's mouth; the guys were absolutely astonished. Paul placed his hand in the stream of water and threw it in his face. Keifer actually washed his entire face and hair. Then he drank so much water that his stomach became puffed. Jamie cupped his hands and said, "Man! This is indeed the best water that I've ever drunk."

After washing our hands, we sat at the table with Mr. Preston. Shortly, thereafter, Cousin Janie entered the dining room with pre-prepared plates of roasted yard hen, collard greens, sweet potatoes, potato salad, sliced ham, cheese biscuits, regular biscuits, peach preserves, grape jelly, and fried chicken feet. Then, she brought everyone a cold glass of kool-aid with sliced lemons. Mr. Preston raised his hands and beckoned everyone to join hands.

Cousin Janie stood between Keifer and Paul as Mr. Preston lead grace. He said, "Blessed and almighty God, we thank you for allowing these young boys to break bread with us this evening. I ask that you guide their path; protect them, and show them the right way. Help them to receive all men in the name of love and respect. Please place a hedge of protection around them as they continue their schooling. Finally, we thank you for the food we are about to eat. Please bless the cook and the ones who are about dine at this table. These and all blessings, we ask in your Holy name, Amen."

Paul, Keifer, and Jamie watched me as I ate. When I picked up a biscuit, they picked up a biscuit. When I took a bite of chicken, they took a bite of chicken. When I drank kool-aid, they drank kool-aid. After about six minutes, I noticed that everyone was eating on their own volition. They were even dunking their biscuits in gravy. The guys were eating collard greens, roasted yard hen, and placing preserves on their biscuits like real southern black people. Paul even grabbed a fried chicken foot and gnawed on it like a genuine connoisseur of chicken feet. Some of the fried chicken feet still had toe nails connected. Nevertheless, Paul eagerly gnawed like a hungry mouse. He smacked his lips and I smiled as I witnessed the guys licking their fingers and placing peach preserves between homemade biscuits. They ate as if each bite and each swallow was truly delectable.

Right at the point when I concluded that the meal was over, Cousin Janie re-entered the dining area with four slices of apple pie. The pie was piping hot and the apples were thick and still smoking. I felt as though I was about to burst. I watched attentively as Jamie, Paul, and Keifer loosened their belts to finish the meal. The meal was hearty and everyone ate with a high level of appreciation. I actually sensed that Cousin Janie and Mr. Preston genuinely appreciated our presence. For some reason the glow in Cousin Janie's eyes and the smile that graced Mr. Preston's face were indicators of joy and appreciation. As I sat at the table and enjoyed the warm embrace, I could not figure out whether Cousin Janie and Mr. Preston were delighted in having company during the work week or whether they were overjoyed because they were having dinner with three young white American males.

The apartheid tradition of Hyde County did not cater to blacks and whites eating together at the same table. In fact, while working in Preston Mooney's cucumber and potato fields, it was not uncommon for whites and blacks to segregate themselves during lunch. Even though the poor whites had spent the entire morning working side-by-side with poor blacks, when 12:00 noon tolled, the ugly face of segregation availed itself. Mr. Preston and Cousin Janie had actually witnessed a paradigm shift and little did they know that this was the beginning of a new societal order. Jim Crow was on the verge of dying and we (society) hadn't even recognized the terminal illness. The apartheid tradition was common place and the advent of a new societal order was at best in its fetal stage. The demise of Jim Crow would not be a quick death; it would be a slow, very slow and a well-fought battle. Even the funeral would be elongated due to the perpetrator's fear of the unknown. Pallbearers would move at a snail's pace and the eulogy would be erratic and poorly scripted. Jim Crow lived a comfortable and privileged life. To discard a life of privilege for the unknown was terribly scary and filled with restlessness.

Cousin Janie and Mr. Preston were survivors of an era when blacks and whites lived in totally different worlds. The apartheid tradition had conditioned them and they had difficulty accepting change. They had witnessed much and they knew when to smile and when to be quiet. They were indeed remnants of a time past and the rebelliousness of the new black American made them uneasy. Cousin Janie and Mr. Preston were by no means Uncle Toms. They were simply products of a different time and their prior knowledge made them apprehensive about a new societal order.

After our hearty meal, we relocated to the swing and rocking chair on the porch. I sat on the left side of the steps and Mr. Preston sat on the right. He periodically spat tobacco juice and used the back end of his thumb to wipe his mouth. No matter how often he wiped, a wet drool of tobacco juice accentuated the right corners of his mouth. Apparently, he had sat on the right corner of the steps regularly because the ground had become a discolored dark brown due to ongoing tobacco spitting. Jamie stood in the yard playing with the chickens as Mr. Preston shared thought-provoking stories about growing up in Hyde County. Jamie meandered to the chicken coop and brought back four eggs and a handful of straw. Mr. Preston allowed his chickens to roam the yard at will; and as such, it wasn't uncommon to step in chicken waste occasionally.

Keifer and Paul swung in the swing and listened attentively as Mr. Preston told us stories of the days of his youth. He was nothing less than a West African griot and everyone appeared mesmerized and captivated with each recollection. Then all of a sudden, Jamie ran from around the house in a state of panic and fright. Abraham, Mr. Preston's red rooster, was right on his heels and appeared to be in an attack mode. Jamie jumped on the porch and Mr. Preston grabbed Abraham. Mr. Preston smiled at Jamie and said, "Young whippersnapper, you almost got your eyes picked out. Old Abraham, don't cater much to strangers. He's not very sociable at all. And he definitely don't cater to strangers going into the chicken coop. Old Abraham can be kinda feisty at times."

I had seen Abraham before and he bristled at me and appeared to monitor my every move. He appeared to be territorial and I wasn't interested in trying to test his temperament. There were times when we didn't have enough eggs for breakfast on Sunday mornings and mom would send me down to Cousin Janie's house and she would gladly send more than mom ever requested. The village and family lineage was powerful and unshakeable. I liked visiting Cousin Janie and Mr. Preston because they would tell me life sustaining stories in the form of parables. When I didn't get the true gist of their narratives; they would simply smile and say, "Just live a little longer and you'll understand just what we are saying."

Nathaniel, Cousin Janie's grandson, moved in with them while in high school. He moved from Delaware to Engelhard and all the young ladies fell crazy in love with him. When I referred to him as Nathaniel, he immediately corrected me and told me that his friends call him Nat and his enemies called him Nathaniel. He was much thicker and stronger than I, so the name "Nat" worked well for me. He loved the adulation that he received from the ladies and took on the persona of Denzel Washington or Billy Dee Williams. Lula Belle, by far, the prettiest girl in high school appeared to really gravitate to him. I often watched her from a distance and I knew she didn't fall for the jive talk that most of the guys personified. However, Nat possessed the repertoire that compelled her to smile from ear-to-ear at times.

He had so many ladies fussing and fighting over him that I wished I could have walked in his shoes for just one day. When he hung with Bob, his first cousin, I was afraid to come within five feet of him. They were terribly intimidating and filled with mischief. I knew I could not beat either of them, so I would quickly do a detour if they were among a crowd of students. Bob was one of those muscle-bound guys who knew he was tough and no one ever bothered him. In addition, he was one of the Mackey boys and everyone knew that the Mackey clan would kick butt in a mere heartbeat. As I reflected, I wished Keifer, Jamie, and Paul could have met Bob and Nat. I especially wished Bob and Nat were near when Donnie and Marshall pushed me down and defaced the beautiful watch. It was a terribly lonely feeling when one is alone against two foes that appeared to take delight in bullying and humiliation.

# CHAPTER 5
# INTRODUCTION TO HOOCH

***The greatest discovery of my generation is that man can alter his life simply by altering his attitude of mind.***

***—William James***

After what appeared to be a Thanksgiving feast, Mr. Preston looked at us and summoned us to follow him. As we walked, he asked, "Are you young grasshoppers a little thirsty? If so, come on, follow me to the feed house. I got something that'll put lead in your pencil and hair on your chest. I tell you, you gotta be a man to handle this!"

We quietly followed as Mr. Preston entered the dark and musty feed house. It was extremely humid in there and dust and spider webs appeared to be everywhere. I sneezed about four times before I sat down on the long wooden bench that extended the length of the back wall. Spider webs, shovels, plows, hoes, pitchforks, and other farm tools made the feed house feel like slave quarters. There were no windows and only one door; an eerie feeling clouded the moment. I felt claustrophobic and incarcerated at the same time. However, Jamie, Paul, and Keifer appeared highly inquisitive and highly enthusiastic about Mr. Preston's mission. I said to myself, "It's amazing how white Americans embrace the unknown."

Mr. Preston disappeared into a nearby back room and returned with two molasses jars filled with a clear liquid. He sat down near Jamie and wrapped his long, dark, hairy fingers around the top of one of the molasses jars. He attempted to twist the lid; however, it would not move. I watched in anxious anticipation as he tried, and tried, to open the molasses jar. Then all of a sudden, Jamie eagerly looked at Mr. Preston and said, "Sir, let me try! Your fingers seem to be a little moist, however, mine aren't. In fact, I have very strong fingers and a strong wrist."

After one seemingly effortless twist, the lid turned and a little of the clear liquid fell on Jamie's right leg. Mr. Preston immediately reached for the jar and drank a big gulp of the clear liquid. After the big gulp, he frowned as if he experienced excruciating pain. His eyes watered profusely and I saw a single tear roll down his wrinkled and aged face. Then he smacked his lips and stated, "You gotta be a man to handle this-here brew. This is what we call white lightning. Some people call it hooch but I call it 'white lightning.' I made this from some of that- there corn over there and it is aging perfectly. Nevertheless, you gotta be a man to handle it. It really ain't for everybody."

Jamie enthusiastically asked, "May I have some? I want to try it; I really do! I've heard of white lightning; however, I've never tasted it. My granddaddy has told me numerous stories about hooch and white lightning. He told me many stories about homemade, illegal whiskey, in the South. Please Mr. Preston, just let me have a sip, okay? I won't waste it; I promise."

Mr. Preston thought for a minute, shook his head, and reluctantly said, "Okay, young whippersnapper! Take just a little swig!"

Jamie anxiously threw the molasses jar to his mouth and took a big swallow. His eyes began to water immediately and his face turned as red as a mid-July tomato. Then all of a sudden he stood up and stomped the floor of the feed house. He turned to Mr. Preston and pleaded, "Sir please, please let me have just one more swallow. That was absolutely remarkable. I gotta have one more swallow Mr. Preston. Please, just one more swallow!"

Mr. Preston shook his head again and said, "Okay, young whippersnapper! You can have one more swig. Just take it slowly because this stuff will sneak up on you like a thief in the dark of night. It'll make you howl like a lonely coyote, meow like a young kitten, and crawl like a young baby. Be careful grasshopper! Be careful!"

Jamie anxiously reached for the molasses jar again. He took a much bigger gulp this time. Again, his eyes watered, and his face turned as red as fire. Then he stomped the floor of the feed house two times and punched a stack of hay three times with his bare knuckles. His eyes became glassy and a great smile consumed his face. Jamie appeared to experience a new high, a new intoxication, and he had no fears and no inhibitions. Apparently, the white lightning was good and bad at the same time. It epitomized an oxymoron in every measure. Jamie appeared to want more and more after each swallow. It appeared to have an immediate addictive affect. His response compelled me to reflect on an occasion when I stole a sip of gin one day while visiting Cousin Nathan. It burned my throat immensely and immediately brought tears to my eyes. If the white lightning was anything like Cousin Nathan's gin, I didn't care to sample it in any fashion.

After noting Jamie's reaction, Keifer and Paul pleaded with Mr. Preston to allow them to take a sip. Mr. Preston smiled at the guys; shook his head and said, "Okay, you young whippersnappers just take a sip because this is some of my best brew. Keifer was the first to take a sip. He totally ignored Mr. Preston's request to take a sip and elected to take a big swallow. His entire head turned apple red and his eyes watered so profusely that I thought he was going to actually cry. Then he grabbed both of his ears and jumped up and down three times. After jumping up and down, he immediately turned to Mr. Preston and asked, "May I please have just one more little sip. That stuff is strong but it is absolutely good. I have never tasted anything like this before in my entire life. Please, just one more little sip."

Before he could respond, Paul interrupted and said, "No Keifer! You have had your chance. Now it's my time."

Mr. Preston responded with, "He's right. Let him have a swig. I have plenty to go around. I'm glad you boys like my homemade brew."

Paul grabbed the molasses jar like a hungry infant in search of his mother's breast. He threw the jar to his mouth so fast that his teeth banged against the glass. I actually thought he cracked a couple front teeth. As with Keifer, he took a big swallow instead of a sip. His eyes began to water as well. Tears trickled down his face like raindrops sliding down a windshield. Paul coughed three times and hit his chest five times as if he was strangled and in need of air. He wiped his eyes and reached in his back pocket to retrieve his handkerchief. After blowing his nose, he turned toward Mr. Preston and asked, "Mr. Preston, may I have just one more swallow? In fact, a meager sip would be just fine?"

I interrupted Paul and said, "Hold up! Hold up! I haven't had a taste, yet. I want to see what it tastes like. Come on now! Don't leave me out!"

Mr. Preston grabbed the molasses jar and adamantly stated, "Junior, I tell you, you are not ready for this. I don't want your dad and mom getting upset with me. You really need at least two more years before you even qualify for a small sip. Trust me, you are not ready. Believe me; if I felt like you were ready, I'd give you a whole jar for you to enjoy. Mark my word, in two years, come back to see me, and we'll celebrate together."

I really felt left out; however, my respect for Mr. Preston was enormous. I didn't care to disrespect him in any manner. He disappeared to a backroom again and returned with an old rocking chair. The chair looked like one that he had retrieved from the Engelhard junk pile and restored. One rocker was white and the other was brown. It appeared that Mr. Preston had replaced one of the armrests as well. He placed the rocking chair near us and began to tell us mindboggling stories about slavery, the Ku Klux Klan, and working in the cotton and potato fields.

During pauses, he would reach down and take big swigs of white lightning and spit tobacco juice. As he shared heartfelt stories, the brown tobacco drool around the corners of his mouth became more pronounced. Then he would pass the jar to Paul, Jamie, and Keifer. They all readily embraced the molasses jar and appeared totally indifferent about the fact that they were drinking from the very same jar of an old toothless black man. It appeared that notions about separation of the races and skin-color were truly insignificant. The only matters of importance were the storytelling and the content of the molasses jar. Paul, Keifer, and Jamie appeared to race for the molasses jar once it left Mr. Preston's chapped, red and black lips. The reality that Mr. Preston didn't have a single tooth in his mouth was a non-factor. The setting appeared to be one of mutual respect and void of race and social class issues.

I couldn't erase from my mind the fact that a major Klan rally was scheduled for the next day. However, Mr. Preston and I were enjoying the new-found friendships of Paul, Jamie, and Keifer. The dinner was nothing less than a feast and I, just as Mr. Preston, had never dined with white Americans before. I discovered that white Americans belch, suck their teeth, get chicken in between their teeth, and have gas just like black Americans. I also learned that there were white Americans who were empathetic and sensitive to the dire conditions of black Americans.

After ongoing storytelling, I excused myself from the setting and went home. It was 8:45 p.m. and mom and dad told me to always make it home before dark. They were afraid that one night the Klan would catch me as I walked home from the Ridge Store. I was compelled to pass by the Amity Church as I walked home. Passing the huge graveyard always gave me an eerie feeling, especially at night. There were several tall graves in the cemetery and Mr. Preston told me that Mr. Gibbs requested to be buried standing up so he could watch the niggras as they passed by. There were always really weird noises as I quickly ran pass the Amity Church. I didn't believe in ghosts; however, there was something unusual about the Amity Church that was mysterious and unnerving. Before leaving Mr. Preston's home, I turned to the guys and told them where I lived. They were so intoxicated that they didn't even respond to me.

Mr. Preston had drunk a little too much as well. However, he looked at me and said, "Junior, you can go on home. I'll look out for these-here boys. In fact, I'll let them sleep it off, right here in the barn tonight. They aren't in any shape to walk anywhere. I'll go in the house and get some blankets from Janie to put over them.

These young whippersnappers ignored me when I told them that my brew would sneak up on them like a thief in the night. And as you can see, it will knock you flat on your backside. They look like three little kittens all snuggled–up like that. Nevertheless, they wanted to drink like real men. Regardless, they're some good boys and I'll look out for them. Just come back tomorrow around 8:00 a.m. I need to get out of here early tomorrow because I have to mow Mr. Norfleet's yard before noon. The sun starts to really burn around 2:00 p.m. and I don't need to get any darker."

I walked on home and reflected on the evening. The dynamics of the evening were almost inconceivable. It was basically unimaginable to believe that three young white males would have dinner with a toothless old black man and his wife. It was essentially inconceivable to believe that three young white males, who were strangers, would protect me from Donnie and Marshall. And finally, it was basically unbelievable to witness three young white males drinking from the same molasses jar of a toothless old black man who chewed tobacco. My evening was one to remember. I witnessed a paradigm shift; a great awakening.

# CHAPTER 6
# NEVER CAN SAY GOODBYE

***The best and most beautiful things in the world cannot be seen or even touched—they must be felt with the heart.***

***—Helen Keller***

The next day I was at Mr. Preston's house at 8:00 a.m. as he requested. The guys had terrible headaches, but were anxious about covering the story of the Klan rally. They were sitting at the breakfast table finishing up a breakfast of scrambled eggs, fried cornbread, sliced bacon, fried potatoes and onions, peach preserves, grits, and coffee. None of them had eaten grits or fried cornbread before, and they were eating like run-away slaves.

Mr. Preston ate rather slowly and appeared rather sad that the experience was about to end. Then all of a sudden, we all heard some hollering and chanting. Keifer astonishing asked, "What in the world is that? It sounds like someone is in pain, seriously moaning."

Mr. Preston responded with, "Oh! That's Dessie, my wife's sister. She is doing her rain dance ritual. She does it every once in a while when the grass turns brown from lack of rain. You see Janie and Dessie's grandparents were full-blooded Indians. Dessie still practices a few of the rituals and ceremonies. I can't say that they work, or that they don't. I do know for a fact, when we had a terrible drought around here, Dessie did her rain dance ritual and it rain for three days in a row. Come on, young whippersnappers; let's go for a walk so you can see the ritual. Now, let me tell you, you have gotta be real quiet. If the spirits sense that someone is making fun of them, they don't take it lightly and you will have bad luck. So whatever you see, just don't laugh! My son, Luke, was laughing and making fun of her and within ten minutes he was grabbing his throat and crying that he could not breathe. I don't bother the Indian spirits, and they don't bother me. You should have seen Luke; he was turning red and foaming at the mouth. I thought I was going to have to take him to see Dr. Liverman."

Mr. Preston led us down the road. After walking about three hundred yards, we saw Cousin Dessie hopping around and chanting something in a language that we could not comprehend. It was similar to the "unknown tongue" that I had heard in church when congregants got really happy and in the spirit. The soil beneath Cousin Dessie's feet was dry and dusty. However, she stomped the ground violently and paused periodically and raised both hands to the heavens. Her beautiful long black hair reached the middle of her back. And a blue and white ribbon circled the middle of her forehead and a chicken feather stood tall in the back of her head. She stomped the ground violently and raised her hands to the heavens relentlessly. I noticed a swirl of red ants, black ants, beetles, and locusts ascend into the air as if they had a divine destiny. Cousin Dessie's eyes were closed and she appeared to be indifferent about who may be watching. Then to our amazement, we heard thunder roaring. Dark clouds began to form quickly and the wind began to blow briskly. It was quite evident, rain was on the way. When we heard the deafening clap of lightning, we had seen enough!

Keifer waved for the guys to come on. None of the guys said a single word during the rain dance ritual. It appeared that they respected Mr. Preston and wouldn't dare do anything that was offensive. As we approached Mr. Preston's house, Keifer appeared speechless and emotional. His eyes began to water and his voice began to crack as he thanked him for the numerous lessons that they learned. He told him that he would never forget him or that evening. Keifer assumed the position of spokesperson and sadly stated, "My friends and I had one of the best evenings and mornings of our entire life. We will never forget you and we really appreciate all your acts of kindness and hospitality. My friends and I have talked; we have sixty dollars that we would like to present to you as a token of our appreciation. Please accept our gift. We really owe you a great deal more."

Mr. Preston wiped tears from his eyes and stated, "No. Young whippersnappers, Janie and I are in our late seventies. You have really made our day. Your money is no good around here. Please, don't hurt our feelings. We will not accept your money. You have to go back to Raleigh; save your money for school. However, I do want you boys to do me a favor. I want you to open the door of the feed house. I have a little going-away-gift for each of you. Please accept my gift in the spirit in which it is given, and enjoy!"

The guys hugged Mr. Preston and Cousin Janie and ran to the feed house. Three small, brown, paper bags sat in the doorway. Each bag contained a half-pint of white lightning. The guys jumped for joy and said they were going to save their brew until they returned to Raleigh. After leaving Mr. Preston's house, Mama gave the guys three gallons of gas and they headed to Engelhard to fill their gas tank. They dropped me off at the Ridge Store after hugs and soul shakes. I looked at each of them and noticed that they had tears in their eyes. As I was about to exit the station wagon, Keifer leaned forward and removed a thick gold chain with a small gold cross from around his neck. He smiled a sad smile and said, "Henry, I want you to have this! My deceased granddaddy gave me this chain as a Christmas gift five years ago. He said that it is blessed and it would protect me whenever Satan is on my trail. Henry, believe me, it works!"

I responded with, "Keifer, come on man; this is very expensive and your granddaddy gave it to you. I can't accept this!"

Paul interjected and said, "Henry, I know Keifer. The gift is from his heart, please accept it. You just don't know how much yesterday evening and last night meant to us. It was as if we spent the entire evening in a different culture. It had all the makings of an episode in the *Twilight Zone* or *The Outer Limits*. Had it not been for you and Mr. Preston, my friends and I would have believed many of the negative stereotypes associated with black people. I am confident that we will receive an 'A' on our project. Our professors are going to be delighted to hear of our experiences. So, Henry, please accept Keifer's gift."

I reluctantly accepted the gift and reached for the doorknob. Jamie embraced me and told me to take care of myself. Then he smiled and said, "Don't be walking these dark roads alone anymore, okay? It really is not safe. It really isn't. Take care Henry, we won't forget you!"

As I got out of the station wagon, Joseph saw me and asked, "Henry, who are those white guys? Damn, you'll ride with the Grand Dragon, himself, won't you?"

I smiled at Joseph and said, "They're friends of mine from Raleigh and they're en route to Engelhard to get some gas. Really, they're students at North Carolina State University, studying journalism. To tell the truth, they're in Town covering the Klan rally today as a class assignment."

Joseph looked at me and frowned. Then he asked, "Henry, are you crazy? Those guys could have been junior Klansmen and they could have taken you somewhere and hanged you. Man, you take too many chances for me. I wouldn't even walk the road from here to Scrouge Town like you do each day. The Klan is just waiting to snatch up a brotha and make an example out of him. Man, to tell the truth, I don't know whether you are brave, or simply stupid!"

I ignored Joseph's remarks and entered the Ridge store. Ben Junior was eating a Honey Bun and drinking a Pepsi. As I looked around, I observed Lonnie, Larry, Sammie, and Raymond sharpening their switchblades and oiling their BB guns. The guys were not doing their customary laughing and joking. They appeared to have on their battlefield faces as they contemplated the unknown. Byron came around the counter with some black shoe polish and we strategically placed war paint under our eyes and cheeks.

I cannot figure out why we elected to put on war paint during bright sunlight. However, we did it without any conversation. Sammie began to do pushups and we all followed along with him. Just as we were about to go outside to assume our respective positions of attack, Lonnie elected to pray. He humbly prayed, "*God, please protect us as we venture out into the unknown. I ask that you place a wall of protection around us as we go out to confront the Klan on this beautiful day. Please guide us and protect us as we endeavor to do your will. We ask this prayer in the name of the Father, the Son, and the Holy Spirit. Amen*!"

Lonnie's prayer was powerful and it had overtures of death and dying. I knew I wasn't ready to die and I didn't want anything to happen to any of my friends. As we exited the Ridge store, we did a final high-five and put on our combat face. A tear rolled down Ben Junior's face as we piled out of the store. He immediately lifted his right hand and attempted to wipe it away. In so doing, he smudged the war paint that he had meticulously placed under his left eye. For a brief moment, he looked more like he was preparing for a Halloween trick or treat excursion than preparing for battle with the Ku Klux Klan.

Mr. George Hill entered the store as Byron grabbed his BB gun and switchblade. He didn't ask any questions; he simply got out of our way. Our weaponry was at best archaic but we didn't really care. Our ultimate mission was to eliminate Klan activity in the black community. My heart was pounding and I sensed that we all had serious concern about the unknown that was about to unfold.

I was the last to exit the Ridge store and my knees trembled terribly. Just as I was about to close the door, I met Reverend Emanuel Johnson. Many of the adults in the community referred to him as "Blind Manuel." My parents would not allow my siblings and me to speak of him in this manner because they said it was terribly disrespectful. Mr. Fred, a black merchant, dropped him off at the store. To be a legally blind man, Reverend Emanuel was one of the most insightful individuals that I had ever met. He spoke with a very slow and extremely clear intonation. And his vocabulary was impeccable. There were times when I actually questioned whether or not he could actually see.

Reverend Johnson wore extremely dark sunglasses and there were times when I would intentionally look through his lenses to get a glimpse of his eyes. Each time that I looked, I would consistently see what appeared to be huge white marbles. I was seriously intrigued with his ability to read Braille. It was amazing how his fingers would slide across the pages of his Bible. There were times when I would compare and contrast the language of his Braille Bible with that of my small testament. He was consistently accurate in every detail. After observing him closely, I concluded that he was indeed totally blind. Needless to say, his other senses were extremely acute.

As I held the door for Reverend Emanuel, he enthusiastically said, "Good afternoon, Brother Johnson! How are you today?"

I responded with, "I am fine Reverend Johnson. I hope you are doing well."

Just as I was about to join Byron and the other guys, he said, "Brother Johnson, my senses tell me that there is danger in the air. Be careful, I can sense danger and death very easily. In fact, I know there are several eyes staring at me right now. In addition, I hear things. I hear a lot. You boys be careful, very careful!"

Reverend Johnson was accurate in a host of ways. Byron, Sammie, Larry, Lonnie, Joseph, Raymond, and Ben Junior were all staring at him, and quietly listening. It was truly amazing how he was so perceptive and cognizant of his immediate environment. He summoned all of us together and prayed a prayer of protection. He told us to hold hands as "brothers and family" as he prayed a semi-long, heart-felt prayer. As we closed our eyes, I thought about Reverend Johnson's endless days of darkness. I empathized and sympathized as well.

After prayer, we briefly strategized and prepared for battle. We gathered at the back of the Ridge store as convoys of cars and farm trucks made their way to MiddleTown to the Klan Klavern. A few patrons gave us the middle finger and shook their fists at us. I remember vividly as one pickup truck passed the Ridge Store en route to the Klan Klavern and a young white male yelled, "Klan Power! Klan Power!"

Sammie immediately balled his fist and yelled, "Black Power! Black Power!"

Several pickups appeared to be loaded with out-of-Towners. A sense of danger and despair consumed me as I pondered whether a confrontation with the Klan was a wise decision. My ultimate concern was our archaic weaponry and the potential danger of getting shot or seriously maimed. I loved my physical mobility and I really did not want to see any of my "Band of Brothers" injured. The long convoy of cars and trucks en route to the Klan Klavern showcased several patrons holding rifles and shotguns. Then again, some of the patrons looked like they were cast members of the *Beverly Hillbillies* as they rode in terribly old and dirty farm trucks. They appeared to be extremely poor and in search of a greater piece of the great American dream. Seemingly, dirt-poor whites had a lower tolerance for blacks than middle-class white America.

I was extremely restless the night before the planned Ku Klux Klan confrontation. I oiled my BB-gun several times and I polished its barrel spotlessly. After listening to the 6:00 p.m. news, I concluded that the Klan were real and they were serious about terrorizing black communities. My sister, Linda, came to my room and asked, "Junior, are you okay? You have been real quiet for the last couple days. What's going on?"

Linda was very perceptive. However, I downplayed my true disposition and gave her the impression that I was simply concerned about my upcoming mathematics test in Mr. Weston's class. She knew that I planned to attend college and I was always concerned about maintaining decent grades. To be absolutely honest, I don't believe I received three hours of sleep the night before our planned attack on the Ku Klux Klan.

## CHAPTER 7

# A SENSE OF BELONGING

***Follow your instincts. That's where true wisdom manifests itself.***

***—Oprah Winfrey***

Word about the Kool Kolored Kidz and our planned confrontation with the Ku Klux Klan began to travel throughout the campus of Davis School. While quietly sitting on the school bus, Charles (Red) whispered to me, "Henry, I want to join the **KKK**. I heard about you guys and I want to join. How much will it cost? I've been saving my Sunday school money to buy a baseball glove. But, I'll give it all to you guys. I just need to know how much it will cost. My Uncle Ben owes me $2.75 and he is supposed to pay me on Saturday. When he pays me, I'll have about $23.75."

I strangely looked at Charles and stated, "Man, I have no idea as to what you are talking about. If you want to join the **KKK**, I suggest that you change your race and become just a little bit lighter. Really, I don't believe the Klan is accepting applications from black people, right now! Yes, you are light-skinned, but as far as I know, the Ku Klux Klan doesn't allow blacks to join their organization. I don't know anything about the **KKK**!"

Charles pleaded, "Come on man, I'm talking about the Kool Kolored Kidz. I hear things, and the word is out. I just want to join to support you guys."

I looked directly at Charles and denied ever hearing anything about the Kool Kolored Kidz. Then I asked, "Charles, how in the world are you going to join any organization when you can't go anywhere but to the mailbox? The only time you are able to leave your yard is the second Sunday of each month, and that's to go to church. You and Dennis are in the same category. Again, I don't know anything about the so-called Kool Kolored Kidz."

He looked terribly bewildered and disappointed. After denying any association with the Kool Kolored Kidz, Bill sat down beside me and whispered, "Look, I got something to ask you! I heard about you guys and I want to join. My cousin, Ben Junior, doesn't like for me to hang-out with him. He says I am too little and too young and I would only slow him down. How much does it cost? B. J. owes me $4.25 and I can get some more money from my grandma, if that's not enough. Look, I know the KKK is supposed to be secretive and I will keep everything just between you and me. I swear; I can keep a secret! I want to join you guys, please! "

I shook my head and denied any knowledge of, or association with the Kool Kolored Kidz. When I looked up, I noticed that Charles was staring straight at me. Again, I adamantly stated, I don't know anything about the KKK!"

When I got home from school that afternoon, my sisters, Jackie and Vanessa, teasingly asked me if they could join the KKK. Then they jokingly yelled, "Say it loud; I'm black and I'm proud!" After that, they began to laugh hysterically.

I simply ignored their inquiry and laughter and ate my dinner. Mama walked through the living room and noticed that the Rev. Jesse Jackson was on the evening news. She said the Reverend had a very special way with words and could be a major voice for black people. However, he doesn't compare to Dr. Martin Luther King in any measure. After bringing in water for the evening, I took the shortcut through the swamp to go play basketball at Sammie's house. As I approached Ms. Heddie's house, I met Dennis. Dennis was an avid outdoorsman who roamed the swamps like Grizzly Adams and he knew every thicket or mud hole in the swamp. Seemingly he appeared out of nowhere, attired in homemade camouflage hunting gear. In light of the fact that he couldn't afford to buy over-the- counter hunting camouflage gear, he elected to make his own. He was wearing a Daniel Boone hat with a squirrel ponytail dangling mid-way his neck.

Dennis was smart, very smart, and he could readily discern when someone lied to him. In fact, he was always on the honor roll at Davis School and he was never sent to the principal's office for being disruptive. He was a model student and most of the teachers referred to him as an ideal student when they wanted to make a point. However, on the dirt and muddy roads of the Ridge community, role models didn't fair very well.

All of the guys were consummate daredevils who looked for challenges to keep from being bored. An annual ritual was the stealing of watermelons from Mr. Cecil Silverthorn's melon patch. We would wait patiently until about the second week of July and then we would invade his watermelon patch with utmost tenacity. The annual ritual was a rite of passage, as well as a major high for most of the Ridge guys. Dennis and his brothers didn't partake in the annual ritual because Cousin Ella Mae, his mother, kept a tight leash on her sons. Most of my buddies gained their reputations by being mavericks and denouncing the status-quo. To be quite honest, some of the guys would steal grease out of a biscuit just for the thrill of being defiant. While we stole watermelons from Mr. Silverthorn's farm, Dennis and his brothers often raised watermelons and ate them on a regular basis. Their grandfather,

Mr. Herman, taught Sunday school and served as a stern patriarch for the guys.

Most of the guys on the Ridge attended church and Sunday school on Easter to show off their new clothes. They would show up again on Christmas, to receive a small brown paper bag filled with hard candy, a few nuts, and raisins. Except for those two special occasions, church and Sunday school were not a special place in the hearts of my friends.

Dennis was deemed one of the smart guys who catered to all the sports that black guys didn't really care to explore. Hunting and fishing was okay; however, playing basketball, baseball, and football readily took precedent over all other sports. When my friends and I were engaging mischievous activities on the Ridge, Dennis and his younger brothers were often exploring the woods with a book tightly clinched in their hands. When the bookmobile visited the Ridge community, most of the guys looked at it as if it were a vehicle from Outer Space and wouldn't dare approach it. In fact, the driver of the bookmobile looked at Larry and stated, "It's an absolute waste of perfectly good gas and time to even drive through the black community. Nobody reads around here!"

I later concluded that Dennis and his brothers were the real mavericks. My friends and I were basically stereotypical blacks who didn't care to venture outside our comfort zones. Keyes Junior, Prentice, and Gary, Dennis' younger brothers, readily followed his lead. Kem, the baby boy, was basically a homebody and didn't venture far from the front yard. However, Dennis was a "bad boy wannabe." This was highly showcased in his conniving smile. There was something about his smile that conveyed the message that he was always three steps ahead of you. When I encountered him in the woods near Ms. Heddie's house on the eve of the big Klan rally, he smiled and glowingly asked, "What's up Prez? Man, you better be careful coming through these paths late in the day like this. Besides the Klan, you have to watch out for rattlesnakes and ground bees. I almost stepped on the biggest rattler that I ever saw about two weeks ago."

He indicated that he had been out staking out some spots for the upcoming hunting season. I thanked him for telling me about the rattlesnake incident. However, I had seen numerous snakes and huge spiders on many occasions as I took the shortcut to go to the Ridge to hang out with my friends. I possessed a greater fear of spiders than snakes. There was something extremely eerie about spiders that made my skin crawl. Ground bees had chased me for almost a mile one evening after school as I passed Ms. Heddie's house. I learned to have serious respect for bees.

Dennis loved guns, all kinds of guns, and he often spoke glowingly about hunting and special shotguns and rifles. His eyes would glow with extreme excitement as he shared exciting and venturous narratives. I told him that I wasn't much of a hunter and I didn't know much about high-powered rifles. He spoke as an expert at age twelve when he matter-of-factly stated, "Henry, experience has told me that a rifle is only as accurate as the ammunition being fired in it. Since you are probably a novice hunter, I wouldn't recommend a hard-kicking rifle for you."

I couldn't get a word in as Dennis enthusiastically talked about high powered-rifles. His enthusiasm elevated even higher as he spoke about cartridge choice. He slowed up a bit and said, "Henry, a seven 30-06 shooting the popular 150-grain factory load kicks twice as hard as a 257 Roberts shooting a 117-grain bullet."

I attentively listened as Dennis shared his love of hunting, rifles, and shotguns. For the most part, I knew nothing about a 257 Roberts or a 117-grain bullet. My ultimate goal was that of getting to Sammie's house and going to the makeshift dirt basketball court to shoot some hoops. Hunting just wasn't my thing!

As I was about to walk away, Dennis hollered, "Yo, Prez! I just want you to know that the word is getting out about the so-called Kool Kolored Kidz. If the group is supposed to be secretive, just know that it is not secretive any more. Just for the record, Mr. Boone (Davis School Principal) called me to his office yesterday and tried to interrogate me. Of course, I couldn't tell him anything. I pretended that I hadn't heard of the so-called Kool Kolored Kidz. He tried to intimidate me; but I simply played mind games with him. He asked me who the real ring leaders were. I denied even knowing anything at all about the group."

I used my stern no-nonsense look and voice, and stated, "Dennis, this is news to me! I have never heard of the Kool Kolored Kidz. I do know the Ku Klux Klan is planning a rally in Middle Creek. However, that's all I know about the KKK. I am shocked that Mr. Boone would ask you a question like that!"

Dennis was very perceptive. He smiled and said, "You can't fool me. I know more than you could ever imagine. You can't play me; I know a whole lot. I know these woods like a bird knows its nest. I hear things; I hear a lot of things every day. In fact, my brothers, Keyes Junior and Prentice, heard Geach and Lonnie talking about your next meeting. It's supposed to take place on Wednesday at 4:00 p.m. behind the Ridge Store, right?"

I thanked Dennis for the information and continued my trek to Sammie's house. As I approached Sammie's house, Larry was in his yard chopping wood. He yelled, "After I put this wood on the porch, I'll come to the basketball court."

Judith, Larry's sister, eventually came out of the house to feed a few stray cats. After scraping food off the plate, she asked, "Henry, do you know that Alice really likes you? She talks about you all the time and she wants to be your girlfriend. I told her that she was simply wasting her time because everyone knows that you are crazy about Judy. Yes, I know you are crazy about Judy. I see it every day when she gets on the school bus. It's like you hold a seat especially for her. And when she chooses to sit somewhere else, I can see the disappointment on your face. I know you are crazy about her. You can deny it; but I know the truth."

I did not respond to Judith's inquiry, I simply went to the basketball court and began to practice my dribbling. Larry eventually came to the basketball court and I shared with him what Dennis told me. He immediately asked, "Does he want to join us? Man, he can't join us! Cousin Ella Mae won't even let him leave the yard. I know he is smart, but how can he help us if he can't go any farther than the mailbox? His situation is just as bad a Charles Howard's! This is not a babysitting club!"

I listened to Larry but did not respond. Judith called him to inform him that supper was ready. He told me that he would be back in about twenty minutes to finish the conversation. I continued to practice my dribble while he ate dinner. Then I began to think, Cousin Ella Mae has always been very kind and pleasant to me. My mom thinks a great deal of her and they even visit each other occasionally. This was unusual because my mom didn't visit anyone.

Cousin Ella Mae and my mom were basically single-parent moms who were compelled to play the role of mother and father for five children. She, like my mom, had her hands full and she had to be the great protector and provider for five boys. As I continued to evolve, I readily learned that black boys are special and American society is not always kind to them. As I sat there and reflected on Larry's comment, I remembered that mom had instructed us (her children) to always refer to Mrs. Ella Mae, as Cousin Ella Mae. She said that we were family and family should always respect each other. After about thirty minutes, Larry returned to the basketball court. Larry continued his perspective that Cousin Ella Mae gets upset when the Ridge boys tried to befriend her boys. Ben Junior walked up to the basketball court and sat down. He asked, "What's going on? You guys look like someone stole your dirty little sneakers. What's up? What's going on? We are still going to deal with the Klan tomorrow, right?"

Larry told Ben Junior that the word is getting out about the Kool Kolor Kidz. He said that someone had been talking too much. Then he informed him that Dennis had mentioned the Kool Kolored Kidz to him and that Mr. Boone had called him to the office to interrogate him. Ben Junior suggested that we forget about Mr. Boone and to continue with our plans to deal with the Klan. Mr. Boone had a history of trying to give Ben Junior a hassle. There were times when he would attempt to belittle him in a crowd of students and Ben Junior would simply smile and take the unnecessary verbal abuse. Mr. Adams, the school janitor, said Mr. Boone responded to him as he did simply because he saw potential in him. He was only testing his temperament.

As Larry talked, Ben Junior scratched his head and said, "Really, I have no problem with Dennis joining the Kool Kolored Kidz. He knows the swamps around here like the palms of his hands. We could use his skills as a young lieutenant; you know, as a young officer. In fact, since most of us are in high school, we will need someone to take over when we graduate. Let's make Dennis an honorary member of the Kool Kolored Kidz and give him the rank of lieutenant?"

Larry did not like Ben Junior's perspective and annoyingly suggested, "Come on guys. Let's leave Grizzly Adams in the swamp where he is most comfortable. When he can go a little farther than his mailbox, we'll put his name up for a vote. If he can't leave his front porch, how can he benefit us? He's always trying to hang-out with us older guys and you know Cousin Ella Mae gets real upset when he talks to us. Let's go! I want me a honey bun and a Dr. Pepper. Let's go out to the Ridge Store."

As we gathered our belongings to go to the Ridge Store, we heard someone yell, "Hey, you guys wait-up! I have to go to the store as well and I want to ask you something. What do I need to do to join you guys?"

Larry responded with, "Dennis, you are too young to hang with us. You are tall and big enough, but you are too young. You can't even leave your porch without permission. We are like the

*Minutemen* in the history books. We may need you in a minute's notice. And there are times when you can't even go to your own mailbox."

I smiled at heart because I didn't believe that Larry was paying attention in history class when the *Minutemen* were discussed. The recognition that he knew anything about the *Minutemen* conveyed to me that he was a much better student than what he presented in class. After about thirty minutes of heated exchange, Larry calmed down but insisted that he wasn't going to babysit Dennis in any regard. Then after Larry calmed down, Dennis became upset and indicated that he could "carry his own bone" and didn't need anyone to protect him or hold his hand.

Ben Junior recognized that we were nearly arguing as we walked to the Ridge Store. He stopped and asked, "How are we going to present ourselves as a united front when there is intense bickering within the organization? We need to stop this bickering from within and direct our attention to our upcoming clash with the Klan!"

Everyone agreed with Ben Junior. However, I could see that Larry and Dennis were still at odds with each other. Joseph made an effort to change the mood as we continued our trek to the Ridge Store. He asked, "Henry, are you still being harassed by Donnie and the preacher's son as you walk home? If so, I suggest that we hide behind some of those huge gravestones in the Amity Church and give those guys a great surprise."

I really appreciated the fact that the guys were concerned about my welfare. However, I always ran full speed past the Amity Church and the huge graveyard because the entire church area seemed really spooky. Donnie and the preacher's son picked on me relentlessly and I really wanted to confront them when I wasn't alone. I didn't need the Kool Kolored Kidz to intervene. I simply needed one other person to help me because I knew that I could give Donnie a serious beat-down. Larry sarcastically asked, "Dennis, why don't you go help Henry?"

Then he sarcastically followed with, "Oh! I'm sorry! I forgot; you can't leave your front porch!"

Sammie shook his head and annoyingly stated, "Larry, we are addressing Henry's safety right now, okay? Ease up on Dennis! I am confident that he would come through for us, if we really need him. He is smart enough to cover his tracks and make things happen."

# CHAPTER 8
# AGE IS NOTHING BUT A NUMBER!

***When a friend is in trouble, don't annoy him by asking if there is anything you can do. Think up something appropriate and do it.***

***—Edgar Watson Howe***

Dennis became highly irritated with Larry's constant tease about what he could or could not do. He vehemently stated, "Larry, you are not really grown either. I have heard Aunt Emma tearing your butt up late at night and I have seen and heard you screaming like a little sissy. You see, my brothers and I roam not only the swamps around here, we even move around in this community late at night. Keyes Junior knows almost as much about this area as I do. You guys should consider each of us; and in about two years, Prentice will be a strong candidate as well. He's a better hunter than all of you guys right now and he is only in the fifth grade. Yes, I know you guys call me Grizzly Adams, but that's okay! My brothers and I keep a close eye on the Klan whenever they start messing around on the Ridge. We've even seen them throw pamphlets and other hate materials in certain neighborhood yards.

Sammie interrupted Dennis and adamantly stated, "We recognize that you are sharp in school. And we recognize that you know the swamps around here really well; however, we are contemplating confronting the Ku Klux Klan and this can be a very treacherous mission. We are concerned about your personal safety."

Dennis maintained that he could handle himself quite well. He said he didn't need a babysitter or anyone to hold his hand. After calming down a bit, he proudly stated, "I actually know where several Klan members live. To be absolutely honest with you, you would be seriously shocked if I were to share with you the names of some of the people that I've seen come from under those sheets. My brothers and I know more about Klan activity around here than you guys will ever learn. You see, we have eyes everywhere. Honestly, we are like the CIA!"

Ben Junior asked, "How in the world are you able to know so much when Larry contends that Ms. Ella Mae will hardly allow you to go to the mailbox?"

Dennis indicated that his mom often that he and his brothers are quietly tucked in bed on most nights. However, they are more 'underground' than Superman. Then he smiled, loosened up a bit, and stated, "Keyes Junior and I are the night hawks while you guys are sleeping and having wet dreams. When you guys are snoring late at night, my brothers and I are laying traps and watching every move that the Klan makes. Think about it, the Klan doesn't come within ten feet of our house. We have bear traps and other traps strategically placed along walking paths to our house and around our house."

After almost fussing us out, Dennis calmed down and blatantly stated, "Guess what guys, I know where your so-called secret meeting place is. I even know your monthly dues. In fact, I actually know your oath."

Ben Junior interjected and perplexingly stated, "You say you actually know our oath? If so, let me hear you recite it."

Dennis stood tall and proudly stated:

"Cowards never start,
Weak men never arrive;
In the Kool Kolored Kidz, only the strong survive!"

Ben Junior smiled and said, "He even recited it with conviction. I like that, he brotha definitely has smarts!"

Dennis responded with, "I can take you to your supposedly secret meeting place. In fact, I can take you there in less than five minutes. Your secret meeting place really is not a secret! It's a complete joke!"

Ben Junior stopped immediately and looked inquisitively at Larry and asked, "What did he say? I know he didn't say what I think he said."

Dennis turned around immediately and we all followed him like a mother hen leading her biddies. Sammie looked Dennis straight in his eyes and used a no-nonsense intonation and stated, "If you know so much, prove it!"

Dennis boldly stated, "Yes, I know where your so-called secret meeting place is located and I can take you directly to it. In fact, I know a shortcut to it that you don't even know about. It's real simple and anyone could easily find it."

Lonnie impatiently stated, "I don't believe you. If you know so much, show us!"

We followed him as if he had been named our platoon leader. We crossed two dried-up canals and stomped through a couple acres of recently harvested pea fields and then, right in front of us, stood our secret meeting place. Miguel and Martin were sitting in our so-called secret meeting place going over the agenda for the planned altercation with the upcoming Klan rally.

Martin stopped what he was doing and immediately asked, "Why is Dennis in our 'supposedly' secret meeting place? This place is for initiated members only. This place is not a social outlet for your personal friends. Gosh! I don't understand you guys. Do you even know what the term s-e-c-r-e-t means? I guess the FBI and the CIA will be walking in here at any time, right?"

After Martin finished his sarcastic speech, all eyes were on Dennis. Ben Junior shook his head and said, "He is right. This place is not as secure as I thought. We have got to find another place for our meetings."

Dennis happily stated, "I can show you the perfect place but you've got to let me join the Kool Kolored Kidz. Yes, I know about you guys and your plans to deal with the Klan. Some of you guys just don't know how to whisper. I know a lot about you guys and your plans. However, if you don't let me join you, I won't show you anything. The place I have in mind is perfect, it really is."

We all looked puzzled because we didn't anticipate Dennis giving us an ultimatum. Martin and Miguel walked away from us and whispered for about five minutes. Then they returned to the group and Martin asked, "How do you guys feel about Dennis becoming a member of the Kool Kolored Kidz? He knows these swamps like the palms of his hands and he is indeed very smart. We could use his smarts as we strategically plan to address local Klan activity."

Miguel responded with, "After assessing the intellectual functioning of some of you guys, I firmly believe that Dennis would be an asset to this organization. I firmly believe that many of you guys are at best liabilities and your intellectual worth is at best miniscule. However, Dennis would be a welcomed asset to our vision and mission. He is articulate and he writes well."

Martin responded with, "If you would like for Dennis to join our esteemed band of brothers, raise your right hand."

Everyone raised their right hand, except Larry. Larry stepped forward and vehemently stated, "Dennis is too young to hang with us. He can't even leave his front yard without his mom's permission. He's just too young to join us right now! Think about it, if we should run up against the Klan, he would probably mess-up in his pants. We ain't got time to baby-sit anyone."

We all listened to Larry very attentively. However, Dennis was allowed to become a member of the Kool Kolored Kidz by majority vote. We respected the fact that he was a bit younger than most of the guys; nevertheless, he knew the swamp landscape with perfection and he was undeniably smart. Dennis reminded us that he knew of an ideal spot to use as our secret meeting place. He indicated that he had personally designed it and it was quite possible for outsiders to be right in front of it, and never recognize it as a functional meeting place. He enthusiastically stated that he had personally camouflaged the spot and even the FBI would have difficulty finding it. He indicated that the spot was near Mr. Lincoln's pig farm.

Mr. Lincoln, Lonnie's uncle, had recently installed an electric fence around his pig farm to keep his pigs from roaming around and getting lost in the swamp. We all knew about the electric wire because several of us had tripped over it when we played baseball and football evenings after school. The jolt of electricity really hurt and we didn't care to play near the wire. However, we took our chances. Dennis further stated that he knew how to extend the electric wire around our meeting place to send a message to would-be intruders.

Dennis emphasized the position that every organization should have some form of security to ward off intruders. Then he told us that Keys Junior and Prentice had put together a makeshift booby-trap near the giant oak tree in their front yard. He enthusiastically stated, "On the night of the last Klan rally in MiddleTown, Keyes Junior and Prentice took a large rope and painted it black. They painted it black to camouflage it at night. Then they tied the rope to the giant oak tree. You know, there is a deep well near the giant oak tree where mama catches rainwater to wash our clothes? Well, on the night of the last Klan rally, Keyes Junior and Prentice took the old linoleum rug that we once had on the living room floor, covered it with grass, dirt, and old leaves and then stretched it over the old well. When the Klan came nosing around our house, one of them stepped on the booby-trap rope and it immediately grabbed him by his feet and pulled him up about twenty-five feet in the old oak tree. Man, you should have seen him dangling and swinging in the air trying to find something to grab. He was yelling, "Help me brothers! Help me!"

He was screaming and crying like a small child. It was like a flying trapeze act out there watching him dangling to that old oak. He lost his Klan hat, pocket change, Swiss Army engraved pocket watch, cigarette lighter, solid-gold cross, and Boy Scout knife that night. Then, the other Klansman stepped on the old linoleum rug and it collapsed and he fell directly into the deep well. Man, you should have been there! That was one hilarious night! It was a rather frigid night and that dude almost froze. You should have seen him walking around like a frozen zombie. After that night, the Klan doesn't bother coming to our house at all."

Larry listened very attentively and stated, "Damn, we got another one of those walking-talking dictionaries. I can't stand dudes like that. Why can't they talk like regular folks?"

Miquel smiled at Larry and said, "I can assure you that you don't talk like regular folks. This sounds absolutely amazing. We could use a brother like Dennis and I sense that he could be very instrumental in crafting other mechanisms to augment the goals of the Kool Kolored Kidz. He epitomizes President Kennedy's noted quote, 'Ask not what your country can do for you, but what you can do for your country'. If Bro. Dennis applies this perspective to the Kool Kolored Kidz, we will be a much stronger and more effective organization. I am proud to embrace you as an honorary member of our illustrious organization. And when you are a little older, you and your younger siblings will be accorded official membership."

I really liked the final decision made by Miguel and Martin. Dennis and his brothers would indeed be an asset to our organization. They were extremely quiet, inquisitive, and disciplined. Prentice and Keys Junior were so quiet and introverted that they wouldn't even say hello, unless someone else initiated the greeting. Their younger brothers Kem and Garry were equally as quiet, yet very nice. The guys on the Ridge nicknamed Keys Junior, "Big Money Grip." He was extremely tall and slender with extraordinary huge hands. He wore a size twelve shoe when he was in the seventh grade. Dennis assumed the role of patriarch of his brothers and kept them in line. When necessary, he would use a commanding voice to guide and keep them on the right path. There were times when I would watch from afar as he used "tough love" to monitor their behavior.

Mr. Herman, their grandfather, played a major role in their upbringing. He taught each of them to be extremely frugal with their money. In fact, Keyes Junior was nicknamed "Big Money Grip" because he was so tight on a dollar. When afros became the official look of the Black Power Movement, Dennis and his brothers became neighborhood celebrities. Due to the fact that they possessed what black Americans call "good hair", they stood out in crowds. They instantaneously became the Ridge version of the "Jackson Five." Their thick afros made them unique on the campus of Davis School. Most of the guys on the Ridge had thick nappy hair that was seldom combed. My so-called "afro" was an embarrassment to the Black Power Movement. It was so thin that one could look right through it.

After the brief meeting with Martin and Miguel, Dennis looked at his watch and thanked the guys for their time. He excused himself because he had to hurry home to chop wood and place it on the porch before dark. I had already chopped my wood for the evening and stacked it on right side of our house. In addition, I had given my sisters a dime to bring in water for me. I had saved a few dollars by picking up pecans and selling them to Mr. King Paul, a neighborhood merchant. My sisters were happy to receive the money. We didn't have inside plumbing and that became a serious hardship at times. Nevertheless, we persevered.

Martin and Miguel said they had to thumb a ride back to Engelhard before their moms got off from work. For some unknown reason, none of our parents queried us about our afterschool activities. As long as we completed our chores and did our homework, everything was fine. Our underground ventures were well kept secrets. We were all excited about visiting our new meeting place. Dennis agreed to meet us near Ms. Heddie's house at 4:00 p.m. on the next day. None of us liked passing her house because strange noises were always heard. Larry said the house was haunted. We continued our trek to the Ridge Store and shadowboxed along the way.

We knew Byron was running the store and it was the ideal afterschool hang-out. We laughed and joked at the store as if it were comedy hour at a Comedy Club in Vegas. We were brothers with an unshakable bond. As we approached the Ridge Store, Judy and Dorenda, Byron's sisters, were crossing the road to go home. Byron was like a brother to us; however, his sisters were beautiful. As such, there was an unwritten rule that denounced flirtatious acts with siblings of the brotherhood. We simply waved and smiled at Dorenda and Judy and continued our trek to the store.

I was in the store for about five minutes before Mr. Robert, Byron's dad, entered. He appeared terribly tired and irritable. The look on his face conveyed the message that he wasn't in for any foolishness. His brogan shoes were extremely dirty and his hands were caked with mud and dirt. The heels on his work shoes were so badly worn that the nails connecting the heels to the soles were visible. However, he walked as if the shoes were simply broken-in well. It appeared evident that he wouldn't discard them for a brand new pair. His fingernails were soiled with a mixture of black dirt and engine oil. Nevertheless, his hands were his bread and butter and he didn't mind a little dirt, if it meant that his family was comfortable.

Mr. Robert worked with my dad at a huge logging company called Georgia Timberland. The company paid well; however, the work was strenuous and very dangerous. My dad loved his job because it supplemented his military retirement income. Mr. Robert was a serious entrepreneur who worked on automobiles and lawn mowers to supplement his income. Mrs. Rebecca, his wife, was a consummate money manager. She regularly managed the store and maintained the household. Mr. Robert was a savvy businessman with a vision that superseded his era. As he left the store to prepare for dinner, he sternly stated, "Barlon, the store is a place for business and not a place for horseplay. I hope you understand what I mean! Do I need to spell it out for you?"

Our friend, Richard, was a serious jokester and comedian. He declared that Mr. Robert always called Byron, Barlon. In addition, he was masterful at mocking Mr. Robert's voice and mannerism. Richard would be so funny at times that we cried with laughter. There were times when the Ridge Store had all the makings of a makeshift comedy club. The mood of the store was quite transformative. If I had a bad day at school, the Ridge Store would always uplift me. It was quite therapeutic.

Richard could readily change from Richard Prior to Dr. Martin Luther King, Jr. in a heartbeat. Each day at the Ridge Store was filled with unanticipated excitement. However, we were brothers and we had each other's back. As young children, many of our toys were "Transformers." We would take a two-by-four piece of wood, the top of a Crisco can, and nail it to the two-by-four and "transform" it into the make-believe car of our choice. Being black and poor compelled us to be creative with our meager resources. We viewed hotdogs and hamburgers as fancy feasts and if we were fortunate enough to get a real hotdog bun and real hamburger bun, we would think our parents must have won something from playing numbers. For us, food was food!

## CHAPTER 9

# ALL OF THIS FOR A SIMPLE MOUSETRAP!

***The cost of freedom is always high, but Americans have always paid it. And one path we shall never choose, and that is the path of surrender, or submission.***

***—John Fitzgerald Kennedy***

After laughing and joking with the guys in the Ridge store, I asked Ben Junior to go to Engelhard with me. Mom had given me $5.00 to purchase three mouse traps and a half-pound of cheese. The weather was changing and when temperatures dropped, for some reason mice would roam all over our house. Ben Junior agreed to go with me and we began walking to Engelhard. After walking for about a half-mile, Hatton Junior drove up and stopped to give us a ride. He was driving a beautiful 1968 Dodge Charge. The car was beautiful and the engine roared as if it were ready for the racetrack. When Hatton Junior took off, he took off squealing tires and the car almost got away from him. He asked us if we would like to see 120 and he slammed the accelerator to the floor and it reached120 mph very, very quickly. I had never traveled at that speed before and it was fun.

When we arrived in Engelhard, Hatton Junior asked us if we had a dollar or two for gas. Ben Junior and I explained that we didn't have any money.

Hatton Junior became irritated and said, "You mean to tell me that I showed you boys 120 mph, using all my gas, and you can't even give me anything on gas. I tell you what, if you ever need another ride to Engelhard and you see me coming, don't even try to flag me down, because I won't be stopping."

We smiled and thanked Hatton Junior and walked to Mr. Tony Spencer's General Store. When we entered the store, he greeted us with a very pleasant smile. Then he asked, "What can I do for your boys today?"

I explained that I needed to buy three mouse traps and a half-pound of cheese. Ben Junior and I stood in front of the counter and waited until he could secure the traps and cheese. I could see the cheese as it sat in a round class container and a jar of pickles rested nearby. While Ben Junior and I patiently waited for Mr. Spencer to return to the front counter, I heard the screen door slam, which indicated that someone had entered the store. Three young white boys entered the store and briskly came to the counter where we stood patiently. One of the guys asked us, "Have you seen Mr. Spencer?"

I told him that Mr. Spencer had gone to the back of the store to locate some mousetraps. Then one of the guys asked, "Have you heard that the Klan is supposed to have a big gathering in Middle Creek tomorrow evening. It's a lot of cars in Middleton at the Klan Klavern. I can't wait for tomorrow to get here; I've never been to a Klan rally before. Aren't you boys a little scared?"

Before I could respond, the smaller white guy declared, "Well, I am white and I am a little scared. I was told that the Grand

Dragon is supposed to be here. He doesn't take any mess and he is always heavily armed."

Ben Junior became a little annoyed with the conversation and bravely stated, "I am not worried about the Klan. Tomorrow will be just like any other day for me. I am not going to change anything. I'm not worried about the Klan!"

The tallest and biggest of the young white guys smiled and stated, "I am not going down to Middle Creek for no Klan rally. I have worked side by side with colored people all my life and they have never bothered me."

I listened carefully because I had seen the white guy before. He was standing in line, just like I was, waiting for Ms. Ella Mae Mooney to pay us. Then the shorter white guy said, "In fact, last summer I worked for Preston Mooney Farms and the colored guys there treated me nicely. We never had any problems at all. In fact, we would sit in one of the sheds during lunch and share Vienna sausages with each other. There were times when we even ate out of the very same *pork & bean* can."

Then the largest white guy said, "Come to think of it, there was a colored guy there who was called "Monk Louis." He was one of Preston Mooney's most loyal workers. The Mooney's really loved him and they looked out for him during the winter months when farm work was slow. He had it made with the Mooneyes!"

The shorter white dude said, "Yes. I remember him. Ole Monk was a hardworking man and he was really nice. But on weekends, he would get so messed-up that he couldn't even walk. I carried him home on several occasions. He had a niece who was really fine; I believe he called her Addie.

I watched Sammie's demeanor when he called Addie's name. He walked over and listened carefully. All of the guys on the Ridge knew that Sammie had the hots for Addie. However, he was so big and strong that we wouldn't even tease him. No one cared to take the risk that he would get angry.

The white guy went on to say, "Addie was tall and slender with silky, long black hair. Man, she had the most beautiful dimples that I had ever seen on a colored girl. If I were colored, I would be tapping on that door every weekend."

As he continued with his description of Addie, Sammie reached in his back pocket to retrieve his pearl-handle switchblade. Ben Junior recognized the rage building up within and yelled, "Yo, Chisel, it's all good! No harm done! Don't get all bent out of shape! Save it until tomorrow! "

The white guys were totally accurate about Monk Louis' work ethic. He would work terribly hard from Monday through Friday. However, when Friday night came around, he looked forward to getting his drink on. It was almost as if he received a degree of hope and consolation from the ill-effects of alcohol. Whatever challenges or obstacles he may have had, seemed to have momentarily disappeared while under the influence of alcohol. As much as he loved to drink on weekends, he would never, ever, take a drink of whiskey from a bottle that was already open.

After waiting about three minutes, Mr. Toney Spencer returned to the counter with one mousetrap. He indicated that he had only one trap left, but he will order some more and they should be here in about a week. He apologized and stated that Gilbert Gibbs' Hardware store carried mousetraps as well. I purchased the one mousetrap and the half-pound of cheese and walked directly to the hardware store. As Ben Junior and I approached the store, I immediately noticed that there were three pickup trucks with Georgia license tags, four with Mississippi tags, and three pick-up trucks with Alabama license tags. Each pickup showcased a Confederate/rebel flag either on the front, back, or rear window. Ben Junior and I shrugged our shoulders and entered the store.

Upon entering the hardware store, I readily noticed that there were eight white males in there whom I had never seen before. In fact, they all appeared to be strangers. In addition, they were all wearing coveralls and brogan shoes and they became very quiet when Ben Junior and I entered. Mr. Gilbert was well-known for selling some of the best rifles and shotguns in the county. He even sold ammunition. Black hunters readily purchased their rifles and shotguns from him. He would even allow a few local black hunters to purchase rifles and shotguns on credit. Mr. Gilbert had a thriving business and he was a savvy business man. He knew how to earn a dollar and he knew how to keep a dollar. All of the young guys on the Ridge purchased their rite of passage switchblades from him. I purchased my beautiful pearl handle switchblade from Mr. Gilbert also. He was consistently kind and pleasant to me. When I purchased my first switchblade from him, he only asked, "Are you sure you are old enough to purchase a knife as fancy as this?"

However, on this day when Ben Junior and I entered the store, a different disposition was apparent. He appeared a little nervous, very uneasy. He didn't speak as glowingly and friendly as he normally did and his hands appeared to tremble. He immediately asked, "What can I do for you boys today?"

I immediately responded with, "Mr. Tony Spencer told me that you sell mousetraps and I would like to purchase two. My mom said she believes she heard some mice last week; and I would like to get a couple traps to see if I can catch them."

Mr. Gilbert responded with, "No problem! Give me a second and I will be right back. I just received a new batch of traps last week."

Ben Junior and I stood near the counter and waited patiently. Then one of the patrons reached for one of the new rifles on the gun rack. I assumed that he was simply checking it out prior to purchasing it. However, he looked at his friends and pointed it directly at Ben Junior's head. Then he said, "Look here fellows, I believe this here barrel is warped just a wee bit. What do you think, Earl, is this here barrel a little bit warped?"

Earl responded with, "Even if it is a little warped, I'd still buy it for koon hunting. When I go koon hunting in Alabama, I always take my Remington speedmaster 552 because some koons are rather fast and sneaky. I don't like to take chances when it comes to koons."

Ben Junior slowly, very meticulously, raised his right hand and very methodically moved the rifle from the direction of his head. Then he said, "I don't know about you, but where I'm from, you don't ever point a rifle at anyone unless you plan to use it. Look, I don't play with guns. And I definitely don't play with strangers!"

He didn't mix his words. He was totally stoic and straightforward. The patron stared directly at Ben Junior and stated that he has something very special for him and the rest of his kind. He stated that he had heard about the colored people and their so-called Black Power Movement. He angrily stated, "Yes, I've even heard about the so-called Black Panther Party and Malcolm X, and his supposedly Nation of Islam brotherhood. Believe me; the Klan has something special for those agitators as well. It's just a matter of time and all of them will become ghosts."

Mr. Gilbert slowly approached the counter as they exchanged words. He really didn't know what went down but he knew something had occurred. He looked rather perplexed and said, "I have a special on mousetraps this week. These are free, just take them and leave! I really don't want any trouble in here!"

I reached in my pocket to pay Mr. Gilbert; however, he insisted that the traps were free. It was highly evident that Ben Junior was insanely angry and he was ready to hurt someone. I put my money in my pocket and reached for the doorknob. As I quickly turned the doorknob, one of the patrons yelled out, *"Say it loud; I'm Black and I'm Proud!"* And everyone began to laugh uncontrollably.

I didn't even look at Ben Junior; we simply walked away without saying a single word. We met Doris and Dawn, twins who lived on the Hill Top. They spoke to us as they crossed the road. Ben

Junior was dangerously angry; he didn't even speak to them. Even though he liked their niece, Vanessa, he didn't crack a smile or acknowledge them in any regard. I looked across the road and saw Hatton Junior putting gas in his beautiful blue Dodge Charger. Then I saw a white guy who I had seen when I was working in Preston Mooney's potato fields. Everyone called him Thad and he was driving a beautiful '67 apple red Plymouth Fury. It was a beautiful coupe with a white interior and the Temptations, *I Wish It Would Rain* screamed from the radio. The chromed dual exhaust tips and the engine's roar made the car an eye-catcher. It was a dream car for anyone born with a car gene.

Ben Junior and I simply knew him as Thad and he had given us rides to Engelhard on several occasions. He was always pleasant but didn't say very much to anyone. He was a big Hoss Cartwright type guy who basically stayed to himself and worked his own farmland. His love of the color red was highly evident. He apparently loved the color because his work trucks and cars were all candy-apple red. Hatton Junior was still at Elwood's Esso cleaning his windshield and wiping dust off his car when Thad arrived. Then he lifted his hood and appeared to be checking out his engine. Hatton Junior looked at him and jokingly said, "Smells like to me, you've been running that Mopar. If it runs like my Charger, you got a real land jet on your hands."

Thad responded with, "If I catch you on the road sometime soon, you'll find out what it will do! This is the fastest Mopar that I ever bought. I have a special police interceptor engine in here and when I put my foot in it, I can hardly keep it on the road. I've heard about the Dodge Charger; you are right, they are supposed to be real monsters."

As we walked to the Town Tavern, Mr. Early passed by driving an old, green, and dirty farm truck. He appeared to be in a serious hurry and didn't even respond when I waved at him. Apparently he wasn't paying attention, because he almost hit two cars as he rushed to get to Mr. Tony Spencer's store. When he got out of the truck he yelled, "Look here, you boys need to watch where you're walking. The next time, I just might not see you!"

Ben Junior and I didn't respond to him, we simply kept on walking. Mr. Early was the senior deacon at the Engelhard Disciple of Christ Church and was well respected. It is safe to say that he was an icon and pillar within the Engelhard community. He was similar to an African griot and would often tell compelling stories about struggles of the black community during the Great Depression and World War I. Whenever he spoke, I would give him my undivided attention because I viewed him as a walking/talking history book. This is rather ironic, because as a student at Davis School, I found history classes extremely boring. However, Mr. Early would make the course extremely vivid and more realistic. He wasn't a man with several earned college degrees. However, he was knowledgeable in a host of areas. His down-to-earth southern vernacular and his compassion for the poor were unshakeable.

Even though Ben Junior and I had experienced a horrendous experience at Mr. Gilbert's Hardware Store, we were still deeply rooted into the black American culture that purported respecting and honoring the elderly. This tradition was not limited to the black community; it was applied to anyone who appeared to be of an advanced age. As with the old African griot, a high level of honor was bestowed upon individuals who had withstood the test of time.

Mr. Early had paid his dues and we were not going to disrespect him in any manner. My mom had conditioned me to believe that bad luck would follow young people who disrespected the elderly. I really believed this disposition and Mr. Herman, my Sunday school teacher, often purported the same dictum. As such, Mr. Early had earned our respect and we weren't going to spend any time trying to convince him that he could have run over us as we walked to the Town Tavern.

My day had been truly inundated with challenge after challenge. We met "Mr. Henry Bear" and Ms. Teasle as we meandered to the Towne Tavern. Upon meeting Ms. Teasle, she admonished us by stating, "You boys know Uncle Early can't see very well; you need to watch out for him before it's too late. Even on a bright and sunny day, you need to keep a close eye on him. He doesn't mean any harm; his bark is much greater than his bite."

Ben Junior was still seething from the rifle ordeal and wasn't talking at all. I said, "Yes, Ms. Teasle, we'll be more watchful."

As we continued our walk to the Towne Tavern, 'Mr. Henry Bear,' yelled, "You boys need to be really careful. The Klan is planning a big rally tomorrow evening. It's not safe to walk the roads these days. If Early doesn't run over you; the Klan is threatening to lynch you. Like Teasle said, you boys need to be extra careful."

I began to smell the aroma of fried shrimp and fried fish as I turned the corner to go to the Towne Tavern. The aroma from Mr. Ben's café was relentless and possessed the fragrance of a freshly picked rose. Seemingly, the crowd at the café was larger than normal and I noticed several cars had tags indicating that they were from Georgia, Alabama, and Mississippi. Patrons stood at the front door of the café and appeared to canvass everything within sight. One patron had the audacity to yell, "Hey Buckwheat and Tar Baby, let me hear you yell *Soul Power*!"

Ben Junior and I ignored the insult and continued to walk. Then to our amazement, the front door of the café opened and a patron rushed across the road and snapped a picture of Ben Junior and me. He said, "Boys you are going to be famous tomorrow. This picture will be on the front page of *The News and Observer*."

I was completely befuddled because I had never heard of *The News and Observer*. To this end, I was mystified and could not relate to the patron's statement. Due to the fact that I was poor, buying a newspaper wasn't at the top of my priorities. Maslow's physiological needs were truly real to me. The flow of traffic in Engelhard was extraordinarily heavy. Willie Wallace passed by putting foot in his mom's '69 Dodge Charger *R/T.* For some reason, he was always in a hurry. When he saw Ben Junior and me, he rolled down his window and yelled, "You guys better make it back to the Ridge before it gets dark. The Klan is roaming around everywhere. Be careful!"

I watched as a convoy of out-of-towners paraded through Engelhard. They appeared to be canvassing the entire town. A few cars stopped and took pictures of the Engelhard Bank and Mr. Tony Spencer's General Store. One car abruptly stopped, without giving a signal, and Willie Wallace had to stomp his brakes to avoid colliding with the vehicle. Upon seeing what nearly occurred, the driver stepped out of his vehicle and apologized. Willie Wallace was so angry that he turned Native-American red. He was truly livid! Then the driver displayed his badge and informed him that he was an officer with the FBI conducting surveillance prior to the upcoming Klan rally.

Willie Wallace was one of very few light-skinned brothas at Davis High. He was very likable; however, filled with mischief. Most of the pretty girls adored him. Needless to say, most dark-skinned brothas hated on him. He was cool with me because he liked my sister, Linda. He took me for a ride in his '69 Dodge Charger and almost scared me to death. At about 90 miles-per-hour, he dipped off the road and ended up in Mr. Reginald McKinley's front yard. Apparently, no one was at home, because he backed out of the yard squealing tires and left the scene. Willie Wallace gravitated to the works of Malcolm X and the Black Panthers. However, Dick Gregory was his idol.

It was difficult to distinguish undercover police officers from regular Klan supporters. Several supposedly unmarked police cruisers passed by as Ben Junior and I walked to the Towne Tavern.

There were a few strange black faces walking around in Engelhard. However, we (the black community) didn't know whether they were hunters or fishermen, simply passing through our quaint town. The upcoming Klan rally brought a host of new faces and mystery to the Engelhard community.

## CHAPTER 10
# RALLYING THE VILLAGE

***If by saying that all men are born equal, you mean that they are equally born, it is true, but true in no other sense; birth, talent, labor, virtue, and providence, are forever making differences.***

***—Eugene Edwards***

After Mr. Early nearly hit the two cars and blamed us for his near accident, we continued our trek to the Towne Tavern. I clenched the mousetraps tightly as we entered the Tavern. Since Mr. Gilbert didn't charge me for the mousetraps, I had enough money to buy Ben Junior and me two hotdogs. We didn't have enough money to buy a soda or French fries; however, that didn't really matter to us. We simply loved hotdogs with real hotdog buns. Mr. Coleman, my friend, Meat Ball's dad, ran the Tavern. He immediately placed some napkins on the counter and asked, "What can I do for you boys today?"

I ordered two hotdogs for each of us. Mr. Coleman asked, "What do you boys want to drink?"

I responded that we only wanted the hotdogs because we don't have enough money to buy two sodas. Mr. Coleman shook his head and said, "You know those hotdogs are going to be mighty hard to swallow without something to drink. I tell what, if you boys will pick up the cigarette butts and bottle tops from around the counter and the pool room, I'll throw in some homemade lemonade and French fries with the hotdogs."

There was a significant different inner-feeling by the way Mr. Coleman used the term "boys" versus the way Mr. Gilbert used it. It was hard to explain; however, there was a heartfelt difference. Ben Junior and I agreed to pick up the cigarette butts and bottle tops. This was fine with us; it wasn't anything comparable to picking up white potatoes in mile-long fields in the middle of June for Mooney Farms. After reaching in my pocket to pay Mr. Coleman, I immediately thought about the half-pound of cheese that I had purchased. I remembered that I had left the cheese on the counter at Gilbert's Hardware Store. Gosh! I hated the thought of returning to the store. The thought of walking through those doors again terrified me. I just knew the white guys would be there, just waiting to humiliate me. My heart began to pound rapidly and I began to sweat profusely.

After all that we had been through, I wondered how I was going to tell Ben Junior that I accidentally left the half-pound of cheese on the counter. For a minute, I thought about simply leaving the cheese at the hardware store. Then again, I knew Mom would really fuss me out for coming home with two mousetraps and no cheese. The mousetraps would have been useless without cheese. Then I thought about Linda, Vanessa, and Jackie, my sisters, asking mom if she would make us some homemade cheese biscuits with Sunday's breakfast. I really didn't care to hear my sisters calling me dummy for buying mousetraps and forgetting the cheese. They simply would never allow me to forget the occasion.

I elected to wait until Ben Junior swallowed the last bite of his hotdogs before I told him that I forgot and left the cheese on the counter. When I finally got enough courage to inform him, he simply looked at me, shook his head, and said, "Man, I don't want to go to Mr. Gilbert's store anymore today. You don't know what it's like to look down the barrel of a rifle. I've been humiliated enough for one day."

I responded with, "Okay, I understand. You have been through an awful lot for one day. I understand; I really do! I'll go back to get the cheese. Hopefully, I'll be right back. If I am not back in about ten minutes, just go on and catch a ride home."

I rushed out of the Towne Tavern and slowly walked back to the hardware store. Hilda and Bernice were leaving the Second-Hand Store as I meandered back to Mr. Gilbert's store. Hilda inquisitively asked, "What's wrong Henry? You look like you just lost your very best friend."

I told her that I was fine; however, I needed to go to the Hardware Store and make it home before dark. As I entered the store, I noticed a huge white guy sitting on a tall counter stool with his right leg propped on the counter. He looked at me and asked, "Aren't you one of them-there boys who was in here earlier. You forgot something, didn't you? Well look here, I found this-here cheese and I am enjoying it. It's like you lost it, and I found it!

He was smiling from ear-to-ear and appeared to really enjoy the cheese and crackers. A ten-ounce Coca-Cola rested on the counter near the cash register. Then he said, "Loser's weepers; finders keepers!"

He really irritated me; nonetheless, he was much too large for me to accost. Shortly thereafter, Mr. Gilbert rushed from the back of the store to the cash register. He still appeared rather nervous; however, he asked, "Aren't you one of the boys who was in here earlier. Well, you forgot your cheese and one of my customers found it and began to eat it. I don't sell that kind of cheese because it is known to mess up one's bowels. My customer said it was really good! You must have purchased it from Tony Spencer, right?"

Then he opened his cash register and gave me $3.00. He said, "Here, take this for your trouble and buy some more cheese. If you hurry, you will be able to catch Mr. Tony before he closes for the day."

The white guy, who was sitting on the stool, stood up and angrily shouted to Mr. Gilbert, "Damn, that's the matter with the coloreds. They're always getting a handout or something free. That's why they're so lazy and shiftless. Pretty soon, that same boy will be walking up and down these-here roads balling-up his fist yelling, *Soul Power* and *Black Po*wer! Yes, I have the cheese and I ain't about to give the little 'spook' nothing. You see, in Alabama, we know how to treat the coloreds and we don't have half the problems you people have around here."

I allowed the guy to finish talking and then I thanked Mr. Gilbert again for the mousetraps, and headed for the door. As I reached for the doorknob, the door automatically opened. It was Ben Junior, Big Hurley, Big Jimmy, Big Lightning, Meat Ball, George Thomas, and Jody. Ben Junior had informed them about the dynamics that had occurred earlier in the hardware store and they had come to protect my interest. Everyone appeared serious, very serious. Jody said, "Henry, we brought a little reinforcement to make sure you got your cheese. I hope no one put their hands on you, right? Are you okay?"

Mr. Gilbert was very perceptive. He rushed to the door to close it and informed everyone that the store was about to close, but it would reopen at 8:00 a.m. on the next day. It was only about 5:22 p.m. and the store normally stayed open until 6:00 p.m. The white guy sat down and teasingly ate the cheese. He didn't appear intimidated to the least bit. A mischievous smile consumed his face as he chewed on a toothpick. He appeared ready for battle. He slowly carved bite-sized parcels of the cheese and used his toothpick to meticulously place it on Saltine Crackers. Then he stood, clapped crumbs from his hands, and stabbed the hunk of cheese in dead center. His knife stood tall from the thickness of the cheese. The white guy smiled as he stared directly at Jody. He appeared terribly angry and unafraid of the unknown. He towered over him and was much thicker. Little did he know that Jody had the strength of a pit bull and he was as quick as lightning.

The size difference really didn't mean much to me because I had seen him slam numerous guys who towered over him. As always, Jody began to gnaw on his fingernails and his eyes began to water. I knew from experience, he was getting mentally psyched to brawl. His Joe Frazier demeanor instantaneously kicked into first gear. My cousin, Ervin, asked, "Cuz, are you okay? If not, we will stay here and make sure all is well."

Then all of a sudden, the crowd standing outside began to stand aside. The scene was similar to the movie version of Moses crossing the Red Sea. Merendale and James M., noted gangsters, who had moved from Engelhard to Brooklyn, New York stepped to the front of the crowd. Word had circulated that they had shot two cops at a bar in Manhattan. Merendale looked at Meat Ball and asked, "Why are you guys standing out here acting like you are watching a prize fight at Madison Square Garden?"

Meat Ball slowly walked to the front of the crowd and whispered in Merendale's ear. James M. frowned and said, "Man, you gotta be kidding! Tell me you're kidding! That's why I left the South! Is this mess still going on?"

Merendale shook his head and pointed at the lone white guy still sitting on the stool. He continued eating his cheese and Saltine Crackers. His knife was still stuck in the hunk of cheese and a ten-ounce Coke rested near an ashtray. Ashes surrounded the tray like residue from a volcano. Merendale's eyes possessed a degree of viciousness that commanded respect. I had heard numerous stories about his fascination with death and dying. Everyone in the black community knew that James M. and Merendale weren't afraid of anything. My cousin, Howard, who lived in Brooklyn, knew them well. While in the barbershop one afternoon, he told a host of breathtaking stories of how they would periodically play Russian roulette with each other to gain a serious emotional high. From appearance, the sheer thought of dying didn't bother them at all. They gravitated to death defying acts with little to no concern.

Shortly after James M. and Merendale arrived at the scene, Mr. Gilbert nervously reminded the crowd outside that it was closing time. He informed them that the store would reopen at 8:00 a.m. on the next day. Meat Ball was still whispering to Merendale when he all of a sudden said, "Man, tell me you're lying! Are you serious? He did what? He pointed a rifle at Ben Junior? You mean to tell me, that dude, sitting on that stool, did what?"

Merendale and James M. pushed the door open to Mr. Gilbert's store and slowly walked in. The white guy looked directly at Merendale and didn't say a single word. It appeared that his eyes told the story. There was a deep coldness about his eyes that conveyed the message that he did not play. James M. pulled another stool up to the counter and sat right in front of the white guy. He didn't say a single word; however, he unstuck the knife from the center of the cheese and meticulously carved three thin slices. After eating a couple bites, he quietly reached for the nearby napkin canister and slowly wiped the cigarette ashes off the counter as he gazed directly at the lone white guy.

Everyone quietly watched as he murmured to himself. The white guy towered over James M. and he was much heavier and more muscular. However, after looking into the eyes of James M., he appeared to get nervous, very nervous. The crowd outside grew larger and larger by the minute. The crowd was morbidly silent. Then James M. said with a smirk on his face, "You know, we don't get cheese like this up North. It sends me straight to the bathroom, but that's okay. I use it to clean out my system. A man needs to clean out his system every now and then. Don't you agree?"

There was so much silence in Mr. Gilbert's store that it felt rather eerie, really strange. I really believe if a needle had fallen to the floor, everyone would have heard its impact with the floor. I glanced out of the huge window and observed that the crowd was getting larger and larger by the minute. Cars slowly passed by and rubbernecked to try to figure out what was going on. Then, all of a sudden, I heard the voice of Ruthie screaming, "James M., don't you and Uncle Merendale do anything crazy. We got to live here long after you guys go back to New York."

Wardella, Ruthie's older sister, responded with, "That's right. And we are tired of cleaning up after you guys. Seems like everywhere you guys go, somebody gets shot or ends up dying. It's time for you guys to grow-up!"

Jody responded with, "Ladies, I don't mean no harm, but you all need to go on home. We are simply handling our business. We don't try to tell you how to handle your business, so don't tell us!"

I watched from afar as he gnawed on his fingernails. He was getting mentally prepared for battle. Everyone at Davis School knew it was wise to relocate when Jody placed his fingertips in his mouth. I wondered if the other out- of- town Klansmen were going to suddenly reappear. If so, it was going to be a bloody mess. I kept looking out of the large window for the arrival of other Klan members. I was scared, real scared!

I watched as Jody and Meat Ball whispered as they focused on the beautiful new rifles resting in the gun rack. The lone white guy maintained his indifferent demeanor. He didn't appear to fret at all during the whole ordeal. I was so afraid that my knees were knocking and I wasn't even sitting on the hot seat. James M. had a smirk on his face as he reached for the ashtray to dump the cigarette butts. When he reached, he accidentally knocked over the remains of the ten-ounce Coke and it splashed on the shirt of the lone white guy. He apologized and offered to buy him another Coke.

The white guy didn't smile, he angrily stated, "That's okay boy! It had gotten hot anyway. Then again, I shouldn't be drinking dark sodas. It simply ain't healthy!"

When he used the term "boy", my heart began to pound so rapidly that I just knew I was on the verge of fainting. The crowd outside began to murmur loudly. Some of the spectators dispersed immediately. As several dispersed, I heard murmurs like, "I'm gettin outta here befo Sheriff Cahoon comes."

Then I heard someone say, "I ain't gonna be a witness to nothing. This ain't my fight anyway! You can stay here if you wannna. I'm carryin my black ass home!"

Then I heard Meat Ball say in a very slow and serious intonation, "I know he didn't refer to James M. as 'boy.' Somebody is going to die tonight and it ain't gonna be me. James M. don't play that 'boy' stuff. That dude definitely chose the wrong Negro! "

I could tell on Mr. Gilbert's face that he was ready to close the store and go home. The thought of other Klansmen returning to the store left the door wide open for a serious blood bath. The Klan Klavern was located about four miles away and numerous out-of-Town Klansmen were seen traveling en route to MiddleTown for the upcoming rally. The crowd out front of Gilbert's Hardware Store was simply a group of innocent bystanders curious about the dynamics surrounding Ben Junior and the rifle incident. They weren't prepared for a skirmish of any type. About two weeks before the planned Klan rally, Sheriff Cahoon instituted a ban on the selling of firearms to anyone except members of his office. To this end, blacks would be potentially going to a gunfight with pocketknives.

Mr. Gilbert didn't discriminate, if someone desired to purchase a rifle, shotgun, or ammunition, he'd sell it without reservation or interrogation. The announced Klan rally in MiddleTown had the Engelhard community extremely uneasy. Elwood's Esso station was extremely busy during the week of the planned Klan rally. Nearly every car or truck that frequented the gas station showcased a Confederate flag. The proliferation of Confederate flags made blacks extremely angry and uneasy. Blacks viewed the Confederate flag as a signature that the bearer was a proud and unwavering member of the United Klan of America.

The showcasing of the Flag was allegedly reminiscent of southern states withdrawing from the Union. Black patrons who frequented the Towne Tavern watched with disdain as out-of- Town Klansmen paraded their Confederate flags. Even though the flag was allegedly crafted to symbolize the secession, blacks viewed it as a call for a return to slavery, white supremacy, and bigotry. The lone white guy sitting on the counter stool never displayed any sense of anger or fear. He appeared totally comfortable even though Merendale and James M. held the crowd in utter suspense. No one had any indication of what the climax may entail.

## CHAPTER 11

# META PEARL AND PEARLY MAE

***Being considerate of others will take you and your children further in life than any college or professional degree.***

***—Marian Wright Edelman***

Mr. Gilbert became extremely uneasy as the outside crowd murmured continuously. He nervously stated, "I am so glad you boys like the cheese. I tell you what, I have some that's even sharper than this in my storage area. I'll get you a large sample and you can share it with your friends at the Towne Tavern. In fact, I'll even send Coleman a nice thick slice. Tell Coleman that I said hello and I'll be over there during lunch tomorrow for a couple of his hotdogs. And since it's getting late, I'll go on and close the store now, okay!"

Before James M. could respond, Merendale reached on the gun rack and coincidentally removed the very same rifle that the white guy had pointed at Ben Junior. He appeared to check the weight of the rifle as he bounced it up and down. The crowd stood quietly in wonderment and anxious anticipation about the unknown. Everyone watched attentively and wondered what was going to happen next. I hadn't witnessed anyone get shot before and I didn't want this to be my first time. James M's reputation as a known "gangsta" preceded him and I was scared.

Then I heard William Earl yell, "Shoot him Uncle Merendale! Go on; blast a cap in that fool! Go on; set an example for the rest of the Klan!"

Ruthie screamed, "No! No! Don't do it! Please! Please! Leave him alone and let him go! The Bible says; *Thou shall not kill*!"

Merendale curiously looked down the barrel of the rifle. Then he lovingly and passionately stroked its stock. He adamantly stated, "James M., I believe this rifle is a little crooked. Really, the barrel seems a little warped. I have no use for a warped rifle. Here, take a look and tell me what you think."

James M. reached for the rifle, bounced it up and down a few times, and then said, "Let me take a look at the barrel. The front sight seems a little off center to me. That's why I like my pistols. Pistols are so much easier to handle. When I shoot someone, that's what I use. They are so much more convenient."

James M. opened his jacket and pulled out two pearl handled pistols. One pistol was snugly tucked in his waist on the left side of his jacket and the other was hidden in his back area, right above his buttocks. He gently placed them on the stool where he was initially sitting. Then he delightfully smiled and picked up the pistol on his right and affectionately said, "I call this one Pearly Mae."

After picking up the pistol on the left, he proudly and affectionately stated, "I call this one, 'Meta Pearl.' In fact, I named her after my favorite aunt. Aunt Meta has always been reliable and protective. She has never let me down."

James M. looked at the crowd and said, "I never leave home without at least one of these. I might not have any drawers on, but I'll always have 'Meta Pearl' with me."

I looked closely at the grip of each pistol and each had the letter "J" beautifully initialed in dark blue. The letter "J" really stood out on the beige/pearl grip panels. The pistols looked like they were brand new. They actually sparkled and glistened in the dusk of the evening. Everyone was extremely quiet and the crowd outside stood motionless and acted as if they were watching an outdoor drama. The *Lost Colony* outdoor drama had nothing on this evening. An element of mystery and climax governed the approaching night. The white guy sat quietly on his stool and began to sweat profusely. He slowly glanced to his right and then to his left. However, he didn't utter a single sentence. I watched as he looked like a small child who had been placed in time-out. The coolness that once exuded his persona had departed. I sensed he could smell the stench of eminent danger.

Then James M. said, "Merendale, you are absolutely right! The barrel or front sight is a little off center. It's a beautiful rifle though. I wonder what a rifle like this cost? Needless, to say, that's the main reason I love my pistols. That's why I love Meta Pearl!"

Merendale, responded with, "Oh! I forgot to check out the trigger. Do you reckon it has a hair-trigger? I wonder if the rifle is loaded, or if it is empty. Oh! Hell, there's only one way to find out."

The makeshift drama became even more terrifying and suspenseful as Merendale took the rifle and pointed it directly at the white guy's zipper area. He inquisitively asked him, "Do you think this rifle is loaded? I don't really know! There just might be a bullet in the magazine. You see, this rifle is brand spanking new. Maybe someone placed a bullet in the chamber, I just don't know! Then again, this rifle is brand spanking new! Maybe, just maybe, it is empty!"

Then all of a sudden, a loud commotion was heard and the people who gathered outside began to move aside. Mable, Merendale's wife, had arrived at the scene. She was angry, extremely angry and hostile. Her sisters, Linda and Mary stood right beside her and they appeared equally as angry. Mable looked at Merendale in a very no-nonsense manner and stated, "You mean to tell me that you'd rather be out here messing with the Klan than to be at home spending time with your two sons. The boys haven't seen you in three months and this is what you choose to do? I had to pay Mr. Roytan a whole dollar bill to come down here. You are going to pay me my dollar back, you hear me? Times are tight and I don't have money to waste trying to keep you out of trouble! You are a grown man, when are you going to grow up?"

The white guy slowly and calculatingly crawled off the stool and headed for the front door. The seat of his coveralls was wet and a trail of urine drained from his right pant leg. He moved with the urgency of an escaped convict. Apparently, God had miraculously intervened. There were those in the crowd who chanted, "Go home Mable! Go home Mable! Go home Mable! Go home Mable!"

The white guy had parked his truck across the road near the East Carolina Bank. It was so funny watching him plow through mud holes and puddles of water as he ran to his truck. He kicked up mud, rocks, and gravel as he made his great escape. Mable continued to fuss Merendale out as he stood holding the rifle. He held the rifle in his left hand as he jingled the coins in his right pocket. Instead of chewing his fingernails as Jody did, Merendale was known to jingle his pocket change when he became extremely angry. When this occurred, someone was sure to experience excruciating pain.

James M. collected his pistols and said, "Man, you know I got your back. I'll go to hell and back with you! We've been through a lot together! However, Mable is a bit too much for me. You need to handle your business. She needs to be put in her place. I tell you what; you can find me in the Towne Tavern if you need me. I'm going to shoot a little pool until I settle down a bit. I gotta do something; my trigger finger is itching terribly. Maybe after eating a couple of Coleman's hotdogs and a few games of pool, the itch will go away. Later!"

It was obvious that Merendale was extremely angry. He looked at Mable, shook his head and said, "Woman, you need to learn your place. I'm coming to see the boys! In fact, I brought them some new school clothes and new sneakers. Now get on out of here; this is grownup business. You need to learn how to control your lip!"

I was shocked, truly astonished that Mable got by with talking to Merendale as she did. Honestly, I was terribly afraid that he was going to take that rifle and pop a cap in her. It was really funny and scary at the same time. However, she was his wife and wives tend to get by with things that other people cannot. Mable held her ground, and thanks to her, no blood was shed. We were momentarily entertained by a serious outdoor drama that did not cost us a single dime. God intervened through Mable, and a life was saved. I readily concluded that God is always amazingly right on time!

Everyone left the store except Mr. Gilbert and a few bystanders waiting around to see if something else was going to go down. I watched as Mr. Gilbert grabbed a mop and swiftly mopped up the urine that leaked from the white guy's pant leg. The Klan members from Alabama, Georgia, and Mississippi didn't return to Mr. Gilbert's store that evening. However, Dirty Harry showed up well after the drama and began talking trash about what he would have done if he had been there. Everyone knew he was more mouth than action. Ben Junior and I went back to the Towne Tavern where many of the bystanders went to simply mingle. As we entered the tavern, Aretha Franklin's *Chain of Fools* bellowed out of the jukebox. Mr. Coleman asked, "Did you boys handle the situation? I didn't want to close down the tavern but if I had I heard any shots fired, I had ole Susie ready. I just cleaned her up last night, so I know she is ready."

I looked at my watch and realized that I needed to go on to Mr. Tony's store before he closed. While walking briskly, we met Cousin Johnnie. He and three white elderly males were standing outside his barbershop. They were looking in the direction of Mr. Gilbert's store trying to figure out what was going on. There were very few blacks in Engelhard who were self-employed. However, Cousin Johnnie was blessed to be one of the select few. He was unquestionably very charismatic and truly pleasant. The apartheid doctrine really availed itself when it came to the haircutting business. The socioeconomics of Hyde County was extremely low.

Blacks, as well as poor whites, rallied to whatever employment opportunities available to maintain a decent living. Jobs were extremely scarce and salaries were at best meager. Cousin Johnnie was insightful enough to go to barber school to avoid a life that was solely dependent upon the hustles of the seafood and the logging industries. It was quite evident that the white status quo monopolized each of the aforementioned employment options. As a means to survive the customary apartheid practices and provide for his family, Cousin Johnnie would cut the hair of white Americans at his mid-Engelhard barbershop, and later cut the hair of black Americans at his home. Whites refused to allow clippers that were used on black hair to touch their head.

Blacks didn't complain about this practice because we all knew that Cousin Johnnie was simply trying to stay afloat just like other blacks. There were valued dividends in going to his home barbershop. As with Mr. Early, Cousin Johnnie was a walking/talking history book. While cutting hair, he would tell jaw dropping stories about life in the 1920s and 1930s with utmost hilarity. Some stories were rather sad; however, for the most part, he worked hard to maintain an optimistic worldview. Honestly, receiving a haircut from him was equivalent to a step-by-step journey into the life and times of the Great Depression.

Cousin Johnnie would speak of President Franklin D. Roosevelt as if he knew him personally. Smiles would govern his face as he addressed his personal perspective on the "New Deal." Stories told in the barbershop were often rendered in parables and my friends and I would be compelled to search for inner-meaning. At times, it was a challenge to gain true meaning from the cerebral hidden messages within his narratives. When his daughter, Linda, cooked muffins, the front door would customarily open and we would receive a much appreciated sweet treat. Everyone loved Cousin Johnnie because he epitomized class and integrity. Linda was always an amazing breath of fresh air. Her smile was consistently invigorating and she always smelled like a most perfect rose. She truly epitomized class and sophistication.

After exchanging pleasantries, Ben Junior and I needed to get home before it got dark. We ran to Mr. Tony Spencer's store to buy more cheese and then caught a ride back to the Ridge with "Big Lightning." Big Lightning smoked a big cigar; therefore, his car smelled like smoke. He was approximately 6' 6" tall and weighed about 365 pounds and could move like a much smaller man.

The guys on the Ridge would jokingly call him Rosey Grier, a professional football who played for the New York Giants and Los Angeles Rams. "Big Lightning" was a gentle giant and we had utmost respect for him. Ben Junior couldn't stand cigarette or cigar smoke because of asthma. However, neither one of us was brave enough to ask him to put out the cigar. Then again, it was indeed his car and he should be able to do whatever he desired to do. I was simply glad to get out of Engelhard in a whole piece.

When we arrived at the Ridge Store, Dallas and Ben Howard were standing near the pole light smoking cigarettes. We considered these guys "big guys" and our mentors. We had so much respect for them that it seemed if they were our older brothers. Dallas always called me "Prez" and he adored my older sister, Linda. He actually treated me as if I were his biological younger brother. He would occasionally buy me Cokes and honey buns while in the Ridge Store. I would always tell Linda, and she would customarily say, "Oh! That is so sweet!"

Ben Howard was a relentless prankster; he always made me terribly nervous. His skinny physique and boney fingers shouldn't have made me so uneasy. However, he was one of the older guys on the Ridge and with that age difference came unparalleled respect. He was a proud member of the group that we called "The Untouchables." Roytan Junior, Claudie James, Roy Lee, Dallas, Ervin, and Boss Hawg were honored members of this elite group. They towered over us and we responded to them as if they were renowned gangsters from Harlem. A simple hello from them meant that we were no longer invisible. We esteemed these guys as if they could were disciples of Christ. They were our mentors and our protectors.

# CHAPTER 12
# IF I COULD TURN BACK THE HANDS OF TIME

***Think like a queen. A queen is not afraid to fail. Failure is another steppingstone to greatness.***

***—Oprah Winfrey***

Ben Junior beckoned me to follow him. We went around to the back of the Ridge Store. There were six large paint buckets lined up against a green storage house. I thought to myself, Mr. Robert must be planning to paint the Ridge Store again. Then Ben Junior lifted the lid of each bucket to show me that each one contained three large balloons filled with urine. He smiled and said, "Man each bucket is coded with the first letter of the owner's name. I don't know about you; but, I don't want to handle anybody else's pee. Really, I don't even want to handle my own. We are really going to surprise the Klan today. Once this day-old pee hits them, they're going to leave Hyde County for good. They'll be like soaking wet skunks. We won't have to worry about the Klan ever again!"

I patted down my pockets and noted that I had left my pack of BBs on the counter in the Ridge store. As I reentered the store, we noticed two old white American males standing in front of Mr. George Hill asking for directions to get to Middleton. Each of them wore green Army camouflage attire. They wore black military boots and white t-shirts. The back of each t-shirt was covered with a picture of a large Confederate flag. The sleeves of each t-shirt were embroidered with the letters KKK in small black letters. Mr. George Hill appeared a rather nervous but painstakingly told them how to get to Middleton. He stuttered several times before he was able to complete a logical sentence. In fact, he reminded me of Dave Junior, my Cousin Hannah's boyfriend. Nevertheless, the white guys politely thanked Mr. George Hill by saying, "Thank you very much for the directions. You boys have a good day."

Joseph was turning the knob to enter the store as the two old guys were exiting. He accidentally bumped into the older man and said, "Excuse me. I didn't know you were trying to come outside."

The two old guys looked at Joseph very hatefully and rolled their eyes. Sammie smiled at Joseph and jokingly yelled, "Gosh! Jid, you are about to get a beat-down by two senior citizens."

Joseph laughed and responded with, "Man, those two old goons don't want none of this. They better creep on to that old station wagon before they forget how to drive."

All of the guys began to chuckle. Mr. George Hill walked to a side window of the store and noted that traffic was extra heavy en route to Middleton. I walked to the window and looked out as well. Cars were slowing down to make the right turn to go Middleton just as Ben Junior had predicted. Sammie enthusiastically asked, "Brothers are we ready?"

The Ridge Store was surrounded by tall corn fields. A small ditch served as drainage during heavy rains. Ben Junior told us to get our paint buckets and place them about eight feet apart from each other. I didn't have a paint bucket. However, I had two slingshots, ten rocks, five oyster shells, and my high-powered BB gun.

We stationed ourselves about eight feet apart from each other. The paint buckets containing the urine were placed at the foot of each respective owner. Ben Junior counted to three and on three everyone stretched out in the small ditch near Highway 264. The long convoy of cars was coming quickly and purposely. After waiting for about three minutes, Ben Junior said, "When I call out ONE! TWO! THREE! I want you to throw your balloons on THREE."

We waited another three minutes and then Ben Junior yelled out very slowly, "ONE! TWO! THREE!"

Everyone threw their balloons and some of them landed on the Klan rally's Grand Marshall. The Grand Marshall was being chauffeured in a white station wagon that was decorated with four highly visible Confederate flags. A huge white German shepherd stood tall in the backseat of the station wagon and appeared to canvass the entire landscape as he barked relentlessly. The German shepherd's stomach area was wrapped in a tailored Confederate flag. The dog looked vicious, barked continuously, and appeared to have a low tolerance for onlookers. He appeared eager and overly anxious to dig his sharp teeth into some black meat.

I had been told that dogs are color blind; however, after experiencing this day of reckoning, I concluded that someone did not complete their research. I watched in anxious anticipation as day-old urine splashed on the Grand Marshall and drenched the windshield. The front seat of the station wagon was left soaking wet. It was a terribly smelly and nasty scene. Some of the urine from the balloons left the head and chest area of the German shepherd soaking wet. The dog blinked and barked more and more aggressively after being drenched in the day-old stinking urine. Then all of a sudden, the dog stood still momentarily and began to shake violently. While shaking violently, the dog was able to shake the urine off him. However, it landed perfectly on the Grand Marshall and he was furious. His face and eyebrows looked as if he had just gotten caught in a terrible rainstorm. It was rather funny watching the urine drip from his earlobes. I watched the Grand Marshall and the German shepherd attentively.

After the balloons landed on the Grand Marshall, the entire Klan convoy stopped immediately. As I hid in the small ditch, I heard tires squealing and doors slamming. I peeped up and saw Klansmen jumping out of the motorcade brandishing shotguns, rifles, and pistols. Ben Junior yelled, "Man, I believe one of those dudes has a hand grenade. I'm out of here!"

It was comparable to the day that President Kennedy was shot. The motorcade had the feel of nobility or presidency. The Grand Dragon personified someone of great royalty and the regular Klansmen appeared to be his armor guard. The Pope, himself, could not have been treated with greater reverence. The motorcade flaunted Confederate flags as if they symbolized a badge of exclusivity and honor. The bodyguards looked like weightlifters or bouncers and showcased a serious no-nonsense demeanor. They appeared to be on a mission to serve and protect.

I was absolutely scared stiff. I didn't know what to do. Then I heard one of the Klansmen say, "I tell you what. Let's let Old Hitler loose and let him deal with these koons. These spooks won't forget this day!"

I was so scared that I was trembling and my legs felt momentarily paralyzed. Larry heard the Klansman and jumped up and took off running. Old Hitler took off after him, barking and eventually grabbed his pant leg. Larry fell down screaming, "Help! Help! Somebody, please, please help me!"

I heard Judith, Larry's sister, crying and yelling, "Let my brother go! Leave him alone!"

Apparently, Old Hitler's owner felt sorry for Larry. He whistled real loudly and yelled, "Hitler, here boy! Here! Here boy! Let that Piccaninny go right now! Let him go!"

Old Hitler completely ignored Larry and ran back to his master. As he returned to his master, Richard, Sammie, Ben Junior, Lonnie, Raymond, Joseph, and Ben Junior took off through the corn field that surrounded the Ridge Store. Byron ran into a green storage building on the back of the store. Mr. George Hill closed the front door to the Ridge Store and hid behind the counter. He appeared to be equally as petrified as we were. I elected to take off through the pea field since the Ridge Store was no longer an option. I was really scared and I honestly didn't know whether the Klan was going to shoot me in my back or sic Old Hitler on me. I was running with all my heart and then I looked around and noticed that a huge white guy was dead on my heels. As I looked around, I lost my balance and fell to my knees. The huge white guy yelled, "Get up boy! Get up! Get up right now and put your hands in the air. I don't want to waste a bullet on you!"

I was so scared that I was trembling uncontrollably. I actually urinated on myself and I wasn't ashamed to the least bit. My young life was at stake and I wasn't ready to die. Then I heard Mrs. Lizzie exclaim, "Oh Lord! The Klan has gotten Johnson's boy. Please help him God; please help him! Almighty God, please spare these boys! They knew not what they were doing! Please help them, Almighty God!"

Seemingly the entire Ridge Community had come together near Rev. Mackey's barbershop. Mrs. Bessie Mackey saw me with my hands raised in the air and walking out of the pea field. She began to pray, "Merciful God, we need you now! We need you to intervene for these young boys. We ask you to protect them from all harm and danger. Please spare the lives of these young boys. They know not what they do! Please place your protective arms around them. I pray this prayer in the name of the Father, the Son, and the Holy Ghost. Amen!"

I looked around and saw Raymond, Lonnie, Joseph, Richard, Byron, Larry, Ben Junior, and Sammie standing in line with their hands in the air as well. We looked like harden criminals in a lineup at a police department. I was too scared to think about my self-esteem. I was filthy dirty from falling on my knees and I had torn a hole in the knee of my trousers when I hit the ground. My drawers were soaking wet from peeing on myself, but that did not matter at all. We all looked like we had just gotten off a slave ship and were en route to a slave trade or auction. Nevertheless, the fear factor compelled me to forget about my state of filthiness. My ultimate interest centered on survival. It was truly an eerie feeling!

Then a huge white guy wearing a blue blazer, white shirt, skinny black tie, and black pants, silenced Mrs. Bessie Mackey and displayed his badge. He politely said, "Ma'am, I am Captain Osborn of the FBI and I am here, undercover, to protect law abiding citizens from the likes of the Ku Klux Klan. However, the KKK has not broken a single law. Needless to say, these boys have, and I have to do my job. You see ma'am, the Klan has a right to assemble and they even have a permit to march. The Second Amendment (Amendment II) to the United States Constitution even protects the right of the Klan to keep and bear arms. You see the right to bear arms is 1 covered in the United Sates Bill of Rights. Even though I may not support some of the Klan's practices, they still have rights. It is my job to protect law abiding citizens and the United States Constitution. I have to enforce the law; that's my job. And I take honor in doing my job well."

Mrs. Bessie Mackey pleaded with the FBI agent as she said, "Sir, please don't take these young boys to jail. They're just boys! They didn't really know what they were doing. Can't you give them a break?"

Then she shook her head and began singing *Amazing Grace.* It was the most meaningful and powerful rendition of the song that I had ever heard. Tears crowded her eyes as she passionately sang, "*Amazing Grace, how sweet the sound; that saved a wretch like me.... I once was lost but now am found; was blind, but now, I see.*"

I lost my composure and began to cry. I couldn't lower my arms to wipe my tears away because I was afraid of being shot by either the Klan or the FBI. I wasn't going to take any chances. I looked around and the black shoe polish that we used as war paint had transitioned into charcoal teardrops. We looked an absolute mess! Captain Osborn became teary-eyed as Mrs. Bessie sang *Amazing Grace.* He listened attentively throughout the song and never interrupted her. He appeared to have a level of Christianity about him. When he regained his composure, he passionately stated, "I'll talk to the head of the Klan and see if they want to press charges. The fate of these boys actually lies in the hands of the Klan."

Richard, Sammie, Ben Junior, Byron, Raymond, Joseph, Larry, Lonnie, and I continued to stand with our hands stuck up straight in the air. My arms were getting tired and heavy; however, I was too afraid to lower them. We were all sweating like run-away slaves and we really didn't know whether we were going to jail or prison. I really didn't want to be handcuffed and placed in a police cruiser. As we stood, I heard Lonnie crying and saying, "I don't want to go to jail! I look too good to go to jail! I know what they will try to do to me, if I go to jail!"

Agent Osborn walked across Highway 264 and talked with three very angry, huge Klansmen. I could not hear them very well; however, hand motions and finger-pointing told me that this was a very serious matter. After about twenty minutes of standing with our hands in the air, Agent Osborn returned and told us that the Klan elected to not press charges, this time. He stated that he had virtually pleaded and begged the Grand Dragon to give us a break. Then he looked at Mrs. Bessie Mackey and stated that we would be released to the supervision of our parents. Just as Agent Osborn turned toward us and was about to give a lecture, a guy in a blue suit rushed to him and said, "Captain, there is a shootout taking place right now near the Klan rally in Middleton. We need to get there; we need to get there in a hurry."

Agent Osborn completely forgot about our skirmish with the Klan and hopped in a black unmarked police cruiser and headed to Middleton. We finally lowered our arms and gave a big sigh of relief. Shortly thereafter, Meat Ball drove up in his old green pickup truck and yelled, "The Klan shot at Betty Lou and Wardella. It's on now! Hell just broke loose! Walter Thomas, George Thomas, Charlie James, Edward Brown, John Thomas, Bobby, and I are on our way there right now to get the Klan straight!"

I was about to hop in the pickup truck and ride to Middleton with Meat Ball when Mr. Herman grabbed my shoulder and sternly said, "Son, this is grown folk's business. You boys better back off. You need more than B-B guns, slingshots, and rocks to deal with the Klan. These are dangerous times."

Meat Ball pulled off in his pickup truck squealing tires and kicking up rocks. Mr. Herman shook his head and said, "I can smell trouble and it is really brewing. This seventy-two year old nose doesn't fool me. Trouble is right around the corner and the smell is rotten. Henry, you need to go on home right now. In fact, take the shortcut by Heddie's house. That's the safest way for you to get home this evening. You don't have to worry about the Klan meeting you through the woods today; they're all in Middleton. Go on now! Run on home and be careful!"

I took off running as fast as I could. Nevertheless, my heart was actually in Middleton and I really wanted to be in the mix. As I looked back, I saw a convoy of cars en route to Middleton. I saw truckloads of black people with shotguns, handguns, and rifles en route to Middleton to retaliate the firing at Wardella and Betty Lou. It was a very strange evening and the eeriness became even more pronounce as the onset of darkness began to blanket the sky. A dark cloud covered the sky and shades of grey governed the galaxy. The dark shades of grey were reminiscent of a solar eclipse. An eerie feeling captured my emotions and the darkness of the afternoon created a sense of despair and restlessness. There was something about this day that was unsettling and uncomfortable. I could not make meaning of this uneasy state of being. I glanced at the chill bumps on my arms and noted that the thin hairs stood tall. My heart palpitated uncontrollably and a cold sweat covered my body. I was terribly thirsty but I had nothing to drink.

As I approached Ms. Heddie's house, I noticed Eunice and Charles (Red) putting wood on her porch. There were two guys in the neighborhood named Charles. One was very short, so we called him "Little Charles." He never bothered anyone and he was very likable. Now the other Charles was very mischievous. We called him 'Red' because he was very light-skinned. Eunice looked up at me and said, "Junior, you better get on home before the Klan gets you. You know they are supposed to burn a cross tonight."

Charles didn't speak to me at all but when Eunice turned her back, he gave me the middle finger on each hand and then show-cased a very conniving smile. The only places that I had ever seen Charles before was in his yard, on the school bus, on the campus of Davis School, and at church on second Sundays. Ms. Jeanie, his grandmother, would allow him to go to church and then he had to return home, immediately. Red was filled with mischief. When I would pass by his house, en route to the Ridge Store, he would throw rocks and oyster shells at me, and then hide inside their outside toilet.

One day, he clocked me real hard with an oyster shell. Then he ran and sat on the porch beside Ms. Jeanie as if he had not done anything. After doing that, he had the nerve to give me the middle finger. Eunice said that her mother thought the neighbor-hood boys were a bad influence of Charles. Even though Red had clocked me with an oyster shell, I ignored the incident because my mind was so centered on the Klan. I could not fathom why the Klan hated black people with such tenacity.

After a night of intense restlessness, I learned the next day that there was a dangerous shootout in Middleton between the Ku Klux Klan and black Americans. The Klan showcased heavy artillery at the shootout. And the blacks appeared to be going on a deer hunt or rabbit hunt expedition. Their weaponry and ammunition was an insult to makeshift warfare. The Klan appeared to have planned and prepared for the unknown. However, the few blacks who had shown up for the skirmish appeared to be without any semblance of a plan. They didn't have enough weaponry or ammunition for a five-minute assault. The Klan had assault rifles, automatic rifles, and semi-automatic handguns; while blacks had single-shot twenty-two rifles, single and double barrel shotguns and very little ammunition. It was almost as if the blacks were bringing knives to a gunfight. The black community was extremely poor, but had the heart of a lion.

Meat Ball said he hid behind a big pine tree as he emptied his twenty-two pistol. He said the Klan was firing automatic weaponry so viciously that bark from the pine above his head covered his cap. He indicated that he was so anxious to get to the shootout that he left his bullets in the glove compartment of his truck. As bullets whistled and roared near his head, he didn't know what to do. He quietly watched as George Thomas and Charlie James fired their rifles at anything that moved. They eventually gave out of bullets and had no choice but to lie on their stomachs until the firing ceased. George Thomas, Meat Ball's brother, described the shootout at the Klan rally as a scene in *Harlem Nights*; a 1989 comedy-drama crime film starring Richard Pryor and Eddie Murphy.

He told me that he wasn't much of a praying man. However, when bullets began to strip bark from the tree limbs above his head, his only option was prayer. George Thomas said branches slowly fell from the old oak like a mid-December snow. And bark popped off the old oak like sparks from a welding torch. Charlie James described the loud noise of fire power was deafening and the thought of dying became really real. He indicated that he momentarily froze for a few minutes and then all of the sudden, gunfire ceased. He said the silence was nothing less than music to his ears.

The Klan could have slaughtered all of the blacks at the shootout; however, God intervened and the skirmish subsided. Several individuals were shot; however, no lives were lost. My friend, Debra Ann, a twelve- year-old classmate of my younger sister, Vanessa, was shot in her thigh. I went to see her the day after the shooting. She was resting at home in the living room with her leg elevated. She looked at me and asked, "Henry, where were you yesterday? You weren't too scared to come out were you? I tell you, if I knew then, what I know now, I would have kept my big butt right here at home with Mom Pencie. It was like watching *The Wild Wild West* or a shootout at the *High Chaparra*l. Henry I was so, so, scared. I actually thought I was going to die."

I asked Debra, "What was it like being shot?

She frowned and sadly stated, "Well, it felt like someone had shot a streak of fire through my thigh. I really didn't know what had happened until I saw the blood! That's when I really got scared and the pain became more real. It was like a streak of fire had run in and out of my thigh. It's nothing that I ever want to experience again. It pains mostly at night when I am trying sleep."

I told Debra Ann that I wanted to go to Middle Creek with Meat Ball but Mr. Herman told me to go home. He said he could smell trouble and it wasn't safe for me to get caught up in that mess. Mr. Herman told me to be obedient and go home. My parents told me to always respect my elders. So I listened and I obeyed."

Debra Ann laughed and shared, "I was told that Captain Harry was shot in his buttocks at the shootout. I don't remember seeing him, but that doesn't mean he wasn't there. Meat Ball said Capt. Harry can't even sit down comfortably to count his money. Well, I know how my thigh aches at times, and if he was shot in his buttocks, I tell you Henry, he is in a lot of pain."

Rumors circulated that Captain Harry was the Klan ringleader in Hyde County. It was hard to believe because he was one of the main employers of black women in the county. He would customarily strut around in his big fancy cars and act as if he owned the entire county. My mom worked at the Engelhard Crab House and I would periodically go there early Saturday mornings to get money for a haircut. Then again, there were times when she would give me money to go out to Mr. Tony Spencer's General Store to pay on her credit account. I really didn't care to be around Captain Harry because he made me feel very, very, uneasy. He would stare at me as if he believed I was going to steal a crab or two. He wouldn't even speak to me or ask me if he could help me. He simply stared at me in a very repulsive manner.

I enjoyed going to the Crab House because all the women would be dressed in white and they would tell mom that I am a good-looking young man. Mrs. Josephine, the head crab picker, would occasionally hug me and put a dollar bill in my hand at the same time. Back in those days, a dollar bill went a long ways. Cousin Mary Jane was a loyal crab worker as well. She would call me over to her working area, ask me about school, and then she would look around and place a dollar or two in my hand. However, Captain Harry would simply look at me in a very revolting manner. On one occasion, he told everyone to stop momentarily, and then he reminded everyone to keep their children out of the working area. He said the inspector would close him down if kids roamed in and out of the workplace. Then he adamantly stated, "This is not a place for kids. It's not sanitary!"

After Captain Harry made his announcement, he cleared his throat, spit some tobacco juice in the middle floor drainage system, and stuck a big cigar in his mouth. He personified Jackie Gleason's role in *Smokey and the Bandit* (Sheriff Buford T. Justice). Captain Harry had his twisted ways; however, there were occasions when he spoke with amazing logic.

During an early Monday morning meeting with his employees, who were primarily black American females, he gave a profound speech about the nature of black Americans. Captain Harry unapologetically stated, "One of the major problems with the colored race is that y'all don't work together. I have seen on many occasions when y'all go to Swan Quarter to pick up your welfare food, y'all won't even look out for each other. Y'all will drive five or six different cars to pick of the food when you could put your monies together and send two cars to get the job done. It's like y'all don't trust each other. It's like you are afraid someone is going to get ahead of you. Well, with us, white people, we may not like each other; however, when it comes to saving a dollar or two, we will work together. Y'all will always be behind the eight ball as long as you act like my crabs, the very same thing that you pick each and every day. Y'all have seen how my crabs act when they are taken off boats and placed in the cooker. They are constantly moving and when one crab is lucky enough to get to the top of the cooker, and is about to climb out, another crab will immediately grab that crab and bring it back with the rest of the crabs. That's just the way, you colored people behave."

Captain Harry made a great deal of sense with his remarks. His choice of words could have been more polished; however, there were absolute truths in his message. He had his low tolerances but he was a man of wisdom as well. After Debra Ann was shot in her thigh and Captain Harry was shot in his buttocks, the relationship between blacks and whites in Hyde County became more tolerable.

Nevertheless, blacks across the nation began to cry *Soul Power* and *Black Power.* The Reverend Jesse Jackson began to assert himself as the central voice for black America. Of course, there were those who denounced Jackson's world view. Needless to say, the late sixties and early seventies were at best a time of relentless turmoil and cries for change. The Vietnam War was at its height and tension between blacks and whites was in its incubation stage.

At heart, I could not fathom why there was a need for the desegregation of public schools. To me, blacks and whites had gotten along quite well in their respective schools. I wondered why, all of a sudden, public schools were being mandated to desegregate. There was a serious fear of the unknown and blacks feared that being compelled to desegregate public schools carried a serious hidden agenda. The idea of desegregating the public schools of Hyde County created a high level of hysteria between the races. Blacks were in the initial stage of embracing the national Black Power Movement and whites were apprehensive about its intent.

My friends and I gravitated to notions about black solidarity and were optimistic that the "new norm" would provide a higher level of equity with regard to race matters. Nevertheless, the prevailing standard of "majority rule" was not going to vanish without challenge. The status quo was not going to give up their privileges and disenfranchised blacks were demanding equity on the new landscape. The late 1960s and early 1970s was an era of relentless national turmoil. The daily tug-a-war between the races was essentially uncompromising.

I watched in amazement as my friends and I adopted the "natural look" and worked extremely hard to model brotherhood and solidarity. This was not a blatant assault on "white America," it was a symbolic tolling of the bell for "black America" to rise up against the "old norm" and embrace a serious paradigm shift. Proponents of the "new norm" were happy with a gradual change in the way America conducted business. This gradual change would begin with miniscule, yet gargantuan, changes such as the practice of having duo waiting areas to see medical doctors, separate water fountains, separate restrooms, and the option to sit wherever one desires when it came to public transportation.

The Ku Klux Klan denounced any scenario that supported the mingling of the races. They advocated the belief that blacks and whites should live in their respected neighborhoods and only interact with each other when deemed necessary to conduct business. Even in such instances, blacks were expected to be passive participants, and whites were to assert themselves as being "in charge." The Klan were inflexible and verbally admonished white Americans who appeared to be "too friendly with blacks." They viewed the relationships as unhealthy and believed they would lead to the demise of the established hierarchical order. The United Klan of America possessed dire hatred for blacks, poor whites, Mexicans, Latinos, and other minority populations.

## CHAPTER 13
# A STATE OF DENIAL

***For unto whomever much is given, of him shall be much required.***

***—Luke 12: 48, KJ***

The late'60s Klan uprising in Hyde County and the entire nation brought about a great deal of hysteria and anxiety within the black community. Black people were in serious search of their place of fit in American Society. After the death of Dr. King in 1968, blacks in Hyde County and the nation as a whole became more vigilant and sensitive to acts of discrimination. The formulation of the Kool Kolored Kidz was simply a means to alleviate the hysteria and uneasiness that often came with the proclamation of planned Klan activity. Even though the formulation of the Kool Kolored Kidz was supposed to be an "underground," secretive organization, most of my friends who lived in area communities wanted to join and become active members. We (the founding fathers) were all in middle school or high school and didn't really know how to respond to all the attention that we were receiving.

Fellow schoolmates would pass us down the halls of Davis School and raise their fists and yell, "Black Power."

Some would ball their fists as a sign of solidarity and yell, "Soul Power!" Others would simply yell, "Power to the People!"

The middle to late 1960s was a serious time of unrest and the redefining of an all-inclusive American society. The black community was restless because we didn't know where we fit the new paradigm shift. We were seeking identity in popular culture that appeared to be at peace with the status quo. In response to the paradigm shift, black Americans, elected to embrace the "natural look."

Afros basically put bootleg barbers out of business. Huge afros gave homage to black American's African ancestry. It was as if there was a grand epiphany that validated the notion that being black was not a curse, it was God's doing. And God didn't make a mistake, it was His will. The showcasing of the raised fist was simply emblematic of black solidarity. It showcased brotherhood and sisterhood with utmost honor. Being black took on new meaning and the notion of acceptance versus tolerance carried unprecedented significance.

Gold medalist, Tommie Smith and Bronze medalist John Carlos created a national uproar when they raised their fist while at the podium after the 200m in the 1968 Summer Olympics. As they turned to face the United Sates flags and heard the *Star-Spangled Banner,* they each raised a black-gloved fist and kept them raised until the anthem had finished. The late 1960s was indeed a time of local and national unrest. Black solidarity was in its embryonic stage.

Mr. Boone, principal of Davis High, became a little concerned about the power and influence of the Kool Kolored Kidz. Davis High was an all-black school and the only school in Engelhard that blacks could attend. In light of this, we (Kool Kolored Kidz) were not interested in creating havoc in our one and only institution of learning. Martin and Miguel had instituted a strict discipline code and each of us pledged to be model students. We didn't care to deal with the wrath of Martin and Miguel because of actions unbecoming of a Kool Kolored Kid.

We prided ourselves on being disciplined and devoid of temptation. Martin had molded us to be caring and conscientious brothers who took delight in protecting the black community. There were occasions when we had our in-house differences in opinion; however, by the end of each meeting, all differences were resolved. Mr. Boone worked tirelessly to infiltrate us, but he could never crack our cover. On most occasions, he would randomly choose someone who really didn't know anything at all about the plans of the Kool Kolored Kidz.

Mr. Boone took a particular interest in interrogating and harassing Ben Junior and Donald White. For some unknown reason, he gravitated to opportunities to antagonize each of these guys. Nevertheless, Ben Junior was always cerebral enough to stay a step or two ahead of him. I will never forget one morning sitting on the school bus next to Ben Junior when he said, "Watch this! When I get off the bus, I'm going to drop my books right in front of Mr. Boone's wingtips. Watch what he says! I guarantee you; he is going to try to belittle me. He is always trying to embarrass me when there is a throng of students nearby."

I could never understand why Mr. Boone sought opportunities to target Donald. There were very few light-skinned brothas at Davis High and Donald was indeed a member of that minority group. His brother, Anthony, belonged to that minority population as well. Donald and Anthony readily stood out among everyone in an ocean of darkness. They were like lightning bugs in the dark of night and when they elected to engage in mischievous behavior, everyone knew about it. Several of my so-called friends actually hated-on them because of their complexion. When they visited O.A. Peay, the area rival black school, mostly all of the males looked at them with utmost disdain. However, nearly all of the females treated them as if they were celebrities. Donald and Anthony never ever bothered anyone. Nevertheless, they received a tremendous amount of lukewarm embraces from blacks who were of a darker hue.

It appeared that black folks in the early 1960s had a serious prejudice against blacks who were born with highly pronounced Eurocentric traits such long hair, thin lips, and light skin. Dark-skinned brothas and sistas were often referred to as Jiggaboos and light-skinned blacks were stereotyped as "white wannabees." I often wondered why Mr. Boone gave Donald and Anthony so much grief. Estelle Boone, his wife, was so light-skinned that she could pass for a white American female in a heartbeat. She was my seventh grade teacher and I truly loved her. Of course, there were many students who didn't my opinion. She intimidated the Jiggaboos as well as the white wannabees. It was without question, Mr. Boone was seriously afraid of her. I believe Mike Tyson would have been afraid of Mrs. Boone. Mathew Lee told me that she unequivocally wore the big "drawers" in that marriage.

One morning, as we got off the school bus, Mr. Boone stood tall near the end of the hall with his huge right hand resting on the ice cream refrigerator. A huge round clock slowly ticked on the wall behind his head. Mr. Adams held the hall mop tightly and patiently waited for us to clear the halls so he could mop away the debris that we brought into the hallway. We all laughed and talked as we made our way to our respective classrooms. The school environment was a social venue as well as a place for academic learning. Smiles graced our faces and a state of innocence resonated from wall to wall. We were young and extremely naïve about the perils of life.

However, the Black Power Movement was in its incubation stage and we were excited about the unknown. Several of my schoolmates began to grow afros and dress like Malcolm X and Angela

Davis. My friend, Donald, had several uncles who lived in New York. They were really into male fashions and styles commonly seen in Harlem. Donald's uncle, Perry, sent him a black plastic Soul Power fist attached to a fake gold chain and he wore it fashionably on a daily basis. There were times when he didn't have a pencil or pen; however, he was never without his plastic "Soul Power" fist. He acted as if it gave him a serious rite of passage.

Anthony, Donald's younger brother, delighted in wearing dashikis and tiny wire-framed sunglasses. Mr. Boone stayed on Anthony's case for wearing his sunglasses down the halls and in class. Anthony declared that he had a visual perception problem, but no one believed him. He looked very militant with his huge afro and tiny wire-framed glasses. He projected the image that most black aspired to portray. Anthony was cool, real cool! Some of my classmates were wondering if he were trying to emulate Ringo Starr of the *Beatles* or Clarence Williams III, Linc, of the popular television show, *Mod Squad.*

Donald and Anthony embodied blackness to the tenth degree. Some of the brothas envied them because when we went on class trips, seemingly all the pretty girls gravitated to them. They unapologetically made their own fashion statements and didn't really care who approved or disapproved. Being poor and living in the "Dirty South" didn't accord us much flexibility when it came to contemporary male fashions. As long as our private parts were covered, we didn't complain about clothes.

It appeared that Mr. Boone looked for reasons to chastise Donald and Anthony. He would purposely target them when they entered the school building. I watched from afar as he often ridiculed the guys by saying, "Alright, you boys get on to class! This is not a time for lollygagging. You should have done that at home! Move it! Get on to class!"

Mr. Boone possessed a very heavy bass voice and it was quite distinctive and intimidating. For the most part, I avoided direct interaction with him. Since I was getting off the school bus and he was standing at the end of the hall, I had no recourse but to pass him. Ben Junior sarcastically said, "Good Morning Mr. Boone! How are you today?"

He responded with, "Phelps, I'm not in for your mess today. I suggest that you get to class right now! And I mean right now! Don't try to play me! I'll send you home packing, quick, fast, and in a hurry! This is not the day to try me! Now, get on to class!"

Ben Junior sadly nodded his head and kept on walking. I concluded that he actually looked up to Mr. Boone and a sense of mutual respect was ever present. When Martin and Miguel got off the school bus, Mr. Boone used his bass voice and yelled down the hall, "Collins and Whitfield, in my office now! I mean right now! Move it!"

Mr. Boone had the persona of Joe Clark. When I watched *Lean on Me* starring Morgan Freeman, I immediately thought of him. I concluded that Joe Clark must have been a disciple of his because their response to "blackness" and stomping out stereotypes were amazingly similar. Joe Clark as well as Mr. Boone refused to accept excuses for mediocrity and they espoused high expectations for all students. Their tough-love leadership style was not wholeheartedly embraced. However, our school halls were not inundated with male students wearing their pants without belts showcasing their underwear. I often reflected on Mr. Boone's disposition when I became an educator.

After he summoned Martin and Miguel to his office, I looked at Ben Junior and he simply shook his head. Then he said, "I guess he is going to interrogate them about the Kool Kolored Kidz. When they finish playing mind games with Mr. Bone, he'll call Mrs. Lula and have her announce on the intercom that today will be an early dismissal. They can handle their own!"

After about twenty minutes, Martin and Miguel were discharged from Mr. Boone's office. They were full of smiles and appeared totally unaffected by the call to the office. A call to Mr. Boone's office always made me perspire heavily. I spoke with Martin about his call to the office and he indicated that Mr. Boone tried extremely hard to interrogate him about the "so-called Kool Kolored Kidz."

Martin indicated that Mr. Boone adamantly stated that he would hold him primarily responsible for any unrest that took place at Davis School. He further encouraged him to walk the straight and narrow because he was going to keep a keen eye on him. Miguel said when Mr. Boone asked him about the Kool Kolored Kidz, he responded with, "Mr. Boone, the notion of strategically organizing an organization of this magnitude would require an in-depth knowledge of public school law and the allowances thereof."

Miguel said that Mr. Boone got really angry with him and admonished, "Miguel, you try to be a little smart rodent. You can use your three and four syllable words; however, I have your number and when you and Martin slip, I am going to ship you out of here before Joe Tex can say, 1-2-3."

I was utterly shocked because I didn't think Mr. Boone knew anything about Joe Tex. Then I jokingly asked Ben Junior, "Do you think he knows about *Skinny Legs and All* and *Hold What You've Got*?"

Martin told me that Mr. Boone asked if Alice and Hilda were culprits in this "dysfunctional group of thugs." He said that he told him that he really didn't know what he was talking about. And that he only sees them at school, just like he sees all the rest of the students. It appeared that Mr. Boone was taking precautionary measures to curtail the potential of anarchy at Davis School. His anxiety was high due to fear of the unknown. The customary compliant Negro had bitten the dust and the new Negro appeared to be "unchained."

The onset of the Black Power Movement made many "old school" black educators very uncomfortable. They became highly pessimistic because "old guard" blacks had made significant strides between the 1940s and early 1950s. It was now the late 1960s and the "new guard Negroes" commonly called *militant blacks* were "off the chain" and ran the risk of usurping pass progress due to their perceived arrogance and lack of respect. The aforementioned disposition made Mr. Boone and his colleagues very, very, uncomfortable. A new day had dawn and they felt like Rip Van Winkle. The resounding question was, "Where is their place of fit?"

# CHAPTER 14
# SOMEDAY WE'LL BE TOGETHER

***If we are going to think black, think positive about it. Don't think down on it, or think it is something in your way. And this way, when you really do want to stretch out and express how beautiful black is, everybody will hear you.***

***—Leontyne Price***

It was quite amazing how the Black Power Movement manifested itself in the dirty south. The brotherhood at Davis School was terribly alarming. Seemingly, everyone was experiencing a renewed sense of belonging and acceptance. Black communities in Hyde County were nothing less than villages of wannabe fraternities and sororities with endless lines of pledges. At the forefront of this new societal order was the Kool Kolored Kidz. We conducted ourselves as serious brothas of purpose and cause. Martin and Miguel worked hard to personify a disposition of intellect, commitment, and undying allegiance.

They did not want the Kool Kolored Kidz to become just a group of guys hanging together engaging in mischievous behavior. Davis School played a vital role in providing a landscape for social change. I will never forget one morning at Davis School when Ben Junior and I were accosted by Alice and Hilda. Alice politely asked, "May I speak with you guys for a few minutes before class begins? Henry, don't try to play any mind games with me. I know how you can be! As with most of the students and some teachers on campus, I've heard rumors about the Kool Kolored Kidz! I know it is supposed to be secretive; however, I hear things! I hear a lot of things! So don't try to play me!"

Ben Junior interrupted her and adamantly stated, "Ladies, I have no idea what you're talking about! Mr. Boone tried to corner me about the same thing yesterday. I wish I could tell you more, but this is news to me as well."

Hilda irritably interrupted Ben Junior and boldly stated, "Look, we aren't trying to infiltrate your organization. Alice and I have been talking and we want to put together a female group or organization similar to your so-called 'underground' organization. Well, to tell the truth, Virginia and Bernice actually came up with the idea. Since you guys don't want any females in your *little* group, we thought we would organize our own. You probably don't recognize it, but black females are terribly discriminated against every single day. You should listen to some of the speeches by Angela Davis. That sista speaks the truth! And we need to organize the sistas before this thing called 'desegregation' occurs."

Alice responded with, "Henry, can't you all just help us get started? We aren't asking for any of your secrets. We're simply trying to put together a little sisterhood before you all are forced to go to Mattamuskeet School. You all aren't going to have the solidarity at Mattamuskeet that you currently having here.

Hilda adamantly stated, "I am sure the white students are going to have their pockets of organized groups. Honestly, if the schools are going to be desegregated, we need a little unity within the sisterhood. Honestly speaking, most of the students love it right here at Davis High."

I was utterly shocked to hear Hilda speak about social and civic matters. She always appeared really happy and free of worries. I had watched her on May Day doing the *limbo rock* and was shocked about how low she could go. She actually won the prize! However, her expression of concern about social and civic matters really shocked me. I concluded; the Black Power Movement is inching its way to Hyde County.

Alice momentarily interrupted Hilda with, "Right now, it looks as though the federal government is going to force all public schools to integrate. Really, just last night on the evening news, there was a commentary about *Brown v. Board of Education.* David Brinkley plainly stated that it is simply a matter of time before all public schools will be integrated. As you know, Hilda and I are seniors. We won't be attending Mattamuskeet School. However, I am concerned about my cousins and friends."

I was about to respond to Alice's statement when Bernice, Hilda's sister, walked up. She was wearing a pair of tight jeans and sporting a huge afro. Her tight jeans made her bowlegs highly pronounced and the round earrings dangling on her earlobes made her look dangerously militant. She had all the makings of Pam Grier in the 1973 movie *Coffy.* Then, I looked at Virginia and almost did not recognize her. I had never seen her fashioned like a sista on a mission before.

Virginia's long flowing black hair had been converted into a beautiful, thick, and puffy afro. Angela Davis had nothing on her on this day. She looked like she was ready to lead the Black Panther Party. Alice enthusiastically asked, "Bernice have you come up with a name for our organization? Since you and Virginia came up with the idea, I didn't want to move too fast. Hilda and I have been brainstorming a suitable name, but nothing really resonates. Have you thought about a name for our sisterhood?"

Bernice smiled and her dimples immediately caved in as she explained, "Well, I've read several speeches by Angela Davis, and she is awesome! After thinking about her position on sisterhood, I thought maybe we should call our organization, 'Sisters of Soul'. The acronym would be (SOS). Our colors will be black and white. Since it looks as though we will be going to Mattamuskeet and the students there will be either white or black, it just seemed logical that our colors would be black and white."

I was in the act of making a statement when all of a sudden Mr. Boone came out of his office and sternly stated, "Let's get to class! This is not the place for a Civil Rights meeting. This is a public institution! This is not a hub for the NAACP!"

Everyone got quiet and scattered like roaches trying to escape light in the dark of night. We hurried to class with a true sense of urgency. Martin sent me a note by my sister, Vanessa. The note read, ***"Henry, meet me at the Ridge Store at 5:00 p.m. on Thursday. Be on time because we have some very important information to discuss! Alice told me that she approached you and Ben Junior about putting together a "Sisterhood" organization as a means to showcase some solidarity when we all end up at Mattamuskeet. Think about this scenario and give me your honest position on this matter. See you tomorrow at 5:00 p.m.***

***Bro. Martin***

I was shocked to receive the letter from Martin and I knew he really meant business. The ride home on the school bus was filled with excitement and apprehension. Our school bus was old and noisy. Fred Junior had become our driver and he was quiet, yet friendly. Rumor had it that he liked Carolyn, my older sister, Linda's, best friend. After chopping wood, bringing in water, and placing wood on the porch, I came in the house to watch *Hullabaloo.* Mama told me to bring in a little extra water because the girls wanted to wash their hair. For some unknown reason, Linda had decided to wash my younger sisters' hair. I felt like something strange was happening because they did not wash their hair during mid-week. Linda loved music and the record player was bumping to the sounds of the *Supremes.* It sounded as if they had a *Soul Train* line going on right in the kitchen. I could feel the kitchen floor vibrating.

Mama must have been extremely tired from a hard day's work at the Engelhard Crab House. She nodded in her favorite chair and never scolded my sisters for being too noisy. On most days, she would have lectured them about being loud and snickering. However, today, she quietly sat in her favorite chair and allowed the girls to go berserk. It was times like this when I missed my older brother, C-R, most. My sisters could talk about girly things together; but, as for me, I had to resort talking to Thad Junior and Van Grey about manly matters. They were two of the most macho guys at Davis School. For the most part, they gave me faulty information and I often made a fool of myself.

My sisters appeared to be doing extraordinary whispering, laughing, and snickering and I could not figure out what was happening. I ignored them and continued to watch *Hullabaloo.* Then all of a sudden, Linda emerged from the kitchen sporting a humongous puffy afro. My two younger sisters, Jacqueline and Vanessa followed suit. Their afros were shiny black and puffy like the *Jackson Five.* They had put together some outfits that made them look like they should have been back-up singers for Diana Ross.

It was like all of a sudden the Black Power Movement had invaded my living room. Before entering the living room, they put on the album, *Diana Ross and the Supremes.* My older sister, Linda, performed a wonderful impersonation of Diana Ross and Jackie and Vanessa really gave true homage to Mary Wilson and Cindy Birdsong. Mama abruptly woke up and appeared speechless as they danced and lip-synced *Someday We'll Be Together.* They looked fabulously ready for the red carpet treatment of MoTown.

As I prepared for school the next morning, Linda knocked on my bedroom door. When I opened it, she smiled graciously and handed me some money to purchase ice cream at school. My pockets were empty and it would be great to have money to buy ice cream. I sensed that Linda had something up her sleeve; however, I went along with the act of enticement. Jackie and Vanessa listened attentively and smiled from ear to ear.

Linda asked, "Junior, will you help Alice and Hilda put together an organization that addresses black female issues. We heard about the so-called Kool Kolored Kidz and we're hoping that you will work with us. We aren't trying to find out any secret handshakes or mottos. We simply think that black females need to be organized just like you black guys. I know you like Virginia and she asked me to ask you. Will you help us?"

I immediately denied knowing anything about the Kool Kolored Kidz. Jackie and Vanessa stood beside Linda and appeared terribly dejected about my response. The sorrow in their eyes made me feel sick in my stomach. They really didn't realize that I was simply trying to protect them from the perils of the unknown. I didn't want them subjected the wrath of Mr. Boone due to the fact that they were my sisters. Mr. Boone was a very smart man and I knew he would eventually summon me to his office for interrogation. However, my sisters were very emotional and I didn't want them harassed in any manner.

I accepted the money to purchase ice cream and told Linda that I would give her an answer right after school. Then I heard a horn blow loudly three times in a row. The school bus was fifteen minutes earlier than normal. This was Fred Junior's third day of driving the school bus and seemingly he was arriving at our house earlier and earlier each day. My sisters and I ran out of the house to catch the bus. As I stepped up on the school bus, Fred Junior said, "I, I, thought, thought, I was going to have to leave, leave you to, to, today."

His speech impediment was more pronounced in the early morning than mid-day. There were times when he would talk to me and I would be compelled to take extra time to actively listen as a means to figure-out what he was trying to say. Nevertheless, he loved Leonard's sister, Carolyn. It was rather strange; whenever he spoke with Carolyn, he spoke plainly, with zero stuttering. It appeared that Carolyn had a special place in Fred Junior's heart, as well on the school bus. Everyone knew better than to sit on the seat directly behind him because it was reserved for Carolyn.

There were days when the school bus would be filled to capacity. I really hated it when I had to stand-up in the aisle of the bus. Our school bus was extremely old and the seats were cracked and at times loose. When Fred Junior changed gears, it wasn't uncommon for students to lose their balance and fall forward or backwards. It was really dangerous riding the "orange death traps."

Fred Junior would customarily take the back road of the Ridge community to pick up students. The road was inundated with holes and huge bumps. As he geared down the school bus, I noticed Alice and Judith anxiously standing on Aunt Emma's porch. To my amazement, just like my sisters, they had elected to put together the natural look over night. Their short curly afros were midnight black and somewhat wavy around the edges. They were wearing black slacks and white tops/blouses and dress shoes. I really did not connect the dots; however, my sisters were wearing the very same combination of black and white. When Fred Junior stopped to pick up Rosa Marie, Hattie Ann, Delphine, Debra Ann, Julia Anna, Lillie Belle, and Jean Carol, they were all wearing black and white and sporting neatly fashioned afros. I have no idea how the sistas pulled off this feat; however, they looked like sorority sisters on a mission. Their sense of togetherness was unparalleled.

Sammie, Anthony, and Larry missed the school bus at their house. Consequently, they had to jump the ditch and cross the field behind Richard's house to catch the bus. When Larry stepped on the bus, he immediately looked around and asked, "Are we all going to a funeral today? If so, Mr. Boone didn't tell me about it. I can't stand going to funerals. Anyway, who died?"

No one responded to Larry's inquiry. The school bus was extraordinarily quiet on this day for some unknown reason. When Fred Junior slowed down to pick up Judy and Dorenda, I immediately noted that they were wearing black and white and sporting short curly afros as well. When Dorenda sat down in front of me, I noticed that she was writing a poem that was lyrically centered on Stevie Wonder's *Blowin In The Wind.* Her poem had a beautiful beginning. It read, *How many roads must a man walk down before . . .* When she noticed that I was reading her work, she immediately closed her tablet.

Byron, her older brother, sat beside me and asked, "Why are all the girls wearing black and white? Did you decide to help them put together their little "girly club?"

I explained to Byron that my sisters had asked me to help them get started, but I hadn't shared any information with them. Byron told me that Judy and Dorenda had been whispering and snickering all night and he could not figure out what was going on. He said, he ignored them and oiled his BB-gun. However, this was an extremely quiet morning on the school bus. All of the females appeared to be in possession of a new worldview and were on a self-proclaimed mission. An eerie feeling resonated throughout the school bus. I had never seen my cousin, Jean Carol, so focused and quiet before. Belvin, Minnie, and Virginia looked like they were ready to join Angela Davis for a Freedom march. I wondered what was up! No one was singing, and no one was joking.

Normally, Jean Carol would start a popular *MoTown* song and before long, the entire school bus would be rocking. I particularly liked it when she sang, *You Can't Hurry Love* by the Supremes. She would sing and tap on the metal behind the school bus seat in front of her and an undeniable rhythm would manifest. She could really sing and her rhythm was phenomenal. Jean had a charisma that made her the life of anyone's party. However, the school bus was eerily quiet today. I felt as though I was riding in a huge orange hearse.

When our bus arrived on the campus of Davis School, Mr. Boone stood at the front door and directed all males to go to the cafeteria. We were all perplexed because we did not know what to expect. After waiting for about twenty minutes, Mr. Boone eventually came into the cafeteria. He stated that he had a restless night trying to figure out whether he should only meet with the males or whether he should speak to the entire student body. Needless to say, he elected to speak solely to the males. We all sat quietly and attentively. Mr. Boone appeared serious, very serious!

He stated that he had concerns about the state of American society, especially the black community. A sense of urgency resonated from wall to wall as he conveyed his dire concerns. I sat in the cafeteria quietly and tried to figure out the nature and rationale for the meeting. As I reflected, I knew it was not uncommon for Mr. Boone to summon groups of black males together and lecture them about the ills of American society and the perils of an unjust society.

However, on this day, he chose a topic titled *Young, Gifted, and Black*. He vehemently stated that there were more black males going to prison than going to college. Then he began to talk about black males and appearances. He denounced puffy afros and Black English.

Mr. Boone blatantly stated that it irked him when he saw young black men, with no education, walking around talking jive, with a huge black pick stuck in the back of their nappy hair. I remember verbatim when he said, "If you think the white man is going to give you a job when you're walking around yelling *Soul Power* and *Black Power* and you can't even conjugate a verb. You need to think again! You are in for a great surprise! If you think the white man is going to give you a job when you are walking around trying to be cool, saying things like, 'Power to the people'; Can ya dig it?; I've gotta split; Yo, I need some bread!' Well, I tell you right now, Mr. Charlie is not looking for some jive-talking Negro who cannot read, write, or calculate."'

I was rather astonished and appreciative of Mr. Boone's soul-to-soul speech. When he stated that there was a terrible epidemic within the black community that a shot won't cure, I was seriously concerned. I knew that I had not experienced sex at that point in my life; however, I was concerned about my friends who had indeed crossed the hot sands of sexual ecstasy. He stated, "Yes, everyone in here was born the triple B-Syndrome. There nothing you can do about; it's in your genes. You are going to die with this highly visible condition!"

When Mr. Boone made that statement, my anxiety level elevated significantly. Everyone showcased a terribly sad face. It was an extremely morbid feeling inside the cafeteria.

Then he said, "The triple B-Syndrome is simply a case of *Being Born Black*! You cannot escape this condition. It will follow you to your grave! *Being Born Black* means that you will be compelled to work extra hard to remove your invisible status. Believe me, this is no easy feat."

When Mr. Boone initially alluded to the "Triple B-Syndrome," I readily thought of a disease that was totally inherent of the black community. I only had casual experiences with white America and the thought that now, black America had a disease that was incurable was very disconcerting. My ultimate question was, how did this happen?

Mr. Boone had everyone in the cafeteria spellbound. It appeared that we all began to self-check to ascertain if we were indeed the stereotypical black male that he grotesquely described. As I reflected, I knew that I did not want to perpetuate any stereotype. Shortly after the meeting, he implemented a schoolwide policy that required all male students to wear neckties on a daily basis.

Several students rebuked the policy and were sent home until they elected to comply with the dictum. Most of my friends hated the necktie mandate. However, I liked feeling like a young professional and the necktie policy gave me a superficial sense of validation. My self-esteem was at an all-time low and I needed to feel worthwhile. For some unknown reason, dressing neatly and speaking well made me feel like a diamond in the rough. It is without question; Mr. Boone's life lectures really impacted my life in a positive manner. They were great epiphanies for me. I embraced his messages as absolute truths.

Some of my friends viewed Mr. Boone as an Uncle Tom; however, I viewed him as a man of great wisdom and understanding. He was unquestionably well-read, a scholar, and a gentleman. His intellectualism superseded most of his era and he was at best an intellectual recluse. I marveled at his intellectual play with words and the sharpness of his mind. A ten-minute conversation with Mr. Boone and our science teacher, Mr. Weston, was nothing less than a brief discourse with Albert Einstein or Socrates. There were occasions when Mr. Boone and Mr. Weston didn't see eye to eye on societal matters. The differences were most notable on matters dealing black resistance to the status quo. The black power movement created high levels of dissension and unrest within the black community.

Mr. Weston, our science teacher, was a staunch Renaissance man. He was a man of many talents and he executed each extraordinarily well. However, Mr. Boone was stuck in an era when black resistance was deemed the road to personal annihilation. He appeared to be overly concerned that blacks would lose footage if they challenged or questioned the status quo. My father had utmost respect for Mr. Boone as well as Mr. Weston. He often spoke of their resilience and ability to stay the course when others viewed the world through a different lens. I simply relished the opportunity to engage their intellect and unequivocal wisdom. To be quite honest, I aspired to take their path; even though it was often the one less traveled.

# CHAPTER 15

# DASHIKI FRIDAYS - SISTERS OF SOUL

***Leadership is the other side of the coin of loneliness, and he who is a leader must always act alone. And acting alone, accept everything alone.***

***—Ferdinand Edralin Marcos***

After the sixty-minute reality check meeting with Mr. Boone, he allowed us to use the restroom before going to our respective classrooms. As I walked to the restroom, I heard a great deal of noise and chaos. When I entered the restroom, I immediately noted Wardell stuck in the metal trashcan. He and Jody had gotten in an altercation and apparently Jody was the winner. Wardell was stuck in the terribly bent trashcan and he could not maneuver himself to get out of it. None of my classmates offered to help him because he had bullied nearly everyone in class.

I wished that I could have seen the incident because he was notorious for picking on me, especially when female students were near. Wardell actually towered over Jody. However, he must not have heard that he was no joke. He was short, muscular, and as quick as lightning. A fight between Jody and Wardell was nothing less than the biblical story between David and Goiliath.

Wardell's biceps and triceps were humongous and he wore a size twelve shoe when he was in the seventh grade. His hands looked like catchers' mitts and he was extremely fast to be a big guy. I smiled at heart as I watched him kick his legs trying to get out of the metal trashcan. To see him kicking his legs in desperation was a real Kodak moment. By the time Mr. Boone arrived, everyone had dispersed.

Donald told me that Jody was in one of the stalls urinating and Wardell decided to use the commode right next the stall that Jody was using. Wardell was a terribly intimidating figure to many guys at Davis High. If I saw him coming in my direction, I would step into a nearby classroom or turn around immediately and go in a different direction. When I asked Donald what happened, he laughed and said, "Man, Jody wasn't bothering anyone. He was simply draining his weasel when Wardell came into the restroom. Man, it was mad crazy, and unnecessary."

I excitedly asked, "Why did Jody give him a beat-down? I don't believe, he jumped on him for no reason at all."

Donald laughed and stated, "Man, it was like this! Wardell burst into the restroom and muscled his way to the empty stall right beside Jody. Pompey, Leroy, and Felton were quietly waiting in line to handle their business. On the other hand, Wardell came in the bathroom in a hurry, holding his zipper-area, and jumped ahead of all those guys. Man, Wardell even laughed as he took his weasel and sprayed Jody's feet soaking wet."

I responded with, "Come on Donald, Joe Frazier wouldn't even do that to Jody. What was Wardell thinking?

Donald scratched his head and stated, "That's the problem! He wasn't thinking. Jody began to gnaw his fingernails. He didn't even wash his hands before gnawing on his nails. He was angry, real angry! Wardell didn't even have time to come out of the stall before Jody grabbed him."

Everyone in class knew that Wardell was as strong as an ox. In addition, everyone knew that Jody was as fast as lightning, and strong. As such, they traditionally respected each other. I asked Donald, "What happened next? Was Wardell caught off guard?"

Again, Donald laughed and said, "Jody hit him so hard that he fell on one of the commodes. Then he grabbed him by his shirt, picked him up, and slammed him in the metal trashcan. He slammed him so hard that he actually got stuck."

As we rushed to class, Donald reflected on Mr. Boone's speech about being *Young, Gifted,* and *Black.* He vehemently stated that the bathroom incident was totally unnecessary. As we walked to Mrs. Collins' class, he stated that he wasn't going to perpetuate the stereotype that Mr. Boone talked about in his speech. He said he was going to attend school regularly, dress well, speak well, and treat everyone decently.

Donald never attended Mattamuskeet School. He moved to New York with his mother and graduated high school in a multi-diverse setting. He missed out on the federal government's desegregation mandate and the southern dissent with the policy. There was serious unrest in Hyde County and the nation in the 1960s. The desegregation of public schools in North Carolina triggered a high level of unrest and turmoil on the black and white landscape. The Black Power Movement made white America extremely uneasy. Additionally, "old school" blacks denounced the arrogance and demands of so-called black militants.

Shortly after the skirmish between Jody and Wardell, I met my sister, Linda, near the water fountain. She smiled and said, "Junior, what I asked you about this morning, forget about it. While Mr. Boone was talking to all the males this morning, Mrs. Bryant was talking to us about female etiquette. She talked a lot about how females should carry themselves and that women should not be reliant upon men to define themselves. She made a great deal of sense and Alice and Hilda decided that we don't really need the so-called Kool Kolored Kidz to determine our mission and vision. We should be proactive as young women to advance our own agenda."

I listened and asked, "Does this mean that I have to return the quarter that you gave me for ice cream?"

Linda responded with, "Junior, you know how I am! If I give you something, it's yours. Enjoy your ice cream!"

Mrs. Anderson was the Home Economics teacher at Davis High and all the students loved her. She was still in her twenties and was a big sister and role model for all of us. During class, when we goofed off, she was only required to look at us twice and we would check ourselves. I really enjoyed her class because she taught about life skills, planning, banking, saving, education, family planning, and honesty. She was much more than a textbook teacher who only alluded to the academics. My older sister, Linda, worshipped the ground that she walked on and looked to her as the big sister that she never had. Ms. Anderson personified class, sophistication, ethics, morality, and resiliency. There were numerous lessons learned in her class that were not in textbooks.

Ms. Anderson later married Mr. Leon Bryant, a homeboy, as well as a Vietnam veteran. He was by far the strongest human being that I had ever seen. He taught shop and on Fridays, if we had been good all week, he would share some heartfelt and terrifying stories about his experiences in Vietnam. Even though he was a giant of a man, tears often came to his eyes when he talked about the loss of a dear friend while in Nam.

His narratives about the realities of Vietnam made the film, *Deer Hunter,* an absolute farce. My heart would grow heavy as he painted grotesque scenes of Vietnam with the artistry of Leonardo Da Vinci. In addition, he was a super-skilled automotive technician who could convert an aged jalopy into a dependable traveling machine. He hands were huge and his heart was even larger. Mr. Bryant embodied the parable of a Good Samaritan in his daily walk. He called Mrs. Bryant, Candy, and possessed an unparalleled love for her and his children. Students simply loved each of them unconditionally. They were like second parents to all students at Davis High.

Alice and Hilda gravitated to Mrs. Bryant as well. After being snubbed by presumed members of the Kool Kolored Kidz, Alice decided to take matters into her own hands. She collaborated with Bernice, Virginia, and Hilda and took the lead in spearheading the direction of the Sisters of Soul Coalition. Alice's intestinal fortitude and will to impact American society in a positive manner was relentless. I sensed that she would someday meet Angela Davis and Rosa Parks and they would collaboratively be a powerful voice for black American women. She was fearless and she possessed a magnetic disposition that compelled others to gravitate to her. When I listened to Angela Davis' speeches, I would say, "That's Alice in the truest sense."

Mr. Boone held Alice in utmost regard. There were times when I felt as though he was intimidated by her high profile and persona. When she orchestrated "Dashiki Friday" at Davis School, I was astounded by her leadership qualities. Lucy, Clara, Evelina, and Virginia looked like ancient Nubian Princesses as they walked majestically down the halls of Davis School. Elmira, Nancy, and Linda's dashikis looked as if they were professionally made. They looked so militant and anti-establishment that I was afraid to speak to them.

On this day, all the sistas wore afros and colorful dashikis. None of the guys knew about "Dashiki Friday" and it was a major hit. Mr. Boone almost went berserk because Alice cerebrally orchestrated this scheme on the very same day that Superintendent Bucklew made his monthly visit to the black schools of Hyde

County. The sistas were extremely crafty as they actually made the dashikis right in Mrs. Bryant's sewing class and Mr. Boone never had any inclination. It was absolutely amazing how the ladies were able to keep "Dashiki Friday" incognito for so long. They were terribly gorgeous as they modeled sisterhood solidarity. Alice stood out as a matriarch of a new norm.

Superintendent Bucklew arrived at Davis School at 8:35 a.m. I watched as he exited his state-owned vehicle and slowly meandered down the hall. It was quite obvious that Mr. Boone was in a nervous wreck. It was rumored that Superintendent Bucklew had an extremely low tolerance for black people and he detested the fact that he was compelled to visit O.A. Peay and Davis School at least once per month. I watched as he peeped in several classrooms before he got to Mr. Boone's office. Whenever, Superintendent Bucklew visited our school, Mrs. Lula would solicit a student to take a #2 red pencil to each teacher. No words were exchanged; the simple red pencil did the talking. Mr. Adams would put an extra shine on the halls and clean windows with perfection. Even the old and rusted school buses were washed to impress the Superintendent. Mr. Boone would be utterly restless!

When Mr. Bucklew looked in Mrs. Bryant's classroom and saw all the ladies wearing dashikis, he turned as red as a mid-July tomato. He didn't say a single word; he simply stomped to Mr. Boone's office in a seething rage. The Home Economics classroom was near Mr. Boone's office and I heard him ask Mrs. Lula, "Is Charles in his office. If so, tell him that Superintendent Bucklew is here and I need to speak with him right now!"

Mrs. Lula responded with, "Sir, Mr. Boone is with a student right now. However, when the student is dismissed, you will be next in line. Please have a seat. In fact, here, take a look at our yearbook while you wait. We are extremely pleased with this year's final product."

Superintendent Bucklew became very annoyed and asked, "Do you know who I am?"

Mrs. Lula smiled and said, "Why yes! You just said your name is Superintendent Bucklew. I didn't forget that quickly."

I simply loved the manner in which Mrs. Lula downplayed Superintendent Bucklew's positional power and sarcasm. She asserted herself with a high level of professionalism and never compromised her dignity or self-worth. All of the students loved her because she was genuine and caring. Mrs. Lula was so down-to-earth that she would actually ride the school bus with us and we were often quite noisy. Like Mrs. Bryant, Mrs. Lula was like a big sister to all students at Davis High. It was without question, she genuinely cared about us.

Mr. Boone eventually came out of his office and extended his hand to Superintendent Bucklew as a gesture of welcome. However, he ignored his hand and angrily asked, "Charles, what kind of school are you running down here? I peeped in the classroom directly across from your office, and all of the students are wearing African clothes. Charles, this is unacceptable behavior, colored children wearing African clothes in a public school! I peeped in another classroom and one boy had the nerve to give me a 'Soul Power' fist. Look, this is America; this is not Africa. Don't your teachers teach geography and history down here? I know right well you and your teachers aren't trying to start a Black Power Movement in Hyde County, are you?"

I could not fathom why Superintendent Bucklew refused to address Mr. Boone with greater respect. He simply referred to him as "Charles" and never respected him as a grown man or as the assigned instructional leader of Davis School.

After Superintendent Bucklew's ranting, Mr. Boone used a very apologetic voice and stated, "Honestly, Mr. Bucklew, I was devastated when I saw what my female students decided to wear today. Normally, I don't have any problems with them. However, it's a different story with my young males. My young male students are turning my hair whiter and whiter each day. They are always trying to defy authority. I have a young Home Economics teacher, Ms. Anderson, excuse me; I meant to say Mrs. Bryant. She recently married Early Bryant's son, Leon. I will speak to her about this matter and I feel confident that this matter will be resolved."

Superintendent Bucklew shook his head and adamantly stated, "If you can't run this school, I'll find someone who can! Do you understand me Charles?"

Mr. Boone tried to calm Superintendent Bucklew down by taking him on an excursion of the whole school. It was Friday and chicken-day in the cafeteria. Mrs. Florene, head cook, had the cafeteria in spotless condition and the smell of fried chicken and boiling beans resonated from wall to wall. There was something special about Mrs. Florene's fried chicken and Great Northern beans. Ironically, on this day, Mr. Weston sent Van Grey to the office to tell Ms. Florene that his class would be about ten minutes late because they were taking a science test.

When Van Grey entered the cafeteria, he was looking down at his test paper and accidentally bumped into Superintendent Bucklew. He apologized but Superintendent Bucklew didn't respect the apology. When he looked at Van Grey, he angrily stated, "That's the same boy who gave me a 'Soul Power' fist. I'll never forget the mischievous grin on his face."

Van Grey immediately picked up on the term "boy" and instantaneously stated, "Boy! My name is Van Grey and don't refer to me as 'boy.' I can't stand it when someone calls me boy. I am a young man; I ain't no body's boy!"

Mr. Boone ignored Van Grey's response and thanked him for bringing the message to Mrs. Florene. Superintendent Bucklew was still terribly enraged. He stood near Mr. Boone's main office door and chastised him for the dynamics of his day. While he stood near the office door, Alice requested to be excused to use the ladies' room. Mrs. Bryant granted her permission and she grabbed the hall pass and headed out of the door. As she approached Mr. Boone, she politely stated, "Good afternoon Mr. Boone! I hope you are having a good day."

Superintendent Bucklew didn't respond to Alice at all. After she walked away, he continued his rant on Mr. Boone. We sat in the classroom and pretended that we weren't paying attention to what was occurring in the hall. However, we were very attentive and we felt sorry for Mr. Boone. Even though he gave us (students) hell, we knew he genuinely cared about us. Superintendent Bucklew never recognized that he was trouncing around on a serious paradigm shift. The intent of *Brown v. Board* of *Education* was in its latent stage and unparalleled change in public education was on the horizon. We didn't see Superintendent Bucklew again until "Black and Red Friday." However, none of us missed him!

# CHAPTER 16
# BLACK AND RED FRIDAY

***Men are born with two eyes, but only one tongue, in order that they should see twice as much as they say.***

***—Charles Caleb Colton***

After the success of "Dashiki Friday" Martin and Miguel felt the need to orchestrate a similar activity to accentuate solidarity of the Kool Kolored Kidz. We met in our new headquarters in the wooded area near Mr. Lincoln's hog pen. Dennis was truly accurate; the new headquarters was perfect and not readily recognizable. It was camouflaged between thick evergreen, tall pine trees, briars, and a shallow pond. Pine straw covered the top of our headquarters and from afar it looked like a military bunker equipped with tunnels. Dennis didn't lie; he knew the swamp well, extremely well. The meeting was called to order by Miguel and everyone became extremely quiet. Ben Junior and Sammie assumed their positions as sergeant- at- arms. If they looked at us sternly, we would automatically self-check. We respected them to the highest degree.

Martin had a no-nonsense look on his face when he stoically stated, "It looks as though the Sisters of Soul are far more organized than we are and we have been meeting 'supposedly' underground for three months. There is something terribly wrong with this picture. We are supposed to be an underground organization; however, every time I turn around someone is asking me about joining the Kool Kolored Kidz. Something is terribly wrong with this picture."

I thought about Martin's opening statement and agreed with him wholeheartedly. For some reason, the guys were talking too much. Nevertheless, the so-called Sisters of Soul were quiet, poised, and focused. They were so tightly knit that I didn't even know if my sisters belonged to the organization or not. They basically knitted their dashikis virtually right under my nose and I was totally clueless.

Miguel suggested that we model after the Sisters of Soul and do a better job of monitoring our voices and conversations. He vehemently stated that we were not to discuss planned activities on the school bus or on the campus of Davis School. Ben Junior and Sammie said if they heard anyone within the organization talking about planned activities, they would experience their wrath. No one cared to upset Ben Junior or Sammie because they were bigger and stronger than anyone in our organization. When they spoke, everyone listened!

Martin announced to the group that the floor was open for discussion. However, the tone of the meeting was so intense that no one initiated discussion. Lonnie eventually stated, "It's amazing how you guys can find everything to talk about on the school bus, but when it comes to serious business, no one has anything to say."

I wasn't about to raise my hand to share a few insights and run the risk of being embarrassed by Martin or Miguel. There was absolute silence in our new headquarters for about three minutes. The lull of silence was eerie and intimidating.

Then all of a sudden, Ben Junior scratched his head and suggested, "Let's orchestrate a so-called 'Black and Red Friday.' I was thinking that we would spread the word all across campus that on 'Black and Red Friday' all male students would be required to wear black pants, black shirts, but red shocks. In essence, the color black, would showcase solidarity; and the color red, would symbolize blood. The red socks would symbolize the bloody shackles that our forefathers experienced during slavery."

Ben Junior went on to suggest that we hem our pants one-inch above our ankles to accentuate the red socks. I readily envisioned Ben's suggestion and concluded that we would make a profound statement of solidarity if we could pull off this feat. My ultimate concern was the fact that I did not own red socks. My sisters didn't even wear red socks.

In fact, I hardly ever saw anyone wearing red socks. My pockets were empty and the thought of purchasing a black shirt, and a pair of red socks seemed insurmountable. I knew times were tight for mama and I really hated to confront her with this request. Mom was working extra hard at the Engelhard Crab House to simply keep a roof over our heads and food on the table.

I eventually asked mom if I could go to Mr. Tony Spencer's store to purchase a shirt and a pair of socks. However, I never mentioned to her the color of the shirt to be purchased or the color of the socks. She knew that the play *My Three Angels* by Sam and Bella Spewack was scheduled to take place in May and I had a speaking role. I sort of gave mom the impression that I needed the shirt and socks for the upcoming play. She gave me permission to charge the shirt and socks to her account at Mr. Tony's store.

I felt guilty about misleading her about the true nature of my request. Even today, when I think about the long hours that she had to work to simply earn the $7.86 to pay for my purchase, makes me sad at heart. There were times when her loving hands were swollen, cracked, and sore from numerous crab infections.

Nevertheless, she would faithfully go to the Engelhard Crab House with a genuine smile on her face.

Ben Junior's vision was very well conceived and noble in conceptualization. However, economically, we just didn't have any money to make the vision a reality. I sat in amazement as he articulated his vision. Then again, I knew he enjoyed reading about black history, especially slavery. It appeared that he had envisioned using the color "black" to symbolize unity, and the color, "red" to showcase homage to our ancestry. I thought his vision was a sheer sign of genius. After sharing his vision, Martin began to clap his hands and we all joined in with his enthusiasm. Smiles graced everyone's face and the soulful gesture, "give-me-five" emanated in the meeting. An aura of unity, purpose, and brotherhood consumed the meeting.

We all embraced Ben Junior's vision with exuberance. Martin cautiously noted, "You know, if we wear red socks to school, Uncle Johnny is going to hassle us when we go to his science class. He despises seeing male students wearing red socks. He says it's simply not acceptable for us to do so. Uncle Johnny calls the practice showcasing bleeding ankles."

Mr. Weston, our science teacher, was Martin's uncle and the youngest male teacher at Davis School. He lived right down the road from me and I idolized him to the utmost. He was GQ (Gentlemen's Quarterly) everyday and I aspired to be just like him. Martin was accurate; Mr. Weston had an extremely low tolerance for males who wore red socks. In my opinion, he was the sheriff of the fashion police at Davis School. His conservative mannerism was contagious and most of the so-called smart guys attempted to emulate him.

Mr. Weston epitomized sophistication and class on a daily basis. He consistently wore starched white shirts, fancy ties, blue or black suits, and his shoes were always shining. There were days when he looked more like a banker than a classroom teacher. It was difficult to find him not wearing a navy blue or black blazer. Mr. Weston was Bryant Gumbel before Bryant Gumbel was Bryant Gumbel. His class and sophistication were beyond reproach.

I questioned how we would be able to pull off "Black and Friday" when Mr. Weston was our idolized teacher and mentor. Just as Mrs. Bryant was the mentor for female students, Mr. Weston served in the same capacity for male students. My friends and I gravitated to each of them because they were still in their twenties and they had not been indoctrinated by the established order. Their quiet defiance of the status quo resonated without ever having to raise a fist and shout "Soul Power."

Martin gave us a month to purchase our attire to make "Black and Red Friday" a reality. All of us owned black slacks but few of us owned black shirts. Due to the lack of transportation in the black community, most of our parents shopped in Engelhard at Tony Spencer's General Store. He carried everything from mousetraps to cheese. However, when Ben Junior and I went to Engelhard to purchase a black shirt, he didn't have any. He didn't have any red socks for boys or men either. When I inquired about black shirts and red socks, Mr. Tony looked a bit perplexed and noted, "I've had several requests this week for black shirts and red socks. Is something special going on at Davis School or church this month?"

Ben Junior responded with, "No sir! We're simply tired of wearing the regular colors of blue, brown, white, and paisleys. There's nothing really special happening."

Mr. Tony stated that he placed a large order for black shirts in all sizes and he was able to find a few pairs of red socks for men and boys as well. He indicated that the order should arrive in about five work days. The five work days worked fine for us. We had eleven days left before "Black and Red Friday." Ben Junior and I thumbed a ride back to the Ridge Store with Mr. Thad. He was driving an apple red Plymouth Fury that was absolutely beautiful. The white interior made the car feel extraordinarily clean. The engine roared as if he had a tiger in his tank. He never said a single word to us from Engelhard to the Ridge Store.

Mr. Thad was a man of very, very, few words. It didn't really matter that he didn't say very much, what resonated most to us was the mere fact that he was consistently kind. He always drove dream cars and as such, he was idolized by the poor black kids who lived on the Ridge. However, none of his fancy cars was too good to give the black kids a ride. Word readily spread throughout the black community that Mr. Thad was a good and honorable man.

## CHAPTER 17
# A LESSON ON BRAZIL NUTS

***You gain strength, courage and confidence by every experience in which you really stop to look fear in the face. . . You must do the thing you think you cannot do.***

***—Eleanor Roosevelt***

When we arrived at the Ridge Store, Raymond, Joseph and Sammie were standing around laughing and joking. We eventually went into the Ridge Store to joke around with Byron. As we entered, I noted that Larry's older brother, Anthony, was home. He was attending college in Greensboro, North Carolina at North Carolina A&T State University. Anthony was deemed a bookworm who didn't do much joking and laughing. He was a serious-minded individual who worked hard to keep Larry in line. In addition, he was very protective of his younger sister, Judith. Anthony ordered a honey bun and a Pepsi. He was in the process of popping the top of his Pepsi when a white patron entered in the store. The patron purchased an eight-ounce coke, a bag of peanuts, and a Hershey bar.

After the white patron paid for his purchases, he saw some bags of pecans and asked, "How old are your pecans? My wife really loves pecans, are they relatively fresh?

Byron responded with, "Yes, they are real fresh. I just picked them up from our backyard yesterday. Would you like to sample a few?"

The white patron took his time, cracked three of the pecans with his teeth, threw them in his mouth, and stated, "You are right; they are meaty, really good!"

After sampling the pecans, the white patron asked, "Tell me, do you have any nigger toes? My wife loves them the best. However, it's hard to find them except during the Christmas season. Do you have any?"

When the white patron used the term "nigger toes", Anthony's Pepsi fell to the floor. The Pepsi actually splashed and wet the right pant leg of the patron. Anthony stoically stated, "Sir, the nuts you are alluding to are called Brazil nuts, not "nigger toes." There is no such nut that's called a "nigger toe."

None of the guys in the store recognized the epithet that Anthony addressed. We all called the nuts "nigger toes" and never thought anything about it. Nonetheless, Anthony was a sophomore in college and he was well abreast of the negative connotations associated with such jargon. The white patron apologized and stated that he didn't mean any harm. He further indicated that he really did not know that they're truly named Brazil nuts. Anthony accepted his apology and chastised us for being so ill-informed. I felt like an imbecile for not knowing and swore to myself that I would read more and become more cognizant of historical negative connotations.

After the short lesson on Brazil nuts, we began to talk about "Black and Red Friday." It appeared that all the guys on the Ridge were prepared and excited about the big day. Mostly everyone ordered their shirts and socks from Mr. Tony's General Store. I felt as though Mr. Tony had gotten a bit uncomfortable with so many young black guys ordering black shirts and red socks.

At heart, I wondered if he thought we had misguidedly gotten involved in some type cult that would eventually lead to our demise. Truthfully speaking, there were many within the black community who viewed the Black Power Movement and the Black Panthers as cults that would lead to the eventual annihilation of black people.

Martin encouraged us to be on our best behavior and to do everything possible to avoid bringing unwanted attention to us. He wanted to make a clear statement to the "established order" that change was inevitable and necessary if a more perfect society were to avail itself. Martin wanted "Black and Red Friday" to be a total surprise to Mr. Boone and supporters of the status quo.

We couldn't wait for Saturday to come around so we could pick up our orders! The fact that most of the shirts and socks were to be purchased from the very same store gave credibility to our uniformity. We really wanted to showcase solidarity and brotherhood at an exceptional level. The Sisters of Soul had outclassed us and we were determined to reclaim our superior status.

Ben Junior and I got up early on the Saturday that we were to pick up our shirts and socks. We were able to catch a ride to Engelhard with Mr. Farrow, the owner of the local supermarket. He was the owner and operator of the only legitimate supermarket in Hyde County, the *Red and White.* In light of the fact that he owned the *Red and White,* blacks saw him as a millionaire and a man of great influence. However, he worked extremely hard and he was very resourceful. As I grew in age, I often wondered why he never sought a public office in the county. Everyone admired and respected him to the utmost.

As we rode with Mr. Farrow to Engelhard, he asked us about school and encouraged us to take education seriously. He indicated that a good education is the key to success and we should work hard to learn as much as possible. When we entered Engelhard, I readily noticed Jody, Larry, Leroy, Sammie, and Dexter standing outside waiting for Mr. Tony Spencer to open his store. By the time Mr. Farrow parked, Raymond, Joseph, Lonnie, Leonard, Richard, and Byron had made it to the store as well. It was truly great to see the guys. We were like a "band of brothers."

Ben Junior and I anxiously walked up and began joking with the Engelhard guys. We had to be rather easy with our joking because there were certain turfs within the black communities that had not been erased. One of the last things that we wanted to do was ignite a turf war between Engelhard and the Ridge community. Jody was the leader of the "Hilltop Titans" and Ben Junior was the leader of the "Ridge Rovers."

Our skirmishes basically occurred on Friday and Saturday nights. The guys on the Hilltop didn't care for us coming on their turf trying to gain the attention of their ladies. In addition, we didn't cater to the Hilltop Titans invading our territory either. For the most part, we were all cousins anyway. As such, a great deal of kissing cousins took place.

The Ridge Rovers had enough sense to get out of Engelhard before sundown. However, the Hilltop Titans would customarily overstay their visits and we would be compelled to help them find their way back to Engelhard. Jody simply loved Judith, Larry's sister, and he was determined to see her by any means necessary. He would customarily make his way to the Ridge community at midday on Saturdays and hang around until about 7:00 p.m.

While we, the Ridge Rovers, played basketball, Jody and his posse would be sneaking around trying to see our ladies: Judith, Alice, Delphine, Julia, Deborah Ann, Judy, Jean Carol, Dorenda, Belvin, Minnie, Virginia, Trinta Ann, and Lillie Bell. These ladies were our peers and at times our kissing cousins. To be absolutely honest, several of our own distant cousins actually taught us how to French Kiss. They would dump their mouth of snuff or tobacco and plant a most perfect kiss on us. For the most part, we were so hormonal, it didn't matter. However, the Ridge Rovers were committed to protecting our turf. It was without question, we didn't care to have the Hilltop Titans on our landscape. However, on this day, we were in Engelhard and we would respect their territory. After seeing Jody, Larry, and Dexter whispering, I felt very uneasy. I wondered if they were planning to ambush us. I smiled and kept my eyes on them consistently.

After about three minutes of waiting, Mr. Tony Spencer opened the front doors for patrons to enter. We were extremely anxious to purchase our red socks and black shirts. I looked to the far right of the store and saw a tall slender dude placing items on shelves. He nodded and waved at us and continued restocking shelves. Then Mr. Tony Spencer called to him and said, "R.S., come on over here and help sort these shirts according to sizes. I have several orders for black shirts and red shocks, so it's going to be quite busy for the next couple of hours."

I later learned that the young man was Mr. Tony Spencer's son. He was called R.S. and he was a student in college. Joseph whispered to me, "Yo, Prez, ain't that the dude who blocked your shot when the white guys allowed us to come into the gym to play a game of basketball against them?

I responded with, "I believe you are right, Jid. I thought I had seen that dude before. That dude played real smart basketball and he could really shoot."

The black guys who lived on the Ridge played basketball on makeshift dirt basketball courts. We played ball even when the grounds were muddy and soaking wet. We even played when the grounds were frozen due to cold temperatures. We simply loved a good game of basketball! So, while walking home from Engelhard one Saturday, we walked past the old high school where white students-only, attended. We heard a great deal of yelling and laughter.

The old white school had a nice gymnasium; however, we had not seen one before. My buddies and I were only familiar with makeshift, dirt basketball courts. As such, Sammie, Ben Junior, Joseph, and I decided to peep in to see what the gym looked like. The floors were made of beautiful hardwoods that glistened and the goals actually had nets on them. The floors were shining and looked clean enough to eat a meal. To us, it was comparable to the Boston Gardens. When we peeped in, three tall white dudes came to the door. Two of the guys were twins and the other guy was called R.S. He said, "You don't have to peep-in like you're doing something wrong. Come on in and play a little basketball."

After meeting R.S. and the twins, I met a guy called Tommy. He had a serious stuttering problem, but his jump shot was deadly and relentless. My buddies and I cautiously went into the gym and had a great deal of fun. I met R.S. at the gym that Saturday and didn't see him again for about three years. However, I saw Tommy quite often on Saturday nights as he paraded his beautiful cars across the Engelhard Bridge. The white guys were very kind to us and one of the guys, named Michael, actually bought us sodas and gave us a ride back to the Ridge Store. I was shocked to see R.S. on the Saturday before "Black and Red Friday." I never knew that he was Mr. Tony Spencer's son.

It appeared that "Black and Red Friday" was going to be a great success. Several guys from Slocum (a small Township in Engelhard, North Carolina) rushed into the store so briskly that they knocked over a basket of apples that were strategically stacked for aesthetic appeal. Apples rolled over the floor like roaches trying to find a spot to hide. An elderly white lady who worked for Mr. Tony appeared totally petrified as we enthusiastically made our way to the counter to make our purchases. It was as if she had never seen so many black males in one place at the same time. After the initial shock subsided, she politely asked, "How may I help you boys today?"

Jody and Larry were the first to purchase their shirts and socks. Edward Brown, Jody's dad, sat patiently in his beautiful red two-door '63 Chevy Impala as he retrieved his order. William Henry, Larry's dad, stretched his long legs out of his Chevy and walked over to Edward Brown to chat. He kept his engine running as we admired the roar of his mufflers. The glass pack mufflers were music to our ears. Most of the us, except for Byron, Larry and Jody, didn't have fathers around to take us shopping. Having a father around for support and guidance was a sheer luxury. I was compelled to thumb a ride everywhere I desired to go. I often fantasized how I would respond if my dad were to take me shopping. When I would see the guys and their dads laughing and joking, I would get sad at heart because I missed my dad so badly. There were times when I wished that he would surprisingly show up on the campus of Davis School so I could simply say, "Yo, fellas, this is my dad. He is in the Army and stationed in Germany. Check out his shining shoes and fancy uniform."

As we waited in line to make our purchases, Hilda, Bernice, and Maggie entered the store. Their afros were still puffy and shiny as they strutted in their bellbottom jeans, loose-fitting tops, and African-styled earrings. Joseph and Sammie tried to be a little flirtatious with them; however, they simply ignored their overtures. Bernice was the thickest of the sisters. She had a big butt, tiny waste, bowlegs, and would beat a brotha down if he even thought about touching any part of her. And if a brotha was stupid enough to touch her, Hilda and Maggie would be right there to defend her honor. All three of the sisters were fine; however, few brothas were brave enough to approach them in a flirtatious manner. In addition, they were first cousins to Jody, and no one cared to experience the wrath of him.

Hilda, the oldest of the sisters, basically played the role of matriarch. When she spoke, each of them listened. She was very no-nonsensical and did not bite her tongue when he had a point that she desired to make. Hilda was a mocha-colored, short, and feisty intellectual who didn't fear anyone. She was so intellectually astute that she could minimize a brotha with a few three-syllable words and he wouldn't even know how to respond. Maggie, the younger sister, appeared happy every day of the week. Her smile was quite radiant and contagious. She loved a guy called "Big Willie" and everyone respected her choice. "Big Willie" had huge hands and big feet and he was like Wardell, as strong as an ox.

After we made our purchases, we meandered to the Town Tavern to simply hangout a bit. Some of the guys wanted to follow Hilda, Bernice, and Maggie on the Hilltop. However, no one wanted to take the risk of a possible confrontation with Jody and Larry. I wanted to go on the Hilltop to see Cathy; however, Larry liked her as well. To this end, I didn't care to take the risk of getting a beatdown from the Jody and Larry duo. Cathy was fine and possessed a mesmerizing smile. Nevertheless, the Hilltop was Jody's and Larry's turf and I wasn't known for winning many fights. I would fight in a heartbeat; however, I customarily ended up getting beatdowns as my cohorts laughed uncontrollably.

Mr. Coleman had a special on hotdogs; whereas, one could purchase two hotdogs and French-fries for two dollars. Ben Junior and I put our remaining monies together and ordered the special. We elected to go outside to sit on the bridge and watch the young white guys cruise in their beautiful cars. The notion of someday actually owning a car seemed totally impossible because we didn't even own bicycles.

We were dirt poor and to sit on the bridge and watch the beautiful cars parade across the bridge was compelling. I would sit on the bridge and simply dream of the day when I would buy my first new car and then I would cruise across the bridge with Jo Ann. I envisioned putting on creased slacks, a starched white shirt, a skinny tie, and penny loafers and heading straight to Jo Anne's house for an evening of relentless sophistication and class. I even imagined splashing on some Old Spice aftershave lotion. My daydreams and night dreams were nothing less than incentives to achieve. I dreamed of owning my own car and having money so I could own many of life's amenities just as the young white guys. As such, the young white guys gave me exorbitant incentive to achieve.

After seemingly hours of cruising, the young white guys would enter Ben Midgette's café for fine dining. When the front doors opened, the smell of fried shrimp, fried oysters, fried chicken, and soft-shelled crabs resonated. Mr. Ben kept a jukebox near the front door and it wasn't uncommon to hear soundtracks of Sam Cooke, Otis Redding, Percy Sledge, and Aretha Franklin blasting from speakers. I would watch from afar as young white guys exited their beautiful cars, wearing penny loafers, argyle socks, and khaki pants. Quite honestly, it was nothing less than a scene from *Happy Days.* As I sat on the bridge and observed, it became quite apparent to me that blacks and whites lived in two different worlds. My world was inundated with strife, poverty, and socioeconomic challenges. I wanted so much more than what I had. I hated being poor!

The six days before "Black and Red Friday" were the longest six days of my life. We had done an excellent job of keeping the plan undercover. I ran into some problems with hemming my pants correctly. However, my older sister, Linda, hemmed them for me and did not ask many questions. The one-inch above the ankle stipulation made my only pair of black slacks look far too short. The shortness of my slacks made the red socks highly visible. I felt like a genuine nerd when I looked down at my feet. I was simply glad that Ben Junior didn't mention suspenders. If he had mentioned suspenders and thick glasses, I would have been compelled to challenge his vision.

Well, "Black and Red Friday" finally arrived. When I came out of my bedroom, en route to school, my sisters looked at me and began to laugh hysterically. I hadn't even seen them laugh at Flip

Wilson with such intensity. Linda, asked, "Junior, did the weather man forecast that the tide is going to rise today? If so, you definitely don't have to worry about rolling up your pants. You can save that energy!"

I simply ignored my sister and tried to make it to the door before the school bus arrived. My baby sister, Vanessa, laughingly exclaimed, "Junior, your pants are too long to be called shorts and too short to be called pants. What in the world are you wearing? You look like you're wearing clown pants"

Again, I ignored the tease. I thought the teasing had subsided when all of a sudden, my middle sister, Jackie, asked, "Junior, did you cut your ankles? If so, you have time to go back in the house to change those bloody-red socks before the school bus arrives!"

The school bus finally arrived and when I stepped on the bus, I received a big applause. Jimmie, Edward, Donnie, Melvin, Walter, Jerry, and Kenny Junior were all decked out in their black and red. As our bus reached the Ridge community, I saw Sammie, Larry, Ben Junior, Joseph, and Raymond all decked out in black and red. All of the guys met at Sammie's house and entered the school bus at the same time. Their stoic demeanor gave the impression that they were paying attention at the last meeting. None of the guys showcased a single smile. They appeared serious and totally focused. The guys were as serious as pledges trying to join a college fraternity.

Martin and Miguel had been extremely adamant about us governing our behavior on "Black and Red Friday." A sense of urgency graced everyone's face. Ben Junior and Sammie were our leaders and we were to model after their behavior. In fact, the school bus was eerily quiet. As the bus slowly rolled, I felt as though I was attending a funeral on wheels. By the time we arrived at Byron's house, I felt as though I was sitting beside a busload of pallbearers. In my mind's eye, the school bus had transitioned into an elongated hearse and we were en route to the church for a powerful "home going" ceremony. A mysteriously morbid feeling consumed the atmosphere as my sisters and the other female bus riders inadvertently transitioned into flower girls. There was something special about "Black and Red Friday" and the aura could not be denied.

When our bus arrived on the campus of Davis School, I readily noted that Superintendent Bucklew's car was parked right behind Mr. Boone's beautiful Thunderbird. All of the guys remained in their seats as the ladies exited the bus. Dorenda was the last female to exit and then we all stood to exit as a tightly knit group.

Alice and Hilda stood at the front entrance of Davis School as we continued our trek to class. Bernice and Virginia appeared truly astonished that we had transitioned into a cohesive group of young men in a mere twenty-four hours. I must admit, the black and red looked amazingly cool. The red socks moved down the halls like spokes in a bicycle as we rushed to our respective classes. We epitomized solidarity and on this day, the Sisters of Soul were compelled to respect the audacious brotherhood.

I met Martin and Miguel near the water fountain. They were ecstatic that we were able to pull off the plan with such artistry. Just as we were in the process of going to class, the front office door to Mr. Boone's office opened. Mr. Boone and Mr. Bucklew were in the process of taking their monthly tour of the school campus. Mr. Adams was mopping the halls as Thad Junior and Van Grey were returning to class after parking their school busses. With an exception of Mr. Adams, we were all decked out in our beautiful black and red. When Superintendent Bucklew looked up and recognized the commonality in colors. He was so astounded that he dropped the yellow legal pad that he customarily carried. He turned as red as a strawberry and anger ensued immediately. Mr. Boone's head dropped immediately as he shook his head in utter surprise.

When Thad Junior and Van Grey approached Mr. Boone and Superintendent Bucklew, they politely said, "Good Morning! Have a good day!"

Mr. Boone was still in a state of shock, he did not respond at all. However, Superintendent Bucklew disappointingly looked at Mr. Boone and asked, "Charles, what kind of school are you running down here? Every time I come down here, it's something new. I don't have to worry about this at O. A. Peay. Phillip runs a tight ship and I expect the same from you. Tell me, what's going on? Everywhere I turn, I see black boys wearing black and red. And what's up with male students wearing red socks? Is there some type cult or gang affiliation going on down here? If so, I can call Sheriff Cahoon and we can nip this in the bud right away. I just know that this is not a bastion for the Black Panthers or the Black Power Movement."

I felt really sorry for Mr. Boone. However, we were not trying to sabotage his leadership in the face of his superior. The Black Power Movement was in its infancy stage and the Kool Kolored Kidz endeavored to showcase at least a meager semblance of solidarity. We knew that it was simply a matter of time before the desegregation of public schools in Hyde County and we had a serious fear of the unknown. Mr. Boone simply happened to be the leader at Davis School and we were simply trying to model a degree of solidarity among the black males.

When Ms. Piland discovered that we could hear the entire exchange between Mr. Boone and Superintendent Bucklew, she closed the door immediately. The last thing that I heard Superintendent Bucklew say was, "Charles, I suggest you run this school. If you cannot run it, I guarantee you; I'll find someone who can!"

During lunch, in the cafeteria, Mrs. Lula sat at the table with Martin, Miguel and me. She complimented us on our behavior and our attire. Then she chuckled a bit and said, "I didn't know who was going to have a heart attack first, Mr. Boone or

Superintendent Bucklew. Nevertheless, you guys made a serious statement today. Wow, I am so proud of you boys!"

When Lucy, Clara, and Evelina made a special trip to my table to say hello, my mouth was so full of Great Northern beans that a few fell out of my mouth and rolled down my shirt. I could not speak and I felt like an absolute nerd. However, Evelina touched my hand and simply smiled. I was so accustomed to being ridiculed by my peers that I didn't know how to respond to complimentary statements. My self-esteem was at an all-time low and I needed to feel appreciated and significant. The white bean stain on my shirt looked really nasty. When I went to the restroom, I took a handkerchief and cleaned it perfectly. I didn't want anything to mess up this special day. For the first time in my life, I didn't feel invisible.

It was quite apparent that the Kool Kolred Kidz had made an impact at Davis School and we bathed in the adulation. Fridays were always special at Davis School because it was customarily called "Chicken Day." The old adage and stereotype that black people love chicken would have would have manifested itself on this day. However, on this Friday, Ms. Florene cooked the chicken extra crispy, just the way I like it. She even smiled at me and gave me an extra chicken wing. As I dove into the hot Great Northern beans, Donald rushed to the table and announced that Wardell had thrown a baseball to Thomas and accidentally smashed the windshield of Superintendent's Bucklew's car. He said Mr. Boone was really upset.

I crammed my remaining food in my mouth and rushed outside to see what was happening. By the time I reached Superintendent Bucklew's car, Thomas and Wardell were sitting in Mr. Boone's office with Superintendent Bucklew. Mrs. Lula eventually came outside and walked around the car with a yellow legal pad appearing to assess damages. Mr. Adams followed her as he took a small brush and cleaned glass from the dashboard and front seat. I felt sorry for Wardell and Thomas because they were in deep trouble and I felt as though the superintendent had a low tolerance for blacks. Mrs. Lula tried to keep a straight face as she said, "You boys know better than to play ball around these cars. And now you've messed up the superintendent's car. Mr. Boone is really upset right now. I suggest you boys be on your best behavior for the rest of the day!"

Mrs. Lula was loved by all the students because she worked hard to keep us out of trouble. There were time's when she would reach into her pocketbook and give students money to purchase ice cream. However, there were days when Mr. Boone appeared to be bipolar. It was difficult to read his daily mood. Some days he would come to school really chirpy and excited about teaching and learning. Then again, there were other days when he appeared to hate his job and the people that he was expected to lead. Mrs. Lula knew Mr. Boone's disposition quite well and she could readily tell when he was in a bad mood.

At Davis School, the "haves and the have-nots" determined status and recognition. The entire school population was extremely dirt poor; however, there were different echelons of poor. When I did not have money, my self-esteem really suffered. I detested not having money, especially when it came time to purchase ice cream. I really appreciated my sister, Linda, giving me money on "Black and Red Friday."

Wardell and Thomas were not allowed to purchase ice cream after breaking the superintendent's windshield. If I had gotten into the ordeal that they experienced, I am confident that I would have needed a medical specialist. After surviving jokes and ridicule from my siblings, I would have had to deal with the wrath of my parents. My mom and dad did not play when it came to mischievous behavior. As such, I was compelled to walk a tightrope. I did everything in my power to avoid having them spend extra money. Every dollar was designated for something in my household.

Mr. Boone did not suspend Wardell and Thomas for breaking the windshield of Superintendent Bucklew's car. However, they were required to pick up paper on campus and the clean the restrooms for two months. "Black and Red Friday" was a day of torment for Mr. Boone and Superintendent Bucklew; nevertheless, it was a day to be remembered for the Kool Kolored Kidz. Strutting around on campus in a vibrant colors was a beauty to behold and never forgotten. The symbolism of our chosen colors and the cohesion within the brotherhood created a fabric that could not and would not be duplicated.

When the bell rang for the dismissal of school, Alice, Hilda, and Mary Lee approached Martin and Miguel and complimented them for a great execution. They suggested that we work together cooperatively to assure that there would be a semblance of cohesion when Hyde County schools become fully integrated. Martin embraced Alice's suggestion and informed her that we would discuss the potential collaboration at our next meeting. He was very apprehensive about discussing the focus of the Kool Kolored Kidz on the school bus parking lot.

Alice and Hilda had assumed leadership in transitioning "The Sisters of Soul" into a legitimate sisterhood and when they spoke, everyone listened. As we slowly walked to our respected school buses, Alice suggested that the quality of life for black students at Mattamuskeet School would be centered on our personal levels of toleration. I listened without interruption and concluded that there was merit to Alice's vision. At heart, I was concerned about going to Mattamuskeet School and being subjected to deeply rooted racism and lukewarm acceptance. Fear of the unknown created high levels of anxiety and apprehension when it came to the desegregation of Hyde County Schools. I learned that "fear" has the potential to thwart progressive change.

Lucy and Clara died in a terrible auto accident a year after "Black and Red Friday." Then six months later, my older sister,

Linda, died while away in college. Seemingly, my entire world turned up-side-down. I couldn't figure out where I fit on planet, Earth. The loss of my sister was terribly devastating. It was difficult to smile and embrace sunshine for a great while. Shortly, after Linda passed, my classmate and friend, Larry drowned. The world seemed dark and cold to me and I didn't have an answer. Losing my sister was the greatest pain that I had experienced. To some degree, I was left numb and bitter. I just didn't know how to handle the excruciating pain. I needed a sense of belonging and the Kool Kolored Kidz filled the deep void in my heart.

# CHAPTER 18
# MEAT BALL GOES TO COURT

***Every area of trouble gives out a ray of hope, and the one unchangeable certainty is that nothing is certain or unchangeable.***

***—John F. Kennedy***

After my friends and I, the Kool Kolored Kidz, had our altercation with the Ku Klux Klan, it wasn't safe for black Americans to walk the roads of Hyde County. White Americans who had a low tolerance for blacks began to disseminate pamphlets and brochures announcing the return of the Klan. The Klan engaged most of their activity during late night or early morning hours. Most blacks ignored the threat of Klan activity and continued life as if the organization was non-existent.

Mr. David Spencer, a tall, skinny, no-nonsense black man who lived on the Hill Top, declared that he would pop a cap in anybody who threw "Klan papers" in his yard. All the kids in the neighborhood called Mr. David the "Jolly Black Giant." He had the biggest and longest feet that I had ever seen on a human being. His size 16 (sixteen) shoe made his feet look as though he wore clown shoes. In fact, on most occasions, Mr. David had to cut the ends out of his shoes so his feet could fit comfortably into them. He loved small babies and little children and the love was mutual. Children gravitated to Mr. David as if he had some type divine magnetism. Truthfully, as much as Mr. David cussed, essentially every time he opened his mouth to speak, he would never cuss or be rowdy around young children. He loved animals a great deal as well, especially dogs.

Mr. David could not read but he was a master at disguising his illiteracy. One day Mr. David got sick and had to spend a few days in the Beaufort County hospital. He had a great deal of pride and he often tried to cover the fact that he could not read. Kenny, Larry, and Donnie decided to give him a surprise visit as he recuperated in the hospital. They tapped on the door and Mr. David responded by saying, "Come on in. The damn door is open. What do you want me to do, get out of this skinny-ass hard bed and open the door for you?"

As Kenny, Larry, and Donnie entered his room, Mr. David grabbed the dinner menu and gave the impression that he was reading it to select what he wanted to eat for dinner. However, Mr. David was holding the menu upside down and pointing as if he could read. Kenny immediately recognized what was happening, so he asked, "Mr. David, how about some baked chicken, apple sauce, and green beans, would that be okay?"

Mr. David smiled and said, "Damn, I will be so glad to go home so I can get some real food. I started to choose a cup of beans, fried chicken, and French fries but I know fried foods ain't good for me. Come to think of it, when I eat fried food, it tears up my stomach and gives me gas like mad. In fact, if I ate some fried food, you'd have to raise a window up in here."

Kenny, the consummate jokester, responded with, “Well, I tell you Mr. David, judging by the smell of your feet, I believe we need to crack that window just to let a little air up in here.”

Donnie and Larry looked at the menu and readily noted that fried chicken and French fries weren’t even on the menu. They sat and talked with Mr. David for about two hours and then Meat Ball, George Thomas, Charlie James, and Edward Brown entered the room. Meat Ball had gotten a speeding ticket in Washington, which is in Beaufort County, and had to be in court before 9:00 a.m. He was concerned that he might lose his driver’s license, so he asked his brother, George Thomas, to ride with him just in case the judge decided to take his license. Charlie James heard the conversation and asked if he and Edward Brown could ride along because he needed to pick up some spark plugs and Edward Brown needed to buy a new pair of white shoes for Memorial weekend. Seemingly, old school playas weren’t really sharp unless they were wearing their white shoes, white belt, and white socks. It could be mid-December and the old school playas still wore their favorite white combination. Some of the guys looked like they could have gotten starring roles in the *Godfather* movies.

Meat Ball told the guys they could ride along if they were willing to chip in on a little gas. They all piled into the car and headed to the Beaufort County courthouse. Upon arriving at the courthouse, they met Punkin, a homeboy who moved to Washington, North Carolina after living in New York. After customary handshakes and hugs, he said, “I hope you guys aren’t in any real trouble today. Judge Ward is presiding and that dude doesn’t play. He locked me up twice and he told me if I ever enter his courtroom again for public drunkenness, he was going to throw the book at me. He said that he was going to personally make sure that I get some real hard time to sober up. When he said that, everyone in the courtroom began to laugh. It was totally disgusting! They acted as if criminals don’t have rights, too. Man, I was scared, real scared! Don't you know he threw a guy in jail today for failing to pay child support? Can you imagine that? The poor brotha didn't even have a job."

Meat Ball nervously scratched his head and asked, "Man, you've got to be kidding? This judge is that tough?"

Punkin emphatically stated, "Judge Ward is no joke! If I weren't an alcoholic, I wouldn't dare take another sip of liquor for the rest of my life. I just don't know what this world is coming to. Drunkards use to have honor and respect. Look at Otis, on the *Andy Griffith Show*; the whole Town looked out for him."

After pondering Punkin's statements, Meat Ball looked at his watch and said, "Guys, I'd better get on in the courtroom so I won't be late. If Judge Ward is as tough as he says, I don't want to get on his bad side."

As the guys turned to enter the courthouse, Punkin yelled, Hold up! Hold up! Can you guys come up with $2.00? After having to deal with Judge Ward talking smack to me, I need a drink terribly. Come on guys; do your homeboy a favor!"

Edward Brown dug in his right front pant pocket and gave him a balled-up, wrinkled dollar bill. Then Charlie James dug in each of his pockets and came up with four quarters. He asked, "Will four quarters work? I don't have a dollar bill."

Punkin, being the comedic person that he was, stated, "Man, as bad as I need a drink, I don't care if you have one hundred pennies, twenty nickels, or ten dimes. I simply need a drink!"

After giving Punkin the requested $2:00, they almost ran to the courthouse. They were determined to be on time to avoid the possible wrath of Judge Ward. Meat Ball waited in the courtroom for about an hour before the clerk of court summoned him to come forward. He aggressively walked to the front of the courtroom after hearing his name. The prosecutor informed the judge that Meat Ball was traveling east on highway 264 at a speed of seventy-eight miles per hour in a posted speed zone of fifty-five. The judged frowned and scratched his head in a very inquisitive manner.

Judge Ward asked, "Mr. Bowden, why were you in such a hurry on such a wet and dreary night?"

Meat Ball responded with, "Sir, I was alone and I just knew that those chicken-ass Klan boys were chasing me. And wasn't about to allow them to make an example out of me. I was determined to make it to the Hyde County line."

Judge Ward interrupted him and vehemently stated, "Mr. Bowden, that type language will not be tolerated in my courtroom. I suggest you clean up your account on that incident right now. And I mean right now!"

Meat Ball appeared a little astonished about the judge's response. However, he regained his composure and continued his story. He stated that he was trying to make it to the Hill Top in Engelhard where his people lived. After appearing a bit distracted, he calmly stated, "Judge, Your Honor, Her Majesty, my mom always told my brother and me that a good run is always better than a bad stay. I didn't need a bad stay. So, I decided to hall ass! I wasn't going to let them hang me without a fight. You see, Your Honor, Her Majesty, I remembered reading about what happened to Emmett Till in Mississippi. And I wasn't trying to let that happen to me."

Judge Ward prefaced his statement with, "Mr. Bowden, I've already warned you about your foul mouth. Don't force me to remind you again! If you do, chances are, you won't like the repercussions! Are you attempting to make a mockery of this court? You will not convert my courtroom into comedy hour, okay? It is not necessary for you to address me with all those colorful adjectives. Do you understand me, Mr. Bowden? You will not demean me, or this court of law! Again, do you understand me? Are you telling me that you actually thought the Ku Klux Klan were on your trail? You are contending that you had no idea that it was the city deputy was behind you? Mr. Bowden, come on now! That sounds rather strange to me. Can't you come up with a better alibi than that?"

Meat Ball raised his right hand, crossed his chest and stated, "I had just stopped in Belhaven to get some gas and a pack of cigarettes and three white guys smiled at me and then lifted up their white robes to show me that ***KKK*** was boldly written on them. They tried to scare me, but I simply smiled at them and gave them the middle finger and went on in the store. You see Judge; I have long fingers and a couple of young white girls drove up and parked just as I gave them the middle finger. I kinda think they were a little embarrassed."

Judge Ward paused for a minute, frowned, and then stated, "Let me double check to see if I heard you correctly. You contend that three white guys tried to scare you, right? They actually showed you their robes and the letters, ***KKK,*** were boldly embroidered on them. Now tell me in your own words what they actually did? You don't have to be nervous at all. You see, this is my court of law and the only one who's going to be intimidating in this courtroom is me. Do you understand me?''

Meat Ball indicated that when he came out of the store, the white dude sitting behind the steering wheel looked at me and asked, 'Hey, boy, aren't you kinda lost being out here all late like this? You must not be from 'round these parts, right? Me and my buddies are koon hunting. We hate koons with a passion. A koon is the nastiest and filthiest animal to walk the earth. We really hate koons, you know what I mean?'"

Again Judge Ward scratched his head, pondered for a minute, and asked, "How did you respond to the young man?"

Meat Ball was slow to respond to the Judge; however, after coughing three times, he stated that he I peeped into the old truck and saw that each of the guys had shotguns resting between their legs. He said they smiled a stupid smile and acted as if they were about to go on a big hunting trip.

After pondering for a few seconds, he said, "They were chewing tobacco and a nasty-looking spit cup rested on the dashboard as they grinned from ear-to-ear. I really wanted to reach in that old truck and wipe that grin off their face. However, I kept walking to my pickup truck. The driver of the old pickup spit some tobacco juice in the dirty cup and said, 'Look here boy! We don't like your kind around here. So get your gas and get your black ass the hell outta here as soon as possible!'"

"What did you do then, Mr. Bowden?" asked Judge Ward. "As I pumped my gas, a blue 340-Duster drove up and three young white females were in it. They looked at me and smiled. In fact, they actually waved at me in a real friendly way. So, I smiled and spoke to them. I could tell they were probably still in high school because they did a great deal of snickering as they looked down at my shoes. Then the one with the ponytail embarrassingly asked, 'Is it true what they say about black guys and big feet?'"

Meat Ball indicated that he was caught off guard with the question. Then he disappointingly stated, "Before, I could respond to the question, the white dude driving the old pickup truck responded with, 'Yes, their big dirty black feet were made for running. And if you don't stop talking to him, you gonna see the new Jesse Owens tonight. You gonna see just how fast his feet are, in living color.'"

Judge Ward looked perplexed. However, Meat Ball had his full attention. Then he said, "Mr. Bowden, your story is rather fascinating. Tell me more!"

Meat Ball responded with, "Your Honor, the young ladies appeared a little embarrassed and pulled off in that little 340-Duster squealing tires. I really didn't look at the guys as young men. Sir, I looked at them as cowards trying to scare me. In the black community, we call them chicken-asses."

Judge Ward reminded Meat Ball to refrain from name-calling. Meat Ball, turned to the Judge and rhetorically asked, "Why in the world would grown men ride around covered in white sheets? I just don't understand this, at all, Your Honor, Her Majesty!"

The Judge Ward ignored Meat Ball's inquiry and told him to discontinue the rhetorical questions and to continue with his account of the incident of that evening. Meat Ball recounted, "Well, I actually ignored the guys and got in my old truck and drove away. There was a part of me that wanted to come back and pop a cap in each of them. However, I only had one shell for my shotgun."

When Meat Ball indicated that he had only one shell, patrons in the courtroom began to snicker uncontrollably. The deputies and the District Attorney began to laugh as well. Consequently, Judge Ward slammed his gavel on his desk and admonished the patrons for laughing. He angrily stated, "If I hear anymore snickering or loud outbursts, I am going to clear this courtroom and charge everyone in here with contempt of court! Do you understand me?"

The courtroom became eerily quiet. It appeared that everyone knew that Judge Ward did not play. Meat Ball cleared his throat and stated, "Sir, I was outnumbered and I wasn't trying to be a hero. As I took off in my old pickup, I thought about Mr. Glover, my history teacher. He told us about Emmett Till and what happened to him in Mississippi. He was only fourteen years old when the Klan boys got to him."

Judge Ward interrupted Meat Ball by stating, "Mr. Bowden, this is North Carolina, not Mississippi. I can't control what happens in Mississippi. However, I can control what happens in this courtroom. And this is not the time for a history lesson!"

Meat Ball responded with," Yes sir, Your Honor, like I said, I wasn't trying to be Malcolm X or Dr. King. As I pulled off, I noticed that the Klan boys started their engine as well. As such, I was determined to make it to Swan Quarter, or the Hyde County line. I knew my brother, George Thomas, would handle matters, if they were brave enough or stupid enough to come on the Hill Top in Engelhard. Your honor, I truly thought the Klan was chasing me."

Judge Ward rubbed his chin and asked "Why didn't you look in your rearview mirror? You could have seen the patrol light."

Meat Ball looked pleadingly to the judge and stated, "Sir, I don't have a rearview mirror. Your Honor, Sir, my truck is twelve-years- old and the rearview mirror fell off about two weeks before I received the speeding ticket. I was going to get a new one but I had a hole in my muffler and Sheriff Cahoon told me to get my muffler fixed as soon as possible or he would have to ticket me. So, I spent my money on a new muffler and hoped to find an old rearview mirror off a junked car or truck. Sir, I live in the poor black community and I simply gave out of money."

Judge Ward annoyingly asked, "Mr. Bowden is there anything else that you want to share with me about the dynamics of that night before I render my decision?"

Meat Ball indicated that as he put gas in his car the big white guy sitting in the middle of the pickup stated, 'I believe we gonna catch us a koon tonight!""

Meat Ball told the Judge that he ignored the remarks and went on in the store to pay for his gas. After paying for his gas and returning to his pickup, he noticed the guy sitting in the driver's seat. The guy loudly asked, 'Hey, Virgil, what does koon taste like?'''

Virgil responded with, 'Hell, I don't know. They tell me, it tastes just like chicken. You know when Jiggaboos find something that they really like; they always compare it to chicken. If you give a Jiggaboo a piece of chicken or a slice of watermelon, they're in colored folks' Heaven."

Meat Ball told the Judge that the guy sitting to the far right, near the door, looked at me and asked, 'Tell me, you people eat lots of chicken. What does koon tastes like?""

Judge Ward shook his head and asked, Mr. Bowden, how much embellishment are you adding to your account of that evening? The dynamics of that evening are rather bizarre."

Meat Ball crossed his chest and raised his right hand and stated, "I have told you nothing but the truth. That night was a real nightmare for me. To tell the truth, I still have bad dreams about that night."

Judge Ward rubbed the left side of his face and stated,"Tell me more, Mr. Bowden. Your story is filled with drama."

Meat Ball cleared his throat and stated, "Honestly, I looked at them and stated that I hadn't seen any koons. And I didn't give a damn about what it tastes like. I told them that the only thing worth wasting a bullet on was the three stooges sitting in that rusted-ass pickup. Then I suggested that they go on their merry way and try to scare someone else, because it's just not working with me."

Judge Ward asked, "You mean to tell me, after all those alleged insults, you simply walked away and didn't respond in any manner?"

After taking time to blow his nose, Meat Ball indicated that he I walked away. He stated that he was so angry that he thought he was going to explode. Then he stated that he came back and said, 'Look, don't worry about me. Don't be asking me questions about koons. You are supposed to be the hunters; you should have the answer. If I am lost, that's my damn business. You, farm boys, better find some rats to shoot at because I ain't got time to play games with you. Just leave me the hell alone and allow me to get my gas and I am out of Belhaven. Okay?""

The Judge asked, "What did the alleged guys say then?"

Meat Ball's responded with, "Your Honor, Sir, one of the white guys responded with, 'Oh! You're one of those so-called millitant niggras? Damn, Virgil, look at that boy's eyes. He's one of those mixed-koons, ain't he? I really hate mixed-koons most of all. They think they're somebody special. They don't want to recognize that they're still niggras. Tell me, what are you mixed with, rat or dog?""

As Meat Ball told his side of the story, his eyes began to water and his voice cracked three times. He said he found the question, "What are you mixed with, rat or dog?" truly demeaning to his parents. He sniffled and stated that no one insults his parents and gets away with it. That's just not right!

Judge Ward encouraged him to calm down. He said he needed to hear all details about that evening. Meat Ball told the Judge that black people can tolerate a lot, but no one talks about their parents.

The Judge indicated that he was really proud of him for keeping his composure. And indicated if he had retaliated physically, it was highly probable that he would have been charged with a felony instead of a misdemeanor.

After wiping his eyes, Meat Ball indicated that Virgil, the white guy sitting in the middle, angrily, stated, 'It doesn't really matter what you are made of, you are live bait tonight. Boy, you gonna think it's Halloween out here. You betta get plenty gas because you gonna need it. I'm gonna teach you how to have respect for us, white folks. Yes, that's right, we gonna make an example out of you so the rest of the so-called militant niggras will get the message. I promise you, you won't forget this night!""

"Sir, as I was leaving the store, a Belhaven deputy was entering and I accidentally bumped into him." He looked at me and said, 'Boy, you better watch where you're going. Don't be bumping into me, some of that black just might rub off on me.""

Meat Ball indicated that he was going to apologize to the deputy, but after the insult, he simply attempted to go to his car to leave Belhaven. However, the deputy went on to say, 'I was watching the evening news the other night and saw a group of coloreds marching down the streets of Alabama yelling, *Black is Beautiful and Black*

*Power*! Well, I tell you, black ain't beautiful on you people. Do you understand me, boy? I don't play with the coloreds at all. And this-here badge gives me a lot of power. Some white folks try to befriend with you people. I am not one of them.""

The Judge interrupted Meat Ball and asked, "You mean to tell me that you simply accepted those alleged insults and didn't retaliate in any manner, whatsoever?"

Meat Ball's responded with, "Well sir, I looked at him and said, "Boy! The only boys I see around here are the three sitting in that rusty-ass truck outside and you. Tell me, Barney Fife, how big do boys grow in Belhaven? I am not a boy! I am a grown-ass man!"

Judge Ward reminded Meat Ball to cleanup his language. Meat Ball responded with "Sir, I apologize."

The he emphatically stated, "Sir, then deputy stated, 'Oh! I got something for you. You niggras are getting down right too sassy. There ain't going to be no *Black Power Movement* in Belhaven as long as I carry this-here badge. Now don't cause me to take this-here badge off and teach you a real good lesson. I can show you what *White Power* is like real quick, fast, and in a hurry."'

Sir, I looked at him and I said, "If you take that badge off, the only thing you're gonna get is a serious case of whip-ass."

Then the deputy angrily stated, 'You got your gas; now get your black ass out of Town before I really lose my temper."'

"Your Honor, Sir, I didn't say nothing. I simply got into my pick-up and headed to Hyde County. Then, after about ten minutes of driving, a vehicle pulled up on my bumper and tried to ram me from the rear. The vehicle was really, really speeding. Ole Susie, my truck, doesn't have the power that she once had. However, on a long stretch, she needs to be respected.

Jude Ward asked, "How did you respond?"

Meat Ball stated, "I immediately thought about the three Klan boys and the deputy at the gas station. The vehicle that was tailing me began to blink its lights and blow its horn. After seeing and hearing all of this, I mashed Ole Susie to the floor. To be quite honest, I put the pedal to the metal."

Again patrons in the courtroom began to snicker uncontrollably. The District Attorney turned apple red trying to control his laughter. Judge Ward slammed the gavel again, real hard. Then he adamantly stated, "This is your last warning. If I hear any more snickering, I am going to clear this courtroom."

Meat Ball nervously stated, "Like I said, Ole Susie is twelve-years- old. She backfired three times and then I hit passing gear. My steering wheel was seriously trembling and then I hit a bad place on the highway and my left headlight fell to the road. Again patrons in the courtroom bit their lips and turned several shades of red and brown as they fought the desire to laugh. They didn't want to deal with the wrath of Judge Ward.

Meat Ball stated, "I was proud of Ole Susie that night. My steering wheel was trembling so badly that I had to grip it with both hands."

Judge Ward asked, "You mean to tell me that you were traveling at an excessively high speed with only one headlight. You were a danger to oncoming traffic as well as yourself. And you had absolutely no idea that it was law enforcement behind you?"

Meat Ball responded with, "Sir, Your Honor, the vehicle behind me rammed my back bumper three times as if the driver was trying to push me into one of the canals along US-264. After I reached the Hyde County line, the vehicle turned around and went back in the direction to Belhaven, US 264 west. I slowed down to 55 mph and continued my drive to Engelhard. Ole Susie was smoking and my oil light began to flash off and on. I had only one headlight and I could smell exhaust fumes inside Ole Susie."

Judge Ward asked, "You mean to tell me that you didn't pull over to check your oil?"

Meat Ball indicated that he really didn't have a quart of oil to put in his truck. Therefore, it would have been a wasted of time to stop. He stated that he reached into his glove compartment and grabbed an eight-track cartridge and pushed it in his player. The Temptation's, *I Wish It Would Rain* bellowed out of his speakers like a mother singing sweet lullabies to her infant. He said he felt relaxed and at peace. Meat Ball said the music was so soothing and peaceful that he really didn't feel like arguing with anyone. After listening to *I Wish It Would Rain,* he said his eight-track went straight to *I Could Never Love Another* (*After Loving You*). He said he rolled down his window and allowed the wind to blow through my Afro as my left foot tapped to each beat.

Upon approaching Swan Quarter, he immediately noticed lights flashing and a roadblock ahead of him. Meat Ball said he knew that he had done nothing wrong. Therefore, he simply reached into his right front pocket to get my driver's license. As he geared Ole Susie down, three deputies pulled their firearms and pointed them straight at him.

Judge Ward interrupted Meat Ball and asked, "What did you think after seeing the roadblock?"

Meat Ball indicated that he was very relaxed at that point and he didn't know what to think. Then he said as he slowly approached the roadblock, he noticed Sheriff Charlie Cahoon standing in the crowd. He looked at him with a puzzled look on his face and asked, "Meat Ball, why did you try to outrun the Belhaven police? Do you have some illegal whiskey in that truck, or something? I just don't understand it Meat Ball, I thought we were alright with each other. I have never harassed you. Not even when you drove around for weeks with that busted muffler. You know right well that I've never hassled you at all!"

Judge, Sir, before I could respond, Deputy Sheriff Simmons interrupted and emphatically stated, "The Belhaven deputy was simply trying to stop you because you accidentally left your sunglasses on the counter at the gas station. Don't we treat you people with respect down in these parts? Now what are you going to do?

Is that Jesse Jackson or that Golden Frinks gonna come down here and get you out of jail? I guarantee you, singing, *We Shall Overcome* won't get you out of this mess."

As Deputy Simmons continued his preaching, I reached in my shirt pocket and discovered that I had indeed left my sunglasses on the counter of the gas station. Judge Ward, Your Honor, I simply did not know that it was the Deputy behind me. I thought it was them Klan boys doing what they call 'koon hunting.' I made a big mistake. I am sorry. Judge Ward, I just did not know."

Judge Ward looked at Meat Ball and said, "Mr. Bowden, you have shared with me a very interesting story. I don't know how much you have embellished; regardless, the story is interesting. If your account is true, it says a great deal about the fragile state of American society. The dynamics of this story say a great deal about race relations and trust factors in Beaufort and Hyde County. Due to a host of mitigating circumstances, I firmly believe that you did not intentionally violate the law. To this end, I will dismiss this case. Have a good day!"

After hearing the judge's decision, Meat Ball turned to Charlie James and Edward Brown and gave them a "high-five." They left the courthouse and headed to downTown Washington to purchase a pair of white shoes for Edward Brown, and a set of spark plugs for Charlie James. As they entered downTown, a local deputy turned on his police siren and flashing lights, and pulled them over. The deputy slowly approached the car with his right hand resting on the handle of his firearm. He wore dark sunglasses, a large oval police officer's hat and black military-looking boots. The boots were shining like a new fifty-cent piece. Meat Ball looked at Charlie James and rhetorically asked, "What in the hell does he want? I know I wasn't speeding and I know that I gave the right turn signal. Damn, I'll be glad to get my black ass back to Hyde County."

The Washington deputy looked at Meat Ball and said, "Gentlemen, I just left the Beaufort County courthouse and I heard your testimony. On behalf of the Beaufort County Police Department, I just want to apologize for the action of the deputy. Yes, Belhaven is a part of Beaufort County; however, we do things differently in Washington. Believe me, you are always welcome to Beaufort County and if you ever run into any problems in Belhaven, Pantego, Bath, or Washington, just call (9 19) 946-1000 and ask for Officer Robert Smith. I will personally see to it that you are treated fairly. Now, you guys take care and have a great day!"

Meat Ball and Charlie James thanked the officer and headed to Main Street to begin their search for a pair of white shoes. After shoe-shopping, they rode to Beaufort County hospital to see "Long David." Mr. David hurt his back while working for Preston Mooney, a local farmer in MiddleTown. He was asleep when they knocked on the door to his room. Mr. David was sleeping so well that they decided to not disturb him. As such, they decided to return to Engelhard.

# CHAPTER 19
# LESSONS FROM DAD

***Children have never been very good at listening to their elders, but they never fail to imitate them.***

***—James Baldwin***

While Mr. David was in the Washington hospital, my dad and I went to Washington to purchase a lawn mower and a pair of hedge clippers. We stopped at Edgewater Motors to look at the new cars. The dealership was located in Belhaven, North Carolina and sold new as well as pre-owned vehicles. My dad was a loyal customer; whereas, he customarily purchased a new vehicle every three years. Well, the Chrysler Corporation sold Mopar products which were very popular in the late 1960s and early 1970s. My dad was initially a Ford-man, and then he transitioned to Chrysler vehicles. The trek from Engelhard to Washington gave my dad and me excellent one-on-one quality time. When we entered Belhaven, my dad stopped to check out the new cars at Edgewater Motors. The owner of the new car dealership was named Jack. Daddy had purchased several new cars from him. They appeared to have a genuinely respectful relationship. When my dad would drop by the dealership during the Christmas holidays, Mr. Jack would customarily give him a brand new bottle of Jack Daniels. They would laugh and joke as if they lived in the very same neighborhood. Needless to say, Mr. Jack was a white American and of course my dad is black.

When dad drove-up to the dealership, Mr. Jack rushed out of his air-conditioned office, full of smiles, and asked, "Boy, how are you doing? Where you been? I just asked a colored feller about you last week. In fact, he said he had just seen you in church on Sunday. I can't remember that colored feller's name; but I do know is last name is Bryant. He was a real nice boy and I ended up selling him a real nice pickup at a real good price."

Daddy smiled and said, "Jack, I've been doing well. I didn't want anything special. I told my son that I was going to pull over here to see what you have on the used car lot. He should be getting his license in about six months and I promised to buy him his first car. Really, we'll just looking around."

Mr. Jack smiled and said, "Well, I tell you, you came to the right place. I have some real good deals on the 340 Dusters and the much faster and more popular 383 Road Runners. I can give you a real good deal today and you can put it in storage until he gets his license. In fact, if you want to, you can keep it right here and I'll keep it in storage until he gets his license. Just tell me, I'll make it happen!"

Dad shook his head and replied, "No Jack, I am in a hurry today. Then again, it'll be six months before my son even gets his license. As such, I'll come back when I have a little more time."

I was terribly disappointed with Dad's response. However, my respect for him compelled to hide my true feelings. He was always savvy and diligent when it came to money matters. I aspired to be like him in a host of matters. After walking around for about five minutes, Dad concluded that it was time to head on to Little Washington.

Mr. Jack thanked him for stopping by and told him if he sees anything that he wants to test-drive to simply let him know. He told him that he could even keep a car overnight if he desires. I was hoping Dad would allow me to choose one of the blue four-speed 340 Dusters. He checked them out really well and said, "Son, if I were your age, I would go for that blue 340 Duster or that red Road Runner. It's hard to beat a Chrysler product."

After pulling off the car lot, my dad looked at me and stated, "Son, you didn't like the fact that Jack called me 'boy' right? Well Junior, he really didn't mean any harm at all by addressing me like that. Jack and I go way back several years and we respect each other. Yes, I am a grown man and he didn't have to refer to me as 'boy.' You see, I wasn't offended because we have established a friendship. Jack has his ways, and so do I."

I said, "Dad, I just don't like the fact that you are 58 years-old and you have served this country honorably in the United States Army and still you are called 'boy.' Pops, I really don't want to be disrespectful, but that's wrong!"

Dad reached in his shirt pocket, grabbed a cigarette, and simply said, "Son, you've got to learn what battles to fight. Some battles aren't even worth the energy expelled to get your point. You are still very young! However, when you have traveled the roads that I've traveled, you will become more tolerant and understanding. Don't think that all white folks hate black people. That's truly not the case. You've got to learn to choose the battles that you want to fight, carefully. If not, you will spend your entire life fighting!"

I listened to dad and really tried to comprehend his perspective. We drove on to Washington, North Carolina. As we entered the city limits, a policeman pulled Daddy over and requested to see his driver's license. Dad politely handed his driver's license to the officer. The officer perused his license quickly and politely told him to drive carefully and to have a good day. At heart, I viewed the incident as a legitimate act of DWB - "Driving While Black."

My dad viewed the incident as a police officer simply doing his job to protect law abiding citizens. As I assessed the incident, I saw a white American police officer profiling a black male driving an expensive car. He assumed that my dad was engaged in illegal activity. I resented the fact that my dad and I were blatantly profiled. However, my dad took a more friendly and optimistic disposition on the matter. He could have been oppositional and defiant and we would have gotten into the area of diminishing return. Nevertheless, Dad elected to take a passive and law abiding citizen route.

I thought about what my dad attempted to drill into me about choosing the battles that I desired to fight. I had difficulty discerning the difference between passivity and submission to the greater society. It is without question, my dad chose the right path. I asked myself, "Have I become a Rebel without a cause or have I become a Rebel in search of a cause?"

## CHAPTER 20

# THE LAST DAY OF SCHOOL

***Each man must for himself alone decide what is right and what is wrong, which course is patriotic and which isn't. You cannot shirk this and be a man.***

***—Mark Twain***

Living in the Ridge Community was full of excitement and adventure. Seemingly, every single day endeared new exploration and new challenge. None of the guys had expensive toys or fancy clothes. Nevertheless, we were happy and content with our meager means. Most of the guys on the Ridge walked where they wanted to go and never complained about heat, cold, or distance. Some evenings, after school, we would put our pennies together and walk to Mr. Sam's Grocery Store. Mr. Sam was an old white American who loved to call us koons and monkeys when he had drunk too much of King Paul's *Seven Star* wine. His vision was extremely poor but his name-calling never missed a beat. He appeared to simply hate my friends and me and we never did anything to him to warrant his hatred. It was as if he hated us because we were born black.

We grew tired of Mr. Sam's insults and decided to take a stand. Leonard and Ben Junior suggested that we go in the store and order a quarter's worth of two-for-a penny cookies. While Mr. Sam's back was turned, we would take whatever we wanted. We concluded that we would only do this if he greeted us with statements like, "What can I do for you little koons today?"

Mr. Sam was nasty too. He wouldn't even wash his hands before counting out the cookies. He chewed tobacco and there were times when tobacco juice drooled from the corners of his mouth and he would quickly wipe his mouth with the same hand that he counted cookies. He would spit his tobacco juice right on the floor and then take his right foot and slide the spit and tobacco juice between the cracks of the wood floor. Nevertheless, he sold the very best cookies in the neighborhood. I particularly loved the lemon flavored cookies and Ben Junior loved the coconut cookies and Ginger Snaps. There were days when Mr. Sam would drink a little too much wine and he would ask, "What can I get for you little monkeys today, bananas or peanuts?"

After insulting us, he would begin laughing uncontrollably. I would look at his big brown teeth and feel like vomiting. He only had about ten solid teeth and they were heavily stained from years of tobacco chewing. Salesmen came by weekly to reshelf supplies and to introduce new commodities. Mr. Sam would really show-off when white salesmen were present. It was as if he felt more empowered or superior when he insulted us around other whites. There were occasions when the white salesmen would look at us and appear to be very empathetic. In fact, some of the white salesmen appeared embarrassed by Mr. Sam's racist behavior. Actually, on two occasions, the salesmen gave us a whole box of cookies and then encouraged us to take our money somewhere else.

One salesman said, "Look, you young boys don't have to accept his insults. Why don't you take your business to King Paul's

General Store? He won't treat you like this. I don't like the way he treats you boys. This is not right."

The salesman did not know that "King Paul" would drink too much of the cheap wine that he sold, and would occasionally call us names as well. It appeared that we didn't have an outlet. Seemingly, we were being dehumanized from all angles. Mr. Sam could not see very well; therefore, it would take seemingly forever for him to count out fifty cookies. Joseph said Mr. Sam would get real upset if anyone talked to him, or asked questions while he counted. One day, I watched as he attempted to count out a quarter's worth of two-for-a penny cookies. Joseph intentionally asked, "Mr. Sam, how much are those Vienna Sausages?"

Mr. Sam got real upset and said, "I told you boys to never talk to me when I'm counting out cookies. Now you caused me to mess-up. I ain't counting all these cookies all over again. Damn, you boys just don't listen!"

Mr. Sam actually miscounted and gave us twelve cookies too many that afternoon. There were occasions when he would give us ten to twelve cookies too many. There were other occasions when we would be seven or eight cookies short. Regardless, his first count was always final. We decided to visit Mr. Sam on the last day of school. He was very pleasant and asked, "Are you boys out for the summer? Maybe a couple of you boys will come by next week; I have some painting that I need to get done. Don't worry; I'll pay cash money for your time."

None of us elected to accept Mr. Sam's job offer. He was simply too unpredictable and his insults could be terribly demeaning. Nevertheless, it was the last day of school and we were all ecstatic. It was a very, very, hot day and we were dismissed from school early. There was no air-conditioning in Davis High, so Mr. Boone, our principal, decided to end school early. We were extremely happy and excited about the unknown. Leonard and Lonnie sat on the school bus and played cards. Joseph chewed up some paper, threw it, and hit Frankie on the back of his head. Frankie had just moved to our school from Brooklyn, New York. He was a true thug and was well-educated in street life. When Joseph connected him with the spitball, he began to cuss. He immediately turned around and said, "I don't play that. If somebody throws another spitball up here, I am going to punch somebody in their face."

Joseph heard Frankie and he ducked down in his seat and threw another spitball. Frankie became so angry that he threw his entire notebook to the back of the bus and hit Lonnie in his mouth. Lonnie had New York roots as well. He grabbed his mouth and ran to Frankie's seat, grabbed him, and asked, "What's up man? Why did you hit me with your notebook?"

Ervin, the bus driver, heard the commotion and told the guys to stay in their seats. Frankie and Lonnie ignored him. Ervin looked in his rearview mirror and saw that they were still standing and immediately slammed on his brakes. They fell against each other and almost fell to the floor of the school bus.

Joseph saw that a fight was about to ensue, so he said, "Yo, I was just teasing. I threw the spitballs. This is the last day of school. Ease up. There's no school tomorrow. I was just joking around! No harm meant, okay?"

My cousin, Ervin, was a fun school bus driver. He drove down our dirt roads as if he were on a race track. The school bus was very old but he had tampered with it to make it exceed its governed speed. We even passed another school bus one afternoon, and that was unlawful for a school bus. It was the last day of school and everyone was happy. Several students threw trash out of the bus windows and Dallas and Floyd smoked cigarettes and talked about going to Manteo for the summer to work. Happiness was in the air!

Sheila, Martha, Barbara, and Sushie as always sat on the back two seats. They were trend setters and every young girl desired to emulate them. Everyone knew better than to even think about sitting on the back two seats of the school bus. Even if one of them were absent, no one was allowed to sit on their "reserved seats." They were the pretty girls of the community and they wore their self-selected badge of beauty with utmost esteem. I must admit, the girls were pretty and they could sing. They could do a wonderful rendition of Diana Ross' *Come See About Me.* When they sang that song, the whole school bus would be rocking. Martha would assume the role of lead singer and really do a great job of impersonating Diana Ross. It was amazing how she could sensually roll her eyes and move her hands seductively. There were times when the ladies could be embarrassing and mean. Then again, there were days when they could be the loving, kind, and nurturing.

However, on this day, the last day of school, they were happy and they were singing. Barbara noticed Donnie and Abner, two white guys, following our school bus. Sheila looked at Martha and said, "Let's have some fun with these two white boys, okay?"

Martha, responded with, "What do you have in mind? Shall we tease them? Look at them drooling after us! I can tell they are wondering what it would be like to be with a sista. Those white boys have serious case of Jungle Fever!" Donnie and Abner continued to follow our school bus very closely. They smiled and waved flirtatiously at Barbara, Sheila, and Martha. Then Sheila began to throw kisses at the guys. Then Donnie and Abner began to smile and throw kisses back at them. Donnie, who was driving, then pointed to his unbuttoned shirt. He then gestured to Sheila to unbutton her top to expose her breasts.

Sheila looked at Martha and said, "Let's show these two white boys these black twins. Let's show them what they've been missing, okay?"

Not only did they show Donnie and Abner the twins, they pressed them against the school bus back window. Donnie and Abner went berserk! They began laughing and giving each other high-fives. Ervin looked in the rear view mirror of the school bus, heard the students on the school bus laughing, and abruptly hit the bus' brakes. Donnie and Abner were so mesmerized by Sheila and Martha's breast that they ran straight into the back of the school bus and wrecked the hood of their beautiful car. Everyone on the school bus screamed while laughing at Donnie and Abner. I laughed so hard that I wet my pants. After the minor collision, Martha began singing Marvin Gaye's *Too Busy Thinking About My Baby* and every female on the bus began bouncing and singing to the beat. It appeared that every female on the bus was in love and missing someone. When I got home that afternoon, Mom informed me that Aunt Mildred had gotten me a summer job in Manteo. I was really happy because I really needed a new pair of dress shoes and sneakers.

My first job working in Manteo was filled with tremendous excitement and enthusiasm. It was a welcomed transition from working in Preston Mooney's hot potato and cucumber fields. Ironically, the experience of working in mile-long rows of potato and cucumber fields compelled me have a high appreciation for air-conditioned kitchen work. I was hired at the Manteo Motel as a dishwasher and kitchen helper. The work was relatively easy and I could come to work in creased slacked and starched shirts. I didn't have to ride on the back of a pick-up truck at 6:00 a.m. with twelve other people to be transported to a mile-long row to pick up potatoes and cucumbers. Working at the Manteo Motel was indeed a luxury job and I felt as though I had received a promotion from God. I thanked God each day for the blessing and He continued to bless me.

I told Joseph and Raymond that Aunt Mildred had gotten me a good job in Manteo for the summer. All of the guys who lived on the Ridge had nicknames and mine was Prez. Joseph asked, "Prez, What will you be doing? Gosh! I wish I could get away from Engelhard. I'm sick of this country-ass Town!"

I proudly said, "I'll be washing dishes at the Manteo Motel! They're going to pay me $1.60 per hour and I can eat anything that I want in the restaurant except seafood. I can drink all the tea and sodas that I want and I can eat all of the ice cream that I want as well. And check this out; I can have bacon, eggs, toast, jelly, and orange juice every day of the week. I just might gain a few pounds before the summer ends. Man, I can't wait to begin work."

Joseph responded with, "Damn, Prez, you gonna go over there and wash the white man's dishes? You can have that job! I ain't gonna wash nobody's dishes or scrub no damn floors. You can do that if you wanna, I just ain't gonna do it!"

Raymond, stated, "I'd rather wash dishes any day than to work in Preston Mooney's fields. Prez, at least you won't be getting tar-baby- black from working in the hot sun!"

I didn't allow Joseph to steal my joy. As I road my bike, I thought about Joseph's remarks. However, I was still real excited about going back to Manteo. I would be able to hang with my best friends, Harold and Harris Junior. Then I thought about what Raymond said about working in the hot sun and becoming tar-baby- black. I couldn't understand why black people were so preoccupied with skin-color. It appeared that we, as a people, were conditioned to believe that dark skin color was something gross and ugly. Joseph and Raymond were rather dark; however, I loved them like brothers and their complexion was never an issue.

I left Engelhard for Manteo on the first Saturday after the last day of school. Uncle Ran and Aunt Mildred drove to Engelhard to pick up my sister, Linda, and me. We were happy and really excited about going to Manteo and our new jobs. Seemingly, the birds were chirping and a fresh fragrance of new flowers and cultivated soil consumed the air. We were on our way to Manteo, the Mecca to upward mobility and the fun-spot for the summer. I was super-excited about spending time with my brother, C-R. I idolized him and when people said, "Junior, you're beginning to look like your brother more and more each day." I loved the comparison and found it really complimentary.

As we approached Good Luck Street, my heart began to pump with excitement. Good Luck Street was the hangout place to be during the summer months. Most of my friends hung out near La Vada's, a popular nightclub. Uncle Ran slowed down to a turtle's pace as we approached the night club. The parking lot was filled with patrons and people were walking down the street en route to the nightclub. Marvin Gaye's, *Ain't Too Proud to Beg,* bellowed from the jukebox as we approached the parking lot. My heart was thumping with excitement. I was back in Manteo, and I couldn't have been happier.

Uncle Ran spotted my brother, "CR," and blew his horn. He recognized Uncle Ran and Aunt Mildred and then glanced at the back of the car and immediately recognized Linda and me. He immediately grabbed Malinda's hand and headed to Uncle Ran's car. He spoke to Aunt Mildred and Uncle Ran and then kissed Linda on her forehead and said, "Gosh! I have missed you all."

He playfully jabbed me on my shoulder and said, "Sport, how are you doing? Gosh! You are really growing. I believe you are taller than I am."

Malinda, looked at me and said, "Junior, you are really going to be a heartbreaker. Look at you, you are so cute."

Aunt Mildred told "CR" to be sure to come see her because she needed to speak with him about some very important matters. "CR" agreed to drop by on Wednesday. While parked in front of La Vada's nightclub, Robert Ashby rode up on his bicycle and began cussing. "CR" looked at him and said, "Come on Robert, this is my aunt and uncle and my little brother and sister. You don't have to use language like that around them."

Mr. Ashby indignantly stated, "That's *your* family. They don't mean a damn thing to me. He shouldn't have parked in the middle of the road like he's Sheriff Calhoun, or somebody special!"

My brother was known to be very temperamental at times. I could sense that he was getting annoyed with him.

Then Mr. Ashby sarcastically asked, "By the way, what are you calling yourself these days, Cat Man or C-R, I get confused?"

Before my brother could respond, Malinda read my brother's body language and readily knew that he was about to explode. "CR" shook his head and began to walk toward Mr. Ashby. Johnny Pledger, my brother's best friend, yelled, "Cat Man, just ignore Robert! You know how he is when he drinks a little too much. Tomorrow, he won't remember anything he said."

Malinda, looked at Aunt Mildred and Uncle Ran and said, "Mrs. Mildred and Mr. Randolph, it is good to see you. "CR" and I will be by to see you real soon. We need to go to Fearing's Drug Store before 5:00 p.m."

She winked at us and we knew that she was only trying to keep "CR" out of trouble. As Uncle Ran drove off, I saw Geneva, Gwen, Treacy, and Anthony standing near the school talking. They looked at me rather strangely as I waved at them. I was really anxious to head down the street to see my best friends, Harris Junior and Harold. Aunt Mildred fixed Linda and me a quick snack and I headed down the street to find my friends.

I had to pass La Vada's nightclub again to get to Harris Junior's house. Stroller, an ex-convict, with far too much mouth, was coming out of La Vada's as I rapidly walked. He looked at Joe Brooks, Roy, and Wilson and tried to embarrass me. My sneakers were worn terribly and the sleeves of my shirt were too short and my pants were seriously faded after numerous washes.

Stroller, yelled to the guys and asked, "Isn't that Cat Man's nappy- head little brother? Look at him, his pants are too long to be shorts and too short to be pants. He looks like a little welfare boy!"

Joe Brooks and the guys did not laugh. Roy looked at Stroller rather seriously and stated, "Man, you better ease-up on that because "CR" will be out here dragging your little skinny butt through that mud-hole."

Johnny Pledger responded with, "I hope Cat Man does come out here and drag your stinking butt through that mud-hole. At least that would be one way some water would reach your little dirty, rotten, ass!"

I continued my trek to Harris Junior's house. As I walked, I met Geneva, Cora Mae, Cassie, and Debbie. They were all really laughing and joking and I felt a little uncomfortable. I really did not know whether they were talking about my too-short pants or my beat-up sneakers. Regardless, I felt real uncomfortable. They all pleasantly spoke to me and Geneva turned toward me and asked, "Are you in Town for the rest of the summer."

I responded with, "Yes, and I am staying with my cousin, Mary Leary. My sister, Linda, is staying with Aunt Mildred. There wasn't enough room for both of us, so I'm staying with Mary."

Geneva smiled at me and said, "I saw your cousin, Dan, yesterday and I asked about you. He said that he was expecting you any day now. When you see Dan, tell him that I want to talk to him about going to A&T, okay?"

Dan, my cousin, was a junior at North Carolina A&T State University and he worked at Owens Motel and Restaurant every summer. He worked as a busboy and saved his money for school clothes and college expenses. Dan was extremely smart and highly goal-oriented. He was like an older brother to me and I always learned a great deal from him.

I responded to Geneva by saying, "Sure Geneva, I'll tell Dan that you want to speak with him about North Carolina A & T. Well, it is great seeing you all.

I continued my walk to Harris Junior's house. When I got there, he was patching an inner-tube on the front rim of his favorite bike. In fact, he actually had four bikes resting against his house. We simply spoke and didn't hug or anything like that. His hands were filthy and dirty from taking the front rim off his bike and from the glue and dirt that he accumulated in the process. Harris Junior jokingly said, "Henry, I just saw Geneva a few minutes ago and she asked if I had seen you. She said Mrs. Mildred indicated that you would be in Town this weekend for the rest of the summer. She was smiling from ear to ear!"

I responded with, "Yes. I will be staying with my cousin, Mary Leary. You know, Dan's sister. Harris Junior stopped momentarily and appeared a little confused. Then he asked, "Henry, what happened to you?

Then I became confused and asked, "What do you mean?"

Harris Junior responded with, "Mary, Neva Ann, Kevin, and JoAnn are all really light-skinned with pretty hair. Now look at you; you are African-black with nappy hair. Why are you so burnt and they could pass for white? Are you sure y'all are cousins?"

I was about to respond to Harris Junior when Virginia, Geneva's older sister, stopped in front of Mrs. Mabel's house and yelled, "Junior, is that you? Wow! You have really grown. As you get older, you are looking more and more like C-R. Come on over here and give me a hug!"

I ran to the car and she gave me a great big hug. Then see asked, "Have you seen Geneva, yet? I know she is going to be happy when she sees you. Look at you, you even have a little fuzz on your lip and you have those sneaky eyes just like C-R."

Virginia always treated me as if I were a younger brother. I truly embraced the manner in which she responded to me. She never talked *at* me; she always talked *with* me. And when I didn't comprehend the dynamics of the political process, she would talk to me about the typical nature of human beings. I learned that her disposition was grounded on absolute truths. There were times when she would talk to me about school and the need to get a sound education. I would listen attentively because her world view and vision transcended the waters and sand dunes of the Outer Banks.

While in high school, she was crazy about my cousin, Earl. He lived in Columbia; therefore, she basically saw him during the summer months when he worked in Nags Head. Earl and my brother, C-R, were essentially inseparable during their high school days. There were times when I would hear them sitting on the front steps of our house pouring out their hearts about their love for Virginia and Malinda. If they had a six-pack or two, they would be sobbing before they eventually fell asleep. I couldn't fathom how two dudes who presented themselves as super "macho" guys could basically sit on Mom's steps and cry themselves to sleep. One night while sitting on the steps, Percy Sledge's *When a Man Loves a Woman* bellowed out of La Vada's juke joint. As I watched them, I wanted to take their playa's card because they began to sob like small babies. At heart, I wanted to say, "Hold up! Hold up! Playas don't shed tears!"

I learned that love is powerful and it doesn't discriminate. The heart does what it wants to do. Even playas eventually get stung by the powerful sting of love. And when it happens, lives are changed forever!

# CHAPTER 21
# LILLIAN'S INN NIGHTSPOT

***Anytime you see a turtle up on top of a fence post, you know he had some help.***

***—Alex Haley***

The local Ku Klux Klan attempted to terrorize the black communities of Hyde County with vicious tenacity. However, the black communities had its share of internal conflict and rivalry. The black communities of Hyde County were at best seriously disjointed and unsettled. When my mom and dad decided to allow me to hangout on weekends with my friends, I had heard multiple stories about the rivalry between the Slocum guys and the Engelhard guys. In Hyde County, there were no designated teen clubs or teenage hangouts. Everyone partied together, teenagers alongside adults. As such, it was not uncommon to witness fathers and teenage sons and mothers and teenage daughters socializing under the same roof.

The rivalry between the Engelhard guys and neighboring Slocum guys became rather intense at times. For some reason, the guys simply did not like each other. Far too often, the bone of contention centered on competition to gain a female's attention. The guys would tolerate each other at school; but that was it, toleration. I found the rivalry rather strange because all of the guys were black and I could not understand why we could not get along with each other. The rivalry was intense and it was unmistakably real. It was rather bizarre; there were no black/white issues. However, black-on- black rivalries inundated every so-called black neighborhood. The black communities were extremely poor and disenfranchised. There were major territorial conflicts within the communities. The conflicts were comparable to S.E. Hinton's, *The Outsiders* and John Singleton's *Boyz in the Hood.*

My best friends David, Walter, and Louis told me about "Lillian's Inn", a makeshift nightclub located in the Slocum community. David told me that "Lillian's Inn" was like the Wild West. There were notorious fights, bullying, cussing, and shootouts mostly every weekend. Louis said Miss Lillian, the owner of the nightspot, was like Ms. Kitty on *Gun Smoke.* She could be as nice and as kind as the *Flying Nun.* However, it was not wise to get on her wrong side. She kept a loaded double-barrel, sawed-off shotgun, behind the counter and she would use it in a heartbeat. I recall my very first time going to Lillian's Inn; I was happy and petrified at the same time. As I entered the one-door entry, I observed Brenda, my classmate, and Leon, an older guy from Fairfield, swing-dancing. Everyone was fixated on their fancy footwork and their rhythm. They were amazingly smooth and almost choreographic with their dance.

Leon and Brenda were dancing to Wilson Pickett's *Mustang Sally.* Leon's girlfriend, Diane, smiled and waved at me as I entered the nightspot. Louis had already told me that Leon was very, very jealous and he did not like for anyone to talk to Diane, or simply dance with her. I was afraid to speak to Diane; therefore, I simply smiled and waved at her. When I did, Walter appeared a little uneasy and stated, "Man, you better chill on that. Leon is really jealous; I mean jealous to the 10th power. Bra, you don't want to tangle with him; he's a grown-ass man. That dude's much stronger and bigger than you. He works in the log woods every day. Man, believe me; you don't want to make him angry."

My response was, "Look man, I simply spoke to her because she spoke to me. I'm not flirting with her. I know she goes with Leon and he saw me when I spoke to her. It's not like I went over there and kissed her."

David interjected and said, "Henry, you can get caught up in some mess if you want to. You are on your own; we are not going to get hurt trying to help you. We had already told you about Leon's jealousy and you know he is older, bigger, and stronger than any of us. Now, it's up to you. Just know that we are not going to help you out. I ain't trying to get hurt tonight."

I simply shrugged my shoulders and walked away. Little John, Brenda's younger brother, was swinging away with Florida in the far right corner of the nightspot. He was spinning her around and moving to every beat of *Mustang Sally*. The floor appeared to bounce and gyrate to each beat. Florida smiled and appeared totally unconcerned about a plank in the floor potentially breaking. The boards of the wood floor were warped and when the music died down, it was easy to hear the old semi-rotten boards squeak. The dance floor was small and weak; nevertheless, it appeared that patrons had the most fun when they were compelled to squeeze around and bump into each other. Cigarette smoke and the smell of beer and hard liquor consumed the atmosphere. Ms. Lillian didn't possess licenses to sell cigarettes and alcoholic beverages; however, patrons didn't care to the least bit. Happy smiles graced the many faces and loud laughter could be heard from every corridor. I found it hard to believe; I was finally at Lillian's Inn, I was ecstatic.

There were three guys from Pantego visiting the nightspot that night and they appeared somewhat antisocial and rather mean. I had seen them before one Sunday evening at the Hilltop in Engelhard. They were shooting pool and drinking beer as if it were water. I heard them tell Mrs. Meta Pearl that they were from a small country Town called Pantego. Pantego is located in eastern North Carolina and it is equally as impoverished as Engelhard and Slocum. The only asset for Pantego was the mere fact that it was within close proximity of Little Washington, a favorite shopping hub in Beaufort County.

The guys had come to Lillian's Inn because they were working on a boat that was docked in Engelhard. Ms. Meter Pearl's nightspot was not open, so they elected to come to Slocum. I watched them closely as they whispered to each other and laughed loudly. It appeared that they were mocking the patrons as they danced and enjoyed an innocent Sunday evening of fun and frolic. The guys had the roughest skin and the roughest looking hands that I had ever seen. Louis, my cousin, whispered to me, "Henry, watch out for those guys over there. Something is going to go down and you don't want to get caught in the middle of it. I can tell; those guys are looking for trouble."

Just as Little John spun Florida around for the last time, he accidentally bumped into one of the guys. The larger of the two guys grabbed Little John so aggressively that two of his shirt buttons popped off. The big guy hatefully looked at him and said, "Look dumb-ass, stay off my shoes and don't be bumping into me. If you can't see, buy yourself some glasses."

Little John forcefully pushed the guy's hands off of him and apologetically said, "Look man, I don't want any trouble. I didn't mean to bump into you and I didn't mean to step on your shoes. I am sorry. I tell you what, to show you how sorry I am, let me buy you a beer."

The guy towered over Little John and angrily stated, "No, hell no! That's not good enough! I want you to get on your knees and clean the dirt off my shoes."

Everyone in the nightspot appeared shocked with the stranger's response. Then I heard murmurs and whispers that denounced the stranger's request. I watched attentively to see what Little John was going to do.

He disappointingly shook his head and said, "Man, I said I am sorry and I even offered to buy you a beer. I really didn't mean to bump into you. Nevertheless, I am not going to get on my knees and clean your shoes."

The crowd within the nightspot immediately began to applaud Little John's response. It appeared that everyone agreed with his stance. Murmurs and whispers became quite evident again. I looked at David and he put his hand over his mouth to signal me to not say anything. Then the largest of the big guys, looked at his friend and said, "Man, you gonna have to show these backwoods Negroes who's the boss around here. Bra, go on and handle your business. Go on and mop the floor with that little Negro so we can go down to Fred's. I got some business that I want to handle at the "Play Ground."

Little John was in the process of walking away when the guy grabbed him by the back of his collar and pushed him into a pole that stood in the center of the dance floor. The crowd within the nightspot appeared extremely quiet and shocked. Then I heard 'Little Sister' say, "No! Hell no! This ain't right!"

Little John slowly gathered himself; however, he looked a bit perplexed. He appeared to ask, "Man, what's up?"

Florida sympathetically rushed over to him to help him get up. While bending down, she tearfully asked, "Why don't you pick on somebody your own size. He said he was sorry and that should have been good enough. Just because you're big and stupid doesn't give you the right to push people around. I don't blame him; I wouldn't wipe off those beat-up, dirty, cowboy boots either."

Patrons of the nightspot were standing around speechless. Miss Lillian reached under the counter to get her sawed-off shotgun but immediately discovered that she had left it at home. The big guy stared at Florida and boldly stated, "I'm getting tired of you and your big mouth. Don't let me have to close it for you, because I will. I'll kick a woman's butt, just like I'll kick a man's. I'm gettin sick of you really fast. You backwoods, country-ass Negroes, get on my last nerve."

Florida responded with, "You act like you live in some big city or metropolis. Pantego isn't any better than Slocum and Last Chance. If it weren't for Little Washington, you people would have to pump in sunshine!"

When Florida made that statement, patrons began to laugh loudly. I was too afraid to laugh because the other two strangers appeared to be looking directly at me. I didn't want them to mop-up the floor with me. It was quite obvious that the three strangers became annoyed with the laughter.

Florida went on to say, "In fact, you came here; we didn't go there. Nobody made you come to Hyde County and now you feel the need to make fun of us. You three clowns are just as backwoods as we are. Don't think you are somebody special because you aren't. You walk around here wearing those bent-up and out-of- shape cowboy hats, acting like you are Sheriff Cahoon or Matt Dillon. As a matter of fact, you call us backwoods and country; however, if you look around, you'll see that you black hillbillies are the only ones in here wearing cowboy hats and western boots. Now, I ask you, who's more country, you or us? You are just another Negro trying to make it, just like we are. You definitely aren't any better than us."

The big guy angrily looked at Florida and asked, "Who are you calling a black hillbilly?"

Florida responded with, "I didn't stutter! Do you have a hearing problem? Yes, I called you guys black hillbillies; and what about it?"

The big guy stepped to Florida nose-to-nose and said, "Look, nobody calls me black. I ain't black; in fact, I am lighter than you are. It doesn't matter if you are a female or not; nobody calls me black!"

Florida annoyingly stated, "You are one big dumb Negro. You are so dumb that you find it offensive to be called black. Well, let me tell you, you are black and you will always be black. And after listening to your dumb-ass response, you are a *dumb*–black-hillbilly. You are so dumb that you can't even recognize that being called a *hillbilly* is much worse than being called *black*. Apparently, you Pantego *hillbillies* haven't heard of James Brown's record; *Say It Loud; I'm Black and I'm Proud.*"

The big guy embarrassingly looked at Florida and said, "Yes, black is beautiful . . . just not on people."

For some reason, blacks in the mid-sixties had serious problems with being called *black*. It was as if the term *black* made everything profoundly grotesque. I have witnessed students on the school bus joking with each other, and then, when one of them playfully referred to the other as *black*, the entire context of the play changed dramatically. It was as if the term black was the declared line of demarcation and nullified all joking. Truly, calling someone *black*, ranked right up there with talking negatively about one's mother. Each scenario was terribly taboo within the black community. In fact, it carried the very same weight as the N-word.

Finally, the smallest of the three guys decided to speak. He looked at his two cousins and said, "Guys, she is right. We need to respect this place. We are guest and we should act like it."

The largest of the three guys angrily asked, "Man, you gonna wimp out on us? Damn, I ain't tryin to hear no Sunday school lesson tonight. I think we should teach these backwoods Negroes a real good lesson. In fact, I want to teach her a real good lesson about meddling into men's affairs. When I leave here, she's gonna be calling me "Big Daddy." She simply has too much mouth and a sassy black woman irritates the hell out of me. I've had enough! She has gotten on my last nerve."

Florida responded with, "Go ahead Mr. Tough Guy! Just lay one hand on me! I assume you can count that far, right? I guarantee you, you will regret it! Go ahead big man! Please lay one little finger on me! I am standing right here, a simple pinky finger will work!"

When the guy raised his hand to pimp-slap Florida, Leondus, her older brother, walked through the door. The entire juke joint became amazingly quiet. It was as if everyone was waiting to see what was going to materialize. I looked to my right and saw Gregory, Wallace, and Larry starring at Leondus. It was as if, all of a sudden, Sheriff Matt Dillon had arrived in Town to rescue the villagers. Larry was about to take a sip of his brew, but for some reason, he placed it on the counter and quietly waited for the drama to unfold. I immediately looked to my left and noticed Charlie holding on to Vanessa in a very protective manner. Vanessa didn't appear to be concerned at all. She knew that Charlie had her back and he could hold his own. All eyes appeared to be on Leondus and everyone knew he didn't play when it came to his immediate family members.

Leondus was a Herculean guy who commanded tremendous respect. There were those who swore he was as strong as a bear. When he stood erect, his arms nearly reached the top of his knees. His biceps and tricepts were so pronounced that only a fool would challenge him in a physical altercation. Sambo declared that Leondus could have easily been star wrestler in the WWE. His physical strength was amazing and almost surreal.

Ironically, there were those who swore that Otis Lee, his much smaller cousin, could throw him on his backside almost any day of the week. He was much shorter and didn't really showcase an intimidating presence. Otis Lee was said to be clever and faster than a rattle snake. His friends referred to him as a small piece of leather, yet well put together. He dated Sylvia, my older sister, Linda's classmate. She appeared to worship the ground that he walked on.

My Dad and I witnessed Leondus and Otis Lee helping Dr. Liverman one day when he had a flat tire while en route to work. Dr. Liverman was driving a yellow Volkswagen Beetle when he ran across a board on the highway that was peppered with nails. It fattened both tires on the left side of his car and he did not have a jack. He was in a hurry to open his office and did not know what to do. Coincidentally, Otis Lee and Leondus drove up in an old pickup truck. After looking at the Beetle's flat tires, Otis Lee stated, "Dr. Liverman, we can help you with those flat tires. We don't mind handling this for you!"

Dr. Liverman responded with, "I really appreciate your offer. However, I recently purchased this Beetle and I forgot to check to see if the jack was in the trunk. I just found out that I really don't have one."

Otis Lee asked, "Tell me, do you have a lug wrench?"

Dr. Liverman walked to his trunk and held up a lug wrench and said, "Thank God, I do have a lug wrench."

Leondus looked at Otis Lee and stated, "Let's help Doc out. We can check on those crab pots later. He is always helping us. I tell you what, if you'll lift the front-end, I'll get the rear."

Otis Lee said, "Okay, I know I can handle the front-end of a Volkswagen any day of the week without any problems. Are you sure you can handle the back-end?"

Otis Lee grabbed the front-end of the Volkswagen and lifted it like it was the foot of a bed. The veins in his biceps became highly pronounced; however, he didn't appear to strain in any sense. Leondus worked hurriedly to take off the lug nuts. Everything was going well until he got to the very last lug and it appeared frozen on the wheel. Leondus tried and tried again but the lug nut would not turn. Otis Lee became very impatient and disappointingly suggested, "Look man, I am tired of holding up this front-end. I tell you what, I want you to come around to the front and hold up the front-end while I attempt to turn the lug nut, okay?"

Leondus, frowned and said, "Okay, Otis Lee, you can try to turn it and I'll hold up the front-end. If you think you are stronger than I am, give it a shot."

Otis Lee held in his breath and gave the wheel a powerful snatch; the lug nut spun around like a spinning wheel. Leondus didn't say anything; he simply walked to the back of the Volkswagen and grabbed the bumper. He snatched it up and immediately let it fall to the ground. The back-end bounced slightly. Then he looked at Otis Lee and asked, "Do you still have those gloves in the back of the truck? That bumper is rather sharp and it might cut my hand."

Otis Lee went to the glove compartment of his truck and retrieved his gloves. He passed them to Leondus and jokingly said, "If you can't handle this, let me show you how it is done."

Leondus responded with, "Don't forget the engine is in the back not the front. I can handle that front-end with one hand and you were popping sweat like an escaped convict. I got this, you simply get ready to take off the lugs."

After putting on the gloves, Leondus lifted the back-end of the Volkswagen like it was a living room sofa. He didn't appear to strain at all as the back two wheels cleared the ground. A few tourists passed by and took pictures of Leondus as he lifted the Volkswagen and showcased his muscles. There were times when he would show-off by holding the back-end of the car with left hand and make muscles with his right hand. Otis Lee and Leondus were two of the strongest guys I had ever seen. They were nothing less than kind and gentle giants. I could see why they were often called the "Herculean boys."

Dr. Liverman offered to give each of them twenty dollars; however, they would not accept his money. He thanked them and told them if they ever needed anything to simply let him know. When Dr. Liverman offered to give them twenty dollars, Leondus smiled and said, "Doc, you don't owe us anything. You have always been good and kind to our people and you are always willing to help us when we are injured or sick. I am just glad that we were able to help you for a change. Really, a lot of black people really depend on you. You don't owe us anything at all."

Otis Lee interjected and said, "Yes, Doc, you have been a lifesaver for our people and we appreciate you. You don't owe us anything! In fact, we owe you and we can never repay you for all you have done for black people in Hyde County. Doc, have a great day and if we can ever do anything else for you, just let us know."

Dr. Liverman appeared astonished and shocked that he was so well-appreciated by members of the black community. Otis Lee and Leondus were super-strong and kindhearted. Florida was the apple of their eyes and they did not take it kindly if anyone bothered her. They knew that Florida was super strong as well, and she could handle herself without any problems. Nevertheless, she was female and she shouldn't have to fight guys. My friends and I knew Leondus was strong and the guys from Pantego didn't know who they were bothering. When Leondus entered Lillian's Inn, it appeared that the entire nightspot got quiet. Everyone appeared to wonder what was next. They knew that trouble was about to ensue because Florida was well-connected.

Leondus grabbed the big guy's right hand and slammed it into the post that stood in the center of the nightspot. He had a serious speech impediment so no one really understood what he was asking or saying. However, the big guy's hands were so rough and callous from pulling fish nets and other hard work from working on boats that the big guy simply smiled and charged at Leondus. As Leondus was about to tackle the big guy, the smallest of the big guys tripped Leondus and he fell against the jukebox. The guy that Leondus was about to tackle, grabbed a Budweiser bottle and smashed it against Leondus' head. The bottle, filled with beer, exploded on Florida's blouse and Brenda's white hot pants. Florida was speechless because she had never seen her brother in a bloody and savage fight before.

In most cases, Leondus would quickly knock guys out and continue with his playful personality. Leondus and Otis Lee were legendary figures in Engelhard and Slocum. It appeared that all three guys were about to attack Leondus when all of a sudden, Otis Lee and Sambo entered the nightspot. Blood was streaming down Leondus' face like a wounded deer on the first day of hunting season. However, without any explanation, Otis Lee grabbed the guy who hit Leondus with the Budweiser bottle and threw him over Miss Lillian's counter. The glass that sheltered the candy shattered and eventually crumbled. Glass covered the floor as if there had been a head-on collision within the nightspot. The container that housed the two-for-a-penny cookies overturned and cookies rolled on the floor like tiny remote controlled race cars.

Sambo grabbed the smallest of the three guys and smashed his head into the jukebox. The guy stood up momentarily and then withered to the floor like a deer surprisingly shot at a waterhole. Leondus wiped blood from the side of his face and became so angry that he forgot the fact that he was bleeding profusely. The gash on the right side of his head was so deep that the white meat was exposed. A huge knot appeared on the left side of his head. The knot was so pronounced that it made his head look warped. In fact, his head actually looked like it was growing another ear. While Otis Lee was wrestling with the guy who hit Leondus with the Budweiser, Leondus grabbed the other big guy.

The big guy was caught off guard and did not anticipate that Leondus would recover from the blow so quickly. Leondus looked at the big guy and said something. However, due to his renowned speech impediment, the guy looked confused. Nevertheless, Leondus ignored the blood and apparent pain and hit him with an uppercut. The guy hit the floor so hard that the impact broke four boards on the dance floor. The guy grabbed his lower back and slowly climbed to his feet. He rushed Leondus and grabbed his legs and then he put an unbreakable bear hug on him. As he struggled to get Leondus through the small door, Leondus punched him repeatedly in his face. The guy was light-skinned and his face began to redden like a big tomato. By the time they got off of the porch, it was hard to distinguish who was bleeding more; Leondus or the giant guy from Pantego. It was like a scene on *Bonanza* when Hoss Cartwright got caught-up in a saloon brawl.

Otis Lee and the guy that he was fighting made their way through the small door. Patrons attending the nightspot began chanting, "Kick his butt! Kick his butt! Kick his butt!"

Otis Lee had the guy down on the ground pounding him relentlessly with power punches. Dirt and mud covered each of them like hogs trying to find shelter from torrential rain in mid-July. Then all of a sudden a strange woman came seemingly from nowhere and jumped on Otis Lee's back. She rippled off his shirt and began scratching him like a frightened cat. Otis Lee tried to push her off but she was fighting as if it were life or death. Then he heard her say, "Please, please get off my husband. Don't hurt him please. Please don't hurt him. I am pregnant with his child. Please don't kill my husband."

Otis Lee eased up on the guy and stood up and appeared confused. The guy that he was choking embarrassingly looked at his wife and asked, "Honey, are you okay? We're just having a little fun, that's all. I know we should be on the boat resting because we're leaving for Georgia early in the morning. But it's not like I was cheating on you. Honey, we were bored and thirsty, so we came out to drink a beer or two. Are you okay? You are holding your stomach, are you sure you are okay?"

His wife replied, "Yes, I am fine! "No, it's not like you are cheating on me. However, you could have been killed. And what would I tell your son or daughter? Billy, you need to grow up and stop trying to bully everybody. It looks like you met your match to-night. You almost got your brother and your cousin killed tonight over trying to be Mr. Macho. It is time for you grown-ass men to grow up and stop acting like boys. I saved your butts tonight; however, this is the absolute last time. Do you understand?"

After everything calmed down, Otis Redding's *Do You Like Good Music* began to blare out of the jukebox. I re-entered the nightspot and the party mood had resumed. Della Ruth, Deborah, Brenda, and Hilda were laughing and joking about the altercation. I looked to the far right of the nightspot and I saw Kenny Junior, Jimmie, Ralph, Richard, and Little John standing around like gang members waiting for something else to go-down. Kenny Junior loved to brawl and would fight in a heartbeat. Richard, Little John's older brother, was my classmate and had recently moved to Slocum from New York. He was a fast-talker and serious conniver. I eventually learned that he was more bark than bite. Jimmie, Kenny's younger brother, was very quiet but had a temper that could not be denied. He never bothered anyone; however, it was not wise to anger him. Little John, my classmate, was very likable and he loved to dance. He dressed like a consummate city-guy and was always *GQ* in fashion.

I really enjoyed my first night out at Lillian's Inn. My buddies, David, Walter, and Louis were sticking together like white on rice. We were all scared but anxious to explore the dynamics of the adult world. While most patrons drank beer or sipped on fifty-cent shots of illegal whiskey, we ordered soft-drinks and snacks. I bought a Dr. Pepper and held on to it like the other brothas who drank beer. For some reason, I felt more comfortable holding something in my hands. I was too young to drink beer; however, the Dr. Pepper bottle made me feel like I was in the in-crowd.

Walter ordered a Coke and a Baby Ruth and Louis and Walter drank Dr. Peppers and ate honey buns as they watched patrons dance, gulp beers, and smoke cigarettes.

We were all hanging out with the ultimate hope of losing our virginity. Our raging hormones were relentless and overpowering. We were destined to lose our virginity and cross the hot sands to young adulthood. We had no idea who would be first, but we all knew that something lurked in the dark of night that was much better than Honey-buns. We were ready for the rite of passage and our hormones were alerting us every day and night.

When I re-entered Lillian's Inn, I immediately saw Diane from afar. She waved at me and I responded immediately without even thinking about her boyfriend, Leon. Leon stared at me and pulled her closer to his chest. I really did not want to have any problems with him; therefore, I simply went to the counter and ordered a pack of Spearmint chewing gum.

Jimmie and Kenny, Junior took a broom and swept up the broken glass and debris from the fight. I watched as Jimmie put about ten of the two-for-penny cookies in his coat pocket. After they cleaned the floor, Ms. Lillian gave each of them two dollars. Then the jukebox began to scream the latest tunes again. The floor was bouncing because it was party-time again, and everyone was happy. Leon appeared to watch my every move and I kept him within my peripheral vision. I was indeed afraid of him, but I could not allow him to know this as fact.

Diane lived in Fairfield and attended O. A. Peay School, the rival high school. Leon, her boyfriend, was an adult and very insecure. He detested it when Diane laughed and joked with her high school peers. As he maintained eye contact with me, he held her tightly. Then I observed as she pulled him closely to her and whispered something into his right ear.

After kissing her on her cheek and smiling, he reached in his pocket and gave her two one-dollar bills. Then all of a sudden,

Diane walked away from him and came to the counter and ordered a pickled pig's foot. She flirtingly looked at me and asked, "Hello Henry, how are you tonight? You look really nice in that black leather jacket. I have always liked leather, especially on guys. It makes them look kinda rough and tough. You look so, so, cool tonight!"

For some reason, whenever Diane came close to me, I instantaneously got a major woody. My zipper area popped out uncontrollably. My testosterone levels elevated significantly and I could not control the visible manifestation. I was young and full of energy and did not know how to address my innocent adolescent years. Truly, my hormones bounced around like popcorn in an open cooker. My day dreams, night dreams, and wet dreams had me in a quagmire of restlessness. I was trying to find my place of fit; however, it eluded me.

Leon saw Diane talking to me and immediately stormed to the counter. He angrily looked at Diane and asked, "Is this the way you are going to treat me? I gave you two dollars for a pickled pig's foot and then you come over here and start flirting with this little nerd. I should kick your butt and Henry's little skinny ass too. This ain't right! "

My cousin, Ervin, walked up to the counter as he said my name and asked, "Henry, are things okay? Did I hear someone threaten you?"

He stoically looked at Leon and said, "Just remember, if anybody bothers you, I will be outside on the porch talking with Meat Ball, Erskine, and Goose. If anybody, I mean anybody, especially chicken-asses from Fairfield bother you, just let me know. There will be another throw-down out here tonight."

Leon smiled at Diane and said, "Honey, when you get your pickled pig's foot, don't forget to get a couple napkins. I'll be over there standing near the jukebox. Don't take long, okay?"

Diane responded with, "Sure Leon, I'll be right over there as soon as I get my order. I can see you from this spot. Henry is a friend, honestly! Nina talks about him on the school bus almost every day. You don't have to get jealous and bent out of shape. Anyway, he is a true gentleman."

Leon stared at me from a distance that entire night. I kept an eye on him because I found him very intimidating. I just didn't trust him and I didn't want him to clobber me while my back was turned. I felt somewhat secure because I knew Ervin, Erskine, Meat Ball, and Goose were right outside on the porch and they had my back. My first night at Lillian's Inn was filled with excitement and endless drama. As my buddies said, it was like the "Wild West!"

# CHAPTER 22
# DON'T BOTHER THE CHURCH FOLKS

***You see things and you say "Why?", but I dream things that never were and I say "Why not?"***

***—George Bernard Shaw***

Living in the house with three sisters had its challenges. I had no one to play with and on many occasions I felt rather invisible. My sisters played with dolls, skipped rope, played nurse, teacher, and occasionally played church when Mom wasn't around. My sister, Jackie, could do an almost perfect version of Miss Zollie Hill's happy dance. However, if Mom caught any of us mocking church folks, we were in serious trouble. She called it blasphemy.

One day Jackie was mocking Miss Zollie's routine and accidentally knocked over two lamps and broke each of them. I thought I'd never stop laughing. Jackie had her eyes closed, doing a tap dance and spitting just like Miss Zollie would do in church. When the noise from the lamps crashing to the floor occurred, Jackie opened her eyes and Mom was standing right in front of her. I fell to the floor laughing and Mom took Daddy's army belt and gave Jackie a beating that she talks about today. After Mom finished with Jackie, she looked at me and said, "I ought to whip you for laughing."

Mom looked at me with her no-nonsense look and said, "Get on out of here and put some wood on the porch. Don't you know that you can bring curses on yourself for mocking and laughing at people praising the Lord? It's nothing funny about it. Something bad can happen to you for simply laughing. Believe me, there is nothing funny about being in the spirit and praising God. Now, get on out of here before I change my mind and give you the very same thing that I gave Jackie."

Mom didn't have to tell me twice, I eased on outside. After listening to Mom, I became scared and feared that something bad was going to happen to me. I placed the wood on the porch and went down the road to play with Ben Junior. Ben Junior was older, bigger, and much stronger than I. For some reason, we started playing Zorro and sword fighting. We used dried reeds as swords and began to recklessly hit each other's reed. The reeds were similar to cheap fishing poles and we were having lots of fun. I would block Ben's swing and he would block mine. I would charge Ben Junior and he would charge me. This was fun; more fun than playing *Simon Says* and more fun than playing *Hide and Seek.*

The sword fighting became more and more ferocious and we welcomed the confrontation. Sword fighting really heightened a guy's testosterone. *Simon Says* and *Hide and Seek* were girly games and now we were playing tough-guy games. Hattie and Rosa, Ben Junior's younger sisters, eventually came out of the house and sat down as spectators. We now had an audience so the competition became even more violent. Then, all of a sudden, Ben Junior swung at me with tremendous force and my reed broke and stuck in my left eye brow. Blood began to rush down the curvature of my nose. And as I touched it, my fingers became saturated. Ben Junior stood frozen because he did not know what to do. I didn't know whether I had actually loss an eye, or whether it was simply blood oozing out of my eye brow. I was scared, very scared.

Hattie and Rosa looked at each other and then ran into the house. I placed my hand over my left eye brow and began to run home. I cried like a little sissy as I jumped on the porch to get my mom's attention. Mom heard my cry and rushed to the living room to find out what had happened. She knew that something major must have happened because I never, ever, cried. My sisters, Linda, Jackie, and Vanessa rushed to the living room as well. They too, knew something major must have happened because I never cried!

Mom wiped her hands on her apron and then told me to stand still so she could see what was causing the bleeding. She looked at me and said, "Just stand still. You have a nasty cut above your eye brow. I'll put a cold bath cloth on it to stop the bleeding. If it doesn't stop bleeding, I'll get Cousin Janie to take us to see Dr. Liverman. He'll probably give you a shot to stop infection. The blood eventually stopped flowing. However, an ugly scar remains above my left eye brow. I immediately associated my injury with my laughing at Jackie mock Mrs. Zollie Hill. From that incident, I learned that the wrath of God is not to be taken lightly. I wholeheartedly respect the Holy Spirit.

After things calmed down that evening, Mom lectured me with, "You see, Junior, what happened to you for laughing at Jackie mock Mrs. Zolly today. Believe me; you cannot do ugly and think that it won't come back to haunt you. You were less than a half inch from losing your eye today. However, God must have forgiven you for your foolishness and you only loss a little skin and blood."

I honestly never saw Jackie mock Mrs. Zolly Hill again. However, when Mrs. Zolly Hill shouted in church, I would try my best to not look at Jackie. I wasn't going to take the risk of her causing me to laugh. I had learned my lesson, the hard way.

Mom always preached to me about taking charge when she and Linda were not around. She knew that I did not like crowds of people and that I really did not care to talk to strangers or anyone who did not live in the current household. We only had church at our church (Pleasant Grove Baptist) once per month. Every second Sunday was designated as church Sunday and that meant walking a mile to attend Sunday school and to participate in communion during church services.

I really did not like participating in communion because it meant extended time in church. And I was anxious to use the rest of my Sunday school money to buy two-for-a-penny candy at the Ridge Store. Additionally, it meant additional singing and praying. Traditionally, I would sit in church, look at my watch, look at the preacher, listen to the elongated prayers, and become totally disgusted. At heart, I would be saying to myself, "Why don't they just shut up and let the people go home? I need some two-for-a-penny candy like real bad!"

I really did not like participating in communion. The bread tasted absolutely horrible. However, the fake wine was sweet and really good. Just before consuming the bread and wine, Rev. Hilton would always give a long lecture about assessing oneself to see if one were worthy to eat of the bread and drink of the wine. The pre-drink and eat lecture was always scary and it made me very uncomfortable. I knew I had a host of matters to work on to qualify as worthy to partake in communion. The symbolic bread was so nasty-tasting that it was impossible to swallow without having something sweet as a chaser. Geach (Larry) referred to the wine as a chaser because he had seen Uncle David and Mr. Edward do the same thing when they would take a drink of moonshine.

Yes, the bread offered during communion was hardly consumable. The fake wine always left you wanting just a little bit more. It loved grape juice and grape sodas. However, during communion, the usher only gave each member a sip of the juice. During the summer months, especially, I always wanted a great big gulp. Geach offered me a nickel for my wine but I refused to sell it to him. I told myself that when I became an adult, I was going to buy me a whole bottle of that grape juice (posing as wine) and drink every bit of it. Larry said he was going to buy a whole bottle of grape juice and a box to Hershey candy bars and have a personal picnic.

There were occasions during the year when the Pastor and his wife were invited to community member's homes for dinner. Well, it was Mom's turn to extend the invitation, so she accommodated. She lectured my sisters and me thoroughly about demonstrating good manners and being on our best behavior. As for me, I did not see why the lecture was necessary. I viewed the Pastor as simply a man who loved to talk and who got paid for talking, just like teachers. So, I basically said to myself, "I'm going to be me; I ain't going to pretend for this guy that I see once a month."

My Mom and sisters cleaned up the house extra special for the "big day." I had to wear my white shirt, my black pants, and my Sunday shoes. Even though it was October, my sisters wore their best dresses and their little white Easter shoes. I hated my shoes; they were far too large for my little feet. The shoes were actually some hand-me-downs that Aunt Mildred had given me. She worked for the Wises (rich white folks who owned a large super market) in Manteo. Aunt Mildred worked for the Wises for many years and she kept me supplied with khaki pants, loafers, and polo shirts. The Wises' son wore the husky size and I was really skinny. His clothes were always three sizes too large for me and I could not run or walk fast in my shoes because they would slip off my feet.

I was the first kid in my class to sport the over-size look. My pants were sagging on me forty-five years before the style became fashionable. Mom would take up the pants in the waist, put paper in my shoes, and make me wear the clothes as if she had personally purchased them. I really felt as though my Dad could have worn many of the clothes that Aunt Mildred brought me to wear to school. I loved Aunt Mildred dearly; however, when she came with boxes of clothes, I knew that the kids at school would be cracking jokes at me endlessly.

Well, Sunday finally arrived; and Mom lectured again early Sunday morning. She taught me how to maintain a conversation when she was not around. In fact, she actually made up scenarios and asked us to respond to each situation. Mom said that being able to keep a conversation going was a sign of keen intelligence. Then she said, "Junior, with all your good grades and all the good things that teachers say about you, I know that you won't have a problem with this request."

I said, "Yes Mom, I can handle this. I just don't see why we have to pretend. Why can't we be ourselves?"

Mom replied with, "Boy, don't you question what I tell you. If I allowed you, yes, especially you to be yourself, the church would withdraw our membership. I ain't trying to find another church and it is too far for you to walk three miles to Engelhard. You see Junior, I know you. You may have those teachers fooled, but I gave birth to you, and I know you better than you know yourself."

I noticed that Mom had gotten that "fetch-the-belt" look on her face, so I decided to terminate that conversation. The Pastor and his wife were to be at our house at 2:00 p.m. At 2:10 p.m., they arrived sweaty and smelling like a mixture combination of cheap perfume and musty clothes. We all hugged one another and proceeded to the sitting room.

The Pastor looked at Mom and said, "Sista Johnson, you missed a mighty good sermon today. Sista Bessie could not stay in her seat from shouting so much. Sista Gladys sang *Come by Here Good Lord* and Bro. Bud Eure and Bro. Albin Collins were rocking like the Soul Train dancers. Yea, I must say, I really laid it down today. The Lord was straight up in there today! "

I looked at Linda, and she immediately turned her head. Then I looked at my younger sisters, Jackie and Vanessa, and they were biting their lips because they just knew I was going to say something off- the- wall. Linda was smart enough to change the conversation to avoid a moment of hilarity. As such, I thought about Mom's lecture and simply smiled.

The Pastor looked at me and said, "Son, I haven't always been saved. No, not always! Don't let these old arthritic knees and this bad hip fool you. I used to "cut the monkey" with the best of them. Yes, I used to do the jerk, the twist, and the mash potato. I tell you, Youngblood, I was out there on the devil's playground until I saw the light. I still dance; I simply dance to a different beat. I dance for the Lord now and I love every beat and every move."

Then the Pastor said, "Why don't you go get me and the wife a big cold glass of water?" Mom interjected and said, "No, Pastor, I'll get it for you. I have to go in the kitchen to check on the apple pie anyway, I'll bring you some water on the way back. Junior, well he is rather clumsy at times. I don't mind; I'll bring the water on my way back."

Mom looked at me and said, "Junior, keep the Pastor company while I check on the apple pie and get the water. Don't forget what I told you!"

I looked at Mom and smiled. Then, I wondered, what would I say to the Pastor? I don't even like his sermons. He preaches far too long and if you are sitting on the front row, he'll spit on you near the end of his sermon. I never understood what happens. However, right near the end of his sermons, he begins to speak real, super fast, and people begin to shout. They appear to be in a trance, or possibly hypnotized. The mood of the whole church is quite strange.

Some of the people in church even cry and others begin to speak the "unknown tongue." I never understood the "unknown tongue" even though I carefully listened. Cousin Martin said, "Dummy, that's why it's called the unknown tongue. You are not supposed to understand it. It's not for you to understand anyway. When people are shouting and speaking the unknown tongue, they are actually talking to God. Gosh! Henry, for you to get good grades, you are so dumb."

Martin made me angry, but I simply smiled and ignored his put-down.

Regardless, it was rather strange; the people seemed to be in some type of trance or spell during the last five minutes of the Pastor's message. The Pastor would be speaking so rapidly and pounding on the podium at the same that it was frightening. Just before the spitting occurred, a nasty white looking substance appeared in the corners of this mouth. I said to myself, "What do I say to the Pastor? I don't really like him. He'll blow his breath right in your face and it is never fresh. His breath smells like Mr. Lincoln's hog farm? Nevertheless, I must obey mom. I don't want a beating or one of her never-ending lectures.

So I turned to the Pastor, crossed my legs like a legitimate grownup, and asked, "Pastor, what is a 'ho?'" I heard mom talking to Aunt Mildred on the telephone and she said that you work on a bridge in Virginia during the week and that you come home to your wife every Friday evening just like a good husband should do. Then she said that you are a hardworking man, but your wife is a real '*ho*.'"

Pastor, what's a "*ho?*" The Pastor looked at me and then looked at his wife. His wife looked at me with her mouth wide open, grabbed her pocketbook and her big white hat, and ran to the car. Then Pastor looked at me for a second and rolled his eyes. After rolling his eyes in a very mean- spirited manner, he grabbed his brown warped hat and strutted to his car as if he had sat on a hot straightening comb. We still had a festive dinner, even though the Pastor left without uttering a single word. I love hot apple pie with a dip of strawberry ice cream. The Pastor really missed a delicious dinner.

# CHAPTER 23
# UNDISPUTED KINGS OF THE ROAD

***What counts is not necessarily the size of the dog in the fight –it's the size of the fight in the dog.***

***—Dwight D. Eisenhower***

Donnie was the official "King of the Road;" however, Byron and I were no tear drops. We were proud Mopar owners and we welcomed the opportunity to swallow Chevy products. Guys from nearby Towns like Belhaven, Pantego, Columbia, and Manteo had heard of us and they were anxious to meet and challenge us. Donnie, Byron, and I had talked about being very selective about who we raced. In essence, if we raced every guy who came along who supposedly had a fast car, we'd be racing every week. The Boomer brothers from Pantego were the "road kings" of Belhaven and Pantego. The Bailey brothers and cousins of Alligator were the "road kings" of Columbia. And finally, Tink Link, Joe, and Boogie were the "road kings" of Manteo.

The Boomer brothers of Pantego drove '71 340 Dusters. They modified them significantly. They installed headers; high-power carburetors, replaced rear-end gears, and made a host of other modifications to produce maximal power from their small-block muscle engines. Their 340 Dusters were beautiful and commanded respect. They roared and hummed like big-block Mopar muscle engines.

Donnie, Byron, and I never got an opportunity to race the Boomer Brothers because we moved away from Hyde County. Donnie and I attended college and Byron had enrolled in the Army and was stationed in Korea. The late 1960s and early 1970s was an era of high performance cars. American-made vehicles such as the Chevrolet Chevelle, Camaro Z28, the Nova Super Sport, the Plymouth Road Runner, the Dodge Charger, and the 340 Duster ruled southern back roads.

The Ford Mustang was really nice; however, it didn't measure up with the Chevrolet and Chrysler products. My cousin, Alonzo, who lived in New York, bought a 1970 Ford Mustang Mach 1Fastback that was terribly strong on top-end speed. However, it wasn't too impressive to the quarter mile. The Mustang was beautiful, amazingly beautiful, and it had a roar about it that gave the impression that it was a monster on the highway and the race track. It would smoke its tires with very little effort. Alonzo knew how to shift the Mach 1 to get maximum performance and it would embarrass most Camaro and Pontiac Firebird owners.

The Bailey Brothers and cousins of Alligator kept the roads of Columbia and Alligator under wrap. They were consummate back road racers who built fierce reputations as Mopar and Chevy owners. I didn't know the Bailey guys very well; however, Horace, Carl, and Coley had built reputations for themselves in Tyrrell and Dare Counties. They were the "Kings" of Tyrrell County and Donnie, Byron and I respected their turf. However, if they ventured into Hyde County, it was incumbent upon us to test their will. Horace was a diehard Mopar man and he drove a '69 blue Road Runner.

As with the Boomer Brothers, Horace had modified his engine significantly. It roared like a GTX and it would hardly idle due the installation of headers and under-the-hood unmentionables. Horace kept his Road Runner spotless and race ready. Colin, Horace's older brother was a Chevy man. He drove a '71 Chevelle SS 396 that was often referred to as a "Turbo-Jet 396." His Chevelle came from the factory with 375 horses at 5600 rpm and 415 lbs.-ft. of torque at 3600 rpm. His Chevelle SS 396 would fly and whenever I saw him, he would always ask about Donnie and his GTX. He wanted to race Donnie with utmost urgency. They never cross paths; however, it would have been an interesting race.

Carl, Coley's younger brother, was a Mopar-man. Like his cousin, Horace, they marveled at the sound and feel of raw power that came with Mopar muscle cars. Carl was young and restless and he kept his yellow '71 Duster in the wind. His Duster came directly from the factory with 275 horses at 5000 rpm and 340 lbs.-ft. of torque at 3200 rpm. He welcomed opportunities to chew up the Chevy Nova and the Mercury Comet GT. His Duster would proudly travel the quarter-mile in 14.49 seconds at 98.25 mph. Carl declared that it would go from a standing start to 60 mph in 6.5 seconds.

The "Kings of the Road" in Manteo were Tink Link, Noah, and Joe. They loved racing and they loved muscle cars. Tink Link drove a '72 Chevelle SS 396. It was gold and black and harnessed 350 horses and could travel the quarter-mile a shade under 14 seconds. He loved his car and he kept it spotlessly clean. His Chevelle came with a hand-grip shifter, three-speed Turbo-Hydramatic transmission, a special doomed hood and locking pins. It was extra fancy with a left-hand remote control sport rearview mirror, Super Sport "SS" emblems, and a sport suspension on 15 x 7-inch wheels.

Noah drove a '68 Chevelle SS and it came with a 396 –cid V-8 engine. In addition, it came with a heavy-duty suspension, bucket seats, power front brakes, positraction, and accent stripes. It idled roughly but revved ferociously. He welcomed opportunities to race Mopar products. Noah particularly enjoyed racing Dodge Chargers and Road Runners. When he raced, he took delight in taking the money of Mopar owners. Due to the fact that his Chevelle came from the factory with a lusty 375-bhp L78, Noah didn't fear anything on four wheels. When I saw he beat a '69 Corvette to the quarter mile, I knew he was the "truth."

Joe, his older brother, was the Mopar man. He drove a '69 Plymouth GTX and like Tink Link, he kept it spotless. Joe's GTX was a raw street racer with the heavy-duty suspension of Chrysler's police package. The 375-horsepower 440 engine sought competition from the Pontiac GTO, the Chevelle 454, and the Shelby Mustang. Joe was very selective about whom he raced. If the individual had not built a reputable name for himself, he wouldn't subject his car to the unnecessary wear and tear. He kept a white soft towel in the trunk of his car to wipe away beach sand. On most occasions, when he pulled into La Vada's night spot, Curtis, his protégé, would grab his white towel and begin wiping sand off the front end of his muscle machine.

Due to the fact that Joe was a little older than most of the guys who hung out on Good Luck Street, when he spoke, we all listened very attentively. He was always with few words and more about action. Curtis appeared to look up to him as if he were Fonsie of *Happy Days.* Joe never had to brag about how fast his GTX was, because Curtis did all of the talking. It was rather amusing at times because Curtis had a serious speech impediment and when he became excited, it was almost impossible to understand him. He stuttered so badly that it was amusing at times. Curtis was a very amusing character and very well liked.

Joe was the uncontestable "King" of Mopar in Dare County and Donnie was the uncontestable "King of Mopar" in Hyde County. They knew of each other; however, they never ventured out to explore who was absolute king. Like Joe, Donnie was a young man of few words. I had seen Joe get off in his GTX a few times and it was indeed a serious power monster. However, I had actually ridden with Donnie and I knew his GTX was the absolute truth. Joe's GTX had the comparable lion's roar and intimidating tremble of raw power. Nevertheless, the title of absolute king appeared to never really bother them.

Dale Shelton, a homeboy from Hyde County, was a Chevy-man and he had little to no respect for Mopar products. He bought a '72 Chevelle SS 396 and immediately sought Joe and later Donnie to challenge their status as ultimate road kings. Dale's Chevelle was powerful and it was equipped with solid lifters, big-port heads, and an 800 –cfm Holley four- barrel on a low-rise aluminum manifold. Curtis convinced Joe to challenge Dale. The race took place at a secluded spot on east US 264 near East Lake.

Racing had become so popular that guys had to confidently identify the time and place of all races to avoid large crowds and police entrapments. The race between Joe and Dale became highly controversial because Joe's friends swore that he won and Dale's friends declared the opposite. My friends and I took racing very seriously and we all knew that a single loss could have irreparable effect on our reputations.

After racing Joe, Dale began hot pursuit of Donnie. They eventually met and agreed to the challenge. My friend, Richard, road with Donnie and Dale rode alone. Donnie declared that he fairly and unquestionably beat Dale from every angle. My friend, Richard, supported Donnie's position for a while. However, Richard privately told me that Donnie did indeed beat Dale out of the hole. However, when Dale reached second gear, his Chevelle walked away from Donnie. He said by the time Dale reached third and fourth gear, the only part visible to Donnie was the Chevelle's tail lights.

Donnie's brother, Alton, my physical education teacher, bought a '70 blue, four-speed GTX that was absolutely beautiful. He played basketball with the same tenacity that he drove his beautiful GTX. Coach Alton was an absolute terror on the basketball court. He was so fast, strong, and versatile that most guys were embarrassed when they had to guard him. He had all the moves of Earl, "The Pearl" Monroe and could score from any area on the basketball court.

After leaving Hyde County, Coach Alton moved to New York. He welcomed opportunities to return to the back roads of Hyde County so he could exercise the 375 horses of his GTX. Donnie took me for a ride in it and it was awesomely powerful. He took off squealing tires and grabbing the pistol-grip shifter like a professional driver. I could have sworn that the front wheels of the GTX rose up off the asphalt. The GTX spun out of control and headed off the highway before he was able to resume control. I was scared stiff and Donnie appeared petrified as well. He looked at me and said, "Gosh! This car is super powerful. I almost lost it. I better take this car back home to Alton before I wreck it."

Donnie was a masterful shifter and each time that he shifted gears, the front-end raised and then bowed as each gear was perfectly executed. There were times when I watched Coach Alton leave the "Play Ground" and head toward Gull Rock. He aggressively shifted through the gears like Richard Petty and the tires and highway smoked like smokestacks. The engine roared and hummed like a secure and confident road warrior waiting to be pointed in the desired direction. Mopar was king and I was proud to be a Mopar owner.

Donnie's younger brother, Melvin, was not a Mopar-man. He elected to buy a Pontiac Lemans. His car was beautiful; however, it was no match for the Mopar enthusiasts. Melvin modified his engine significantly. He even installed headers and changed the carburetor from a two-barrel to a four-barrel to increase the engine's horsepower. Nevertheless, he could not compete with the factory produced Mopar power monsters. The Mopar muscle machines dominated and GM could not provide an answer to the challenge.

My friend, Marlowe, bought a '72 Duster and he couldn't wait to challenge my '70 Dodge Dart Swinger. His friends, Donnie and Larry, declared that it would run 130 mph easily. I saw his Duster and as my friends said, it was beautiful. Marlowe allowed me to drive it and it was indeed fast. His car was definitely faster than mine on top-end. I knew that my car had a top speed of only 110 mph and I had personally driven Marlowe's at 125 mph. Nevertheless, I could readily reach 110 mph to the quarter-mile and Marlowe's Duster did not have that capability. My transmission was slipping, so, I couldn't race Marlowe. I had beaten Dale Shelton in Manteo while my transmission slipped. However, I didn't think it was wise to accept Marlowe's challenge. I knew his car was newer and definitely faster at top-end speed.

Byron, Donnie, and I came home for Memorial weekend and we couldn't wait to get together to showcase our cars and talk about other cars and the pretty girls that we had met. Ms. Meta Pearl had a live band that Saturday night, so the place to be was The Hill Top. I was the first to arrive at the nightspot and then Donnie rode through. The parking lot was crowded with patrons and a lot of guys were standing outside waiting for the perfect time to go inside to enjoy the band. Truthfully, the pretty girls dictated when, or if we paid the entry fee. Donnie and I were standing outside talking when all of a sudden we heard a powerful Mopar engine. There was something special about the sound of a Mopar engine that was truly unique.

Donnie and I could readily detect its sound without seeing the vehicle. To our amazement, it was Byron. He had just gotten in

Town from Norfolk. He had put headers on his Road Runner and it sounded awesome. The car seemed to be running perfectly and it sounded as if his engine had been super-charged. Byron turned around and then reached for his pistol-grip shifter and then engaged his clutch. His Thrush mufflers roared like hungry lions, and oyster shells and dirt flew up like an unanticipated whirlwind. Byron's car spun out of control and hit two cars and the front-end of his Road Runner rested against a telephone pole. Everybody turned around to investigate the commotion.

Byron had wrecked his beautiful Road Runner right in front of our eyes and we felt so sorry for him. He eventually had his car repaired; however, we never got together again after that night. We went our separate ways. Donnie completed his degree program at North Carolina A&T State University, Byron enlisted in the Army and was stationed in Korea, and I completed my undergraduate degree at Elizabeth City State University. The Mopar era had abruptly come to an end for us and the only thing that we had as a keepsake was enduring memories. For a great while, Donnie, Byron, and I were the "undisputed kings of the road." We were in a league of our own and we were often reckless. Nevertheless, God protected us. I am often reminded of mom's philosophical statement, "God protects babies, old folks, and fools."

# CHAPTER 24
# SUPERSTITION

***Man goeth forth unto his work and to his labor until the evening.***

***—Psalms 104:23***

As a child, I traveled highway US 264 on numerous occasions. The drive from Engelhard to Manteo was always filled with enthusiasm and a compelling interest in the unknown. Deer, snakes, and bears crossed the roads as if humans were indeed invading their pre-selected habitat of demarcation. I have seen huge black bears with two small cubs rushing across the highway to avoid being hit by speeding trucks and cars. I have actually seen white Americans anxiously jump out of their cars and trucks with cameras to photograph and videotape bears and rattlesnakes. They acted as if the bears and deer were celebrities walking down the main streets of Hollywood. In contrast, black Americans who saw dangerous bears and poisonous snakes would slow down, stop, or even turn around and go in an opposite direction to avoid the creatures. Seemingly, the bears and rattlesnakes became more active and visible during the night hours. It appeared that bears felt more comfortable and safe during hours of darkness. Nevertheless, bears are bears and rattlesnakes are snakes and black Americans don't expend any energy trying to befriend them.

I recall riding to Manteo with Hatton Junior, Ben Howard, and William Earl one Saturday night. Hatton Junior had just bought a '69 Dodge Charger and he was anxious to ride to Manteo to show it off. I hopped in the backseat and Hatton Junior took off from the Hill Top squealing tires. The car was dark blue with a fancy white bumblebee stripe circling its rear end. The engine purred and roared as if it knew it was made for the open road and race track. Hatton Junior told us that his Charger had 335 horsepower and fresh air flowed directly to his carburetor to keep his engine ready for competition. He then said that he had personally met Richard Petty and Richard Petty, himself, had declared his Charger was too fast and too powerful to drive on public highways.

Hatton Junior continued to brag about how fast his car was and how he couldn't wait to get to Manteo to see Joe Brooks because Joe thought his '65 Oldsmobile 4-4-2 was God's gift to the fast car world. After traveling for about twenty-five minutes, a huge black cat ran across East Highway 264, right in front of us. Hatton Junior had to stomp his brakes to avoid hitting it. We all knew that Ben Howard was terribly superstitious. When he saw the black cat, he became very upset, extremely uneasy. He shouted, "Damn, turn around! Turn around right now! Don't you know that it's bad luck to cross the path of a black cat? Stop! Stop, let me get out! I don't need any bad luck!"

Hatton Junior didn't respond to Ben Howard's demand and kept on driving. William Earl didn't respond; he simply shook his head. I wasn't superstitious; however, Ben Howard's response made me very uncomfortable. We continued our trek to Manteo even though I sensed a little apprehension. Everyone got extremely quiet and listened to Hatton Junior's eight-track player as it bellowed

*When a Man Loves a Woman* by Percy Sledge and *These Arms of Mine* by Otis Reading.

For some unknown reason, Hatton Junior simply loved songs of love and romance. After about twenty minutes, William Earl asked, "Hatton Junior, don't you have some other music besides love songs? It just doesn't seem right riding through these dark woods with a carload of dudes listening to love songs. It just doesn't seem manly! We are men, and men just don't do that!"

Then all of a sudden, Hatton Junior's dream car began to slow down and lose power. He astonishingly began to depress his accelerator very hard and rapidly; nevertheless, his car would not resume power. Then while in a state of desperation, he began to talk to his car. Hatton Junior pleaded to his car, *Please baby, don't conk-out on me now. Come on baby, I need you. Please don't leave me stranded. Come on baby, please!*

We didn't know what to think. However, it was rumored that Hatton Junior had a history of giving out of gas. His eight-track player was bellowing Sam Cooke's *Bring It on Home to Me* as his beautiful car began to slow down. Ironically, we were in the deep woods, somewhere between Stumpy Point and Wanchese, and Hatton Junior's car, his prize possession, was rolling to an eventual stop. As the car continued to coast, Hatton Junior disappointingly said, "Damn, I forgot to put some gas in the car."

Ben Howard angrily stated, "Damn, you mean to tell me that you have us out here in God knows where and we don't have any gas?"

William Earl was sitting in the back with me and he was a little scared. I was scared as well because it was rumored that the Ku Klux Klan patrolled US 264 between Wanchese and Stumpy Point religiously. William Earl nervously looked at Hatton Junior and asked, "Maybe we can rock the car to move around the remaining gas in the tank and just maybe we can make it to Manteo?"

We all began to shift our bodies from left to right, right to left, and left to right. Ben Howard was sitting on the passenger's side of the front seat. As we shifted our weight around, he suddenly rose up and appeared to be in excruciating pain. He reached down between the car's bucket seats and pulled out two raw chicken feet. When he recognized what he had retrieved, he quickly threw them to the floor. Ben Howard exclaimed, "Damn man, somebody has put a curse on you. I don't know about you guys, but I don't play that voodoo stuff!"

The chicken feet still had their toenails on them and they were painted bright red and black. To no avail, the car rolled to a complete stop. After the car came to a complete stop, we all sat in the car for about thirty minutes. There was absolute silence because we were extremely angry and scared at the same time. Ben Howard was sweating profusely and trembling like an escaped slave. He said, "I told you guys that we should turn around and go back to Engelhard when we saw the black cat. As soon as I saw that black cat, I knew that we were destined for trouble. Not only that, those two raw chicken feet were another sign for me. Hatton Junior, someone has gone to 'Harry Peterson' on you and you have been cursed. However, you didn't want to listen to me. Now look at us!"

Harry Peterson was a well known voodoo man who lived in eastern North Carolina. He would tell his followers what numbers to play and then tell them what to do to assure that their numbers were lucky. Of course, he was well compensated for his prognostication. Harry Peterson had a very strong following and his followers were extremely loyal. On weekends, there were more cars in his yard than in most southern black churches. It was believed that he had communication with the spirits and he could render curses on individuals and perform exorcisms. Ben Howard truly believed in the powers of Mr. Peterson.

We sat in the car all snuggled together because US 264 between Stumpy Point and Wanchese was also known as black bear and rattlesnake territory. It was not a place to walk in the daytime and definitely not in the dark of night. The animals had a low tolerance for us and we weren't interested in adopting any pets. We were in a place of serious danger and we were petrified.

After sitting for about forty minutes, Ben Howard announced that he had to pee. Hatton Junior sadly responded with, "Man, you can get out there if you want to. This car is probably surrounded by snakes. And there's probably a big old bear out there just waiting to get a bite of black meat. Nevertheless, Ben Howard disappointingly said, "Man, I gotta go bad, real bad. I can't hold it any longer. Don't you have a flashlight?"

Hatton Junior fumbled around in his glove compartment and eventually found his flashlight. Then his fingers discovered a white envelope. He politely smiled and stated, "This is probably a surprise love letter from Della Ruth. She is always telling me how much she loves me."

Then he braggingly said, "Henry, read it aloud so all you guys will know how 'ole Hatton' rolls!"

I asked, "Are you sure Hatton Junior? This letter may be very private and I don't want Della Ruth to get angry with me."

Hatton Junior annoyingly stated, "Come on Little C-R, read the letter!"

I reluctantly unfolded the letter and began to read. The letter stated the following:

**Dear Brother Hatton,**
**This is Brother Harry. Turn around! Turn around!**
**And do not tarry. Go home to the wife that you did marry.**
**Now look in your rearview mirror and check out the surprise. You will find a deadly spider and it is alive.**

**Now turn around! Turn around! Change your path. I am warning you now and please don't laugh. The spider watches and is far from dead. Go home right now! And go to bed.**

**Brother Harry has spoken!**

After I finished reading the letter, Ben Howard nervously asked, "What kind of love letter is that? I told you guys, Brother Harry done put a curse on Hatton Junior and we are all caught up in the path. You should have listened to me! You should have listened to me! I told you... I told you. . . I told you."

Then he said, "I got to pee now, worst than ever. Give me that weak-ass flashlight!"

The light was faint because it had been in the glove compartment for quite some time. The faintness of the flashlight did not matter to Ben Howard because he really, really, needed to urinate. William Earl encouraged him to shine the flashlight on the ground with each step that he took. He was nervously sweating and his eyes were as bright as newly minted silver dollars. His neck was soaked with perspiration.

Ben Howard was apparently in severe pain because he desperately gripped his zipper area. He had to shake the flashlight several times to get the meager faint light. Hatton Junior adamantly told him to go to the far right-end of the car because he really didn't care to watch him pee. He was just about to place his right foot down on the ground when all of a sudden he thought he saw something move. We sat quietly as we heard a clicking, rattling noise. William Earl yelled, "Oh hell! That's a rattlesnake! Look at the rattles on that monster! Look at its big head and long fangs. That's an old rattler and he didn't become that large being a fool. I can't stand snakes!"

None of us knew what to do as Ben Howard stood perfectly still. He was a dark-skinned brotha and the whites in his eyes appeared to enlarge and glow second by second. Sweat trickled down his face and around his ears. His long and skinny neck slowly became drenched in perspiration. He stood absolutely motionless with his right hand on the inside of his zipper-area.

William Earl yelled to Ben Howard, "Whatever you do, don't move a single muscle. In fact, you'd better hold that pee until that rattler crosses to the other side of the road. If you don't, this will be your very last pee. Rattlesnakes are very sensitive to movement. If I were you, I wouldn't even breathe. Don't even think about responding to us. Don't say a single word, simply listen to us. We'll do all of the talking!"

Hatton Junior shockingly stated, "I see the snake clearly now and it is a huge one. It's like an anaconda with rattles. Whatever you do, don't move a single muscle! In fact, if I were you, I wouldn't even think."

As Ben Howard stood frozen in time, the snake decided to coil. Then after about two minutes, it uncoiled. It stretched out to about three and a half feet. The rattler began to project its red tongue in and out of its mouth. It appeared to look to the right and then to the left. Its tongue continued to jut in and out as if it served as some type antennae. The jutting of its tongue gave the impression that it was assessing the level of potential danger that lied ahead.

Hatton Junior calmly stated, "William Earl is right. I saw an episode on Bonanza last month when Hoss Cartwright stumbled across a rattlesnake. Little Joe told Hoss to freeze. He told him to not move a single muscle and the snake will eventually go on about its business. However, any type movement will excite it and force it to strike."

The rattler's tongue continued to jut out and in relentlessly. Ben Howard stood helplessly as if he were standing on a mine field in Iraq. The snake was nothing less than an IED (**improvised**

**explosive device) and we didn't care to detonate the bomb.** The snake slowly slithered toward Ben Howard's western boots. Capt. Harry had given the boots to Mr. Eure, Ben Howard's dad. The boots were beautiful and Ben Howard said he liked them because they made him feel taller. He swore that they were very expensive and were made 100% snake skin. They were unique; however, the "brothas" simply did not wear western boots.

Mr. Eure told Ben Howard to never wear the boots to the crab house because Capt. Harry had received them from his son, Harry Junior, as a Father's Day gift. Capt. Harry preferred plain rubber boots because of the moisture in the crab house. The boots were too large for Mr. Eure so he gave them to Ben Howard. As the snake strategically and calculatingly moved, Ben Howard's eyes began to protrude and look like binoculars.

The snake appeared to possess some type kindred spirit with Ben's boots. The kindred spirit was powerful and compelling. Ben Howard stood so frozen that he looked like a manikin. We sat so frozen in the car that one would have thought that the rattler was slithering around in the car. The rattler slowly slithered over and around each of Ben Howard's boots. Then the snake would stare momentarily, and turn around, and gaze at the boots. The boots must have been authentic snake-skin and the rattler appeared to sense something unusual. We sat in the car speechless and wondered if the snake was going to crawl inside of Ben's right boot.

As we sat there mesmerized about what had taken place, we looked up and saw vehicle headed in our direction. I thought, if Ben Howard stands there, he runs the risk of being hit by the approaching vehicle, and if he moves, he runs the risk of being bitten by the rattlesnake. The vehicle was approaching quickly and Ben Howard was still standing on the side of the highway frozen stiff as crocodile tears rolled down his face.

I looked at William Earl and tears crowded his eyes as he appeared to empathize for him. Then, I looked at Hatton Junior and noticed that he was actually crying. We soon learned that the oncoming vehicle was actually an 18-wheeler and the driver sounded its horn three times very loudly as it approached us. The snake apparently felt the vibration of the huge truck and decided to slither quickly across the road and into the woods.

When the snake was free of striking distance, Ben Howard collapsed right in the spot where he was standing. He had urinated on himself before he hit the ground. He was weak and trembling like a ninety-year-old frail man. His shirt was soaking wet and clung to his skin. Ben woefully stated, "Man, that snake scared the absolute piss out of me. I just can't stand snakes!"

After the scary snake encounter, things calmed down. We sat in the car for about forty minutes in absolute silence. I turned to my left and noticed a huge black spider climbing the right shirtsleeve of William Earl's starched white shirt. The huge spider was so pronounced that it looked like a fly in a white bowl. I softly whispered, "William Earl, don't make any abrupt moves. There is a big spider on your right shirtsleeve. Just be calm and maybe it will crawl out of the window. Just don't make any abrupt moves."

Everyone turned around immediately as William Early shook his right arm violently. The spider fell to the floor of the car and I stomped it real hard. I could feel the hard body of the spider on the sole of my right foot. I stomped the spider extremely, extremely, hard. However, when I removed my foot, it had disappeared. I was more afraid of the spider than I was the rattlesnake. Then I rhetorically asked, "How in the world did the spider totally vanish like that?"

Ben Howard responded with, "Man, that's how voodoo works! I told y'all that we should turn around and *not* cross the path of that black cat. I don't fool with black cats! It's simply bad luck!"

After matters calmed down again, Hatton Junior told us that he had an empty gas can in the trunk of his car. Then he suggested that we take the gas can and thumb a ride to Manteo to get some gas. He said he would go himself but he didn't want to leave his car parked, on the side of the road, unattended, because someone would come along and strip it.

Ben Howard wiped sweat from his face and stated, "Hatton Junior, Man, you are crazy as hell if you think I'm walking down those dark roads with a damn gas can. Snakes and bears would eat us alive. If the snakes and the bears didn't get us, we still have to worry about the **KKK**. I tell you what; you take your little crooked ass out there and get the gas, and we'll stay here with the car."

Hatton Junior became profoundly agitated and responded with, "I guarantee you when I get your little skinny, black-ass, back to Engelhard, I will never, ever, give you another ride as long as I am black."

Ben Howard was determined to have the last word. He looked straight at Hatton Junior and adamantly stated, "I would rather take a ride with the Grand Dragon of the Ku Klux Klan, himself, than to ride with you. At least, he wouldn't give out of gas."

## CHAPTER 25

# THE ECU SNAKE MAN

***Old friends are the great blessing of one's later years. . . They have a memory of the same events and have the same mode of thinking.***

***—Horace Walpole***

Just as Ben Howard was about to tell Hatton Junior more, an old dirty-green Chevrolet pickup stopped right beside the car. William Earl yelled, "Oh hell! That's the Klan, what in the hell are we going to do?"

An old, dirty, wrinkled white man rolled down his window and asked, "Are you boys having a problem?"

Hatton Junior responded with, "Yes, sir; I gave out of gas!"

The old white man spoke with a deep southern vernacular and asked, "Do you boys know that this here is Klan territory? A lot of white folks don't like your kind around here. You don't have to worry about me because I ain't one of them! I have always got along good with the coloreds! In fact, one of my best friends is colored! Do you know a colored boy from Engelhard that's called Long David? I don't know his real name, but me and him is good friends!"

I thought to myself, "If you two are truly good friends and you don't really know his real name, there is something mighty unusual about this friendship."

Hatton Junior looked at the old man and asked, "You wouldn't have any extra gas in your truck, would you?"

The old man responded with, "No. I don't have any extra gas but I am going to Manteo and I don't mind giving you boys a lift. By the way, my name is Dave but most people call me, the "Snake Man."

Ben Howard leaned forward and asked, "Why are you called, the 'Snake Man'?"

The old man smiled proudly and said, "I work for the biology departments at East Carolina and Duke University. I catch rattlesnakes and water moccasins and sell them to the universities. Researchers at the universities use the snakes' venom for research. I can easily get twenty dollars for a nice healthy rattler or moccasin."

The old man coughed and spit out seemingly a mouthful of tobacco juice. The corners of his mouth were brown and caked with hardened old tobacco saliva. His eyes were red; his teeth were brown, and his hands were filthy dirty.

He looked at Hatton Junior and said, "I guess I'd better be moving on. I can give you boys a lift if you want one. I have so much stuff inside my truck that only one of you can get in the front."

William Earl rushed to get in the truck's cab. Ben Howard and I climbed in the back of the truck. Hatton Junior stayed with his prized possession car. He appeared to love his '69 Dodge Charger more than his wife. It was a very cold night and Ben Howard and I thought we were going to freeze in the back of the old pickup. The pickup was dirty and smelled like he used it to dump trash. It had an unusual smell about it. Ben grabbed what appeared to be a 100-pound bag of sweet potatoes and placed it over his body to keep warm. I was so cold that I was trembling. I grabbed what appeared to be a rain coat and curled up in it. The rain coat was dirty and smelled like motor oil and gasoline. The old man was speeding and taking curves much too fast. When he would slow down for steep curves, the old pickup would backfire.

William Earl was happy and warm because he was sitting in the truck's cab. He kept looking through the back glass to see if we were okay. The wind chill was breathtaking as I trembled mercilessly. Ben Howard was curled with the bag of sweet potatoes as if it were the love of his life.

Then all of a sudden, he jumped up and said, "Oh! hell, that's not sweet potatoes."

Then he jumped on top of the truck's cab.

The old man geared the truck down and the muffler backfired through each gear. When the pickup finally came to a rest, the old man climbed out of the cab and annoyingly asked, "What in the hell is going on back here?"

Ben Howard struggled with his words but he was eventually said, "I had one of those so-called sacks of sweet potatoes resting on me to keep warm and as I was looking at the sack, I saw some several tiny bright eyes looking right back at me. I thought something was a bit peculiar because I had never smelled any sweet potatoes that smelled like that before. Then I began to feel something wet rolling down my neck. After that, the entire sweet potato sack began to move. It almost scared the hell right out of me."

The old man laughed and said, "Those are not sacks of sweet potatoes. I have my captured snakes in those bags. I've actually had a very good night. I have seventy-five snakes in those two bags. After I catch a hundred, I'll call it a night"

Ben Howard angrily looked at the old man and asked, "You mean to tell me that you put us in the back of your pickup knowing that you had snakes back there?"

The old man responded with, "You asked me for a ride and I tried to help you. That's how I make a living, catching snakes. Did you think that I was going to release my snakes to give you a ride? My snakes are secure in those sacks. If you don't bother them, they won't bother you!"

As they stood in the middle of the highway talking about the snake ordeal, a white hearse rode up and the driver rolled down his window asked, "Are you boys okay?"

The "Snake Man" responded by saying, "Well, I'm just fine. These here boys need a lift to Manteo to pick up some gas for their friend. Can you give them a ride? I need to make about six more stops before I get to Manteo."

Ben looked at me and said, "I ain't riding in no dead man's car. That's creepy as hell."

William Earl responded to Ben Howard by asking, "What would you rather do, ride in the back of the 'Snake Man's' pickup, or ride in this warm and clean hearse?"

Ben Howard thought about his two choices and said, "I'd rather take my chances in the hearse."

William Earl said, "Good! Just pretend the hearse is a station wagon and we're all going on a family trip to Manteo, okay?"

## CHAPTER 26
# THE HEARSE MAN

***I want to be able to live without a crowded calendar. I want to be able to read a book without feeling guilty, or go to a concert when I like.***

***—Golda Meir***

We thanked the "Snake Man" for his help and got into the hearse. It was warm and clean. Ben and I were still terribly cold, so we asked the 'Hearse Man' to turn up the heat. We never introduced ourselves, so Ben introduced himself, then William Earl, and finally, I introduced myself. It was really warm and cozy in the hearse and he had easy listening music playing. The 'Hearse Man' said his name was Sam Lyrch and he lived in Columbia, NC. He said he was en route to Manteo to drop off a body at Twiford Funeral Home and then he would pick up two more bodies and bring them back to Columbia for Rowson Funeral Home.

We were riding along chatting and enjoying the warmth of the hearse when all of a sudden, Ben whispered to me, "Henry, did you fart or are you sick? Damn! Man, something smells rotten. It smells like someone did the number 2."

Then we started thinking and looking at each other. Ben whispered and asked, "Didn't the 'Hearse Man' say that he was en route to Manteo to drop off a body at Twiford Funeral Home and then he would pick up two more bodies and bring them back to Columbia for Rowson Funeral Home?"

I looked at Ben and he looked at me and the terrible stench in the hearse became more and more pronounced as the heat in the car escalated. William Earl sat in the front seat and laughed and joked with the "Hearse Man." He had him laughing so hard that he dipped off the road a few times.

Then William Earl abruptly turned around and said, "Damn! Something stinks. Did somebody back there fart? Man, you guys stink. You are some stinking dudes."

The 'Hearse Man' couldn't hear very well. He looked at William Earl and asked, "Did you say that something smells bad?"

William Earl said, "Yes. Man, it smells like somebody died back there."

The 'Hearse Man' smiled and said, "That just might be old Luke back there smelling. He had been in the canal for three days before anybody found him. The crabs had eaten his right eye and his left ear was half-way eaten. He hardly had any nose left at all. I had a hard time putting him in the body bag because he was so decayed and he was as stiff as a board. You see, when I was in World War II, I had some nerve damage to my nose. I can't smell anything. Everything smells the same to me and I got accustomed to being around dead bodies while in the war. That's how I got this good job!"

Just as the "Hearse Man" finished telling us his story, we noticed a great fire in a cut-out wooded area. The entire sky appeared to be lit and a flaming cross glowed liked a lighted angel on top of a Christmas tree. White robes lined the left and right sides of the rode like a mountain snow in Asheville. As we slowly approached, the "Hearse Man" readily noticed that it was a Ku Klux Klan rally. We were in an area of Tyrrell County commonly called East Lake. The white Americans who lived there were known to have a low tolerance for black people.

The 'Hearst Man' exclaimed, "Damn, if they see you boys, you are in major trouble. It's not safe for you boys to get out and hide in the bushes because of snakes and bears. I just don't know what to do."

William Earl thought for a minute and suggested, "Suppose you tell the Klan boys that I am your grave digger and you have three bodies back there?"

The "Hearse Man" replied, "Brilliant! I tell you boy that just might work. I have two body bags back there. You two boys get in the body bags and I'll just zip them up just a little bit so everything will look legitimate. Now make sure you boys stay perfectly still. Some of the Klan boys swear they can smell a niggra a mile away. Old Luke might get a little ripe back there. However, if you boys want to get out of here alive, you can't move a single muscle. Like I said, I can't smell a damn thing."

Ben looked at the 'Hearse Man' and William Earl and said, "Man, you are crazy. I ain't getting in no damn body bag. Damn the Klan! They will just have to hang me!"

The 'Hearse Man' responded, "You boys better make a decision. We are getting closer and closer to the Klan rally. If I were you, I'd get in the body bags quick, fast, and in a hurry."

William Earl started sweating and trembling as he ambivalently said, "I'll get in the body bag, just don't zip the top too tightly. I am claustrophobic but I'll get in the damn body bag. Henry, you get in the other one."

I didn't say anything; I simply got in the bag. It smelled like a combination of Clorox and new rubber. Ben Howard got in the front seat with the "Hearse Man".

The "Hearse Man" looked at Ben and said, "Boy, you really look like a grave digger. You even smell like one. That other boy, William Earl, was too soft and too pretty to be a grave digger. However, you look like you were born with a shovel in your hand."

Ben Howard took the "Hearse Man's" remark as a compliment. Then he told William Earl and me to stay perfectly still when he stops. After that, he told Ben Howard to allow him to do all of the talking because he knew how to deal with the Klan boys.

The "Hearse Man" slowly pulled off and within three minutes, William Earl raised his head and exclaimed, "Man, 'ole Luke' back here is really kicking. I mean this dude is absolutely rotten. I don't know if I can stand this much longer. This is the worst smell I've ever experienced."

We were about one fourth of a mile from the Klan rally when William Earl raised his head again and asked, "Sir, would you please turn off the heat? The heat is causing 'Ole Luke' to smell worse than ever. Now it looks as though meat is falling off his body and a nasty fluid is creeping out of his mouth."

The "Hearse Man" adamantly stated, "Boy, I'll turn off the heat. However, if you don't keep your head down, we'll all be in a heap of trouble."

Ben Howard turned around and said, "If you pop that pointed head up one more time, I'm gonna take this shovel and give you the worst headache you've ever had. Now pop that head up one more time!"

William Earl was absolutely correct. Old Luke was slowly deteriorating right in front of our eyes. The stench was truly unbearable and the fluid trickling out of his mouth was deplorable.

The "Hearse Man" approached the Klan rally rather cautiously. When we arrived at the cut-out wooded area, he came to an eventual stop.

He rolled down his window and said, "Good evening Brothers of the Fold. How are you all tonight? It is so good to see God-fearing white folks like you working to preserve our history and our dignity. It takes good white folks like you and the other brothers out there, to keep this country honest and clean. If we don't watch it, the niggras will be trying to take over."

The Klansman responded with, "I like the way you think brother! Why don't you park that death mobile and come join us. Brother "Catfish" doesn't bite his tongue at all. You really need to hear Brother Catfish!"

The "Hearse Man" informed him that he had to get to Manteo as soon as possible to pick up a couple bodies. However, the Klansman ignored him and continued talking as he stared directly at Ben Howard. I tightly gripped my pearl-handle switchblade. I was scared, terribly petrified!

He asked, "Did you hear about those niggras in Greensboro who refused to leave the lunch counter so us white people could eat. The niggras were from that colored school called North Carolina AT&T. Can you imagine that, the coloreds named their school after a telephone company? Half of them don't even know how to use a phone."

The Klansman appeared to possess a disposition similarly to that of Donald Sterling, owner of the Los Angeles Clippers. Sweat began to roll down my neck and ears. Then all of a sudden, a big black spider began to crawl near my nose. Honestly, it looked like the very same spider that I stomped in the floor earlier. As such, Ben Howard's statements about voodoo crossed my mid. I wondered, is this a voodoo spider? After crawling near me, it crawled up on William Earl's body bag and sat motionlessly. A car passed as the "Hearse Man" sat on the road and talked with the Klansman. When the headlights flashed on William Earl's body bag, the spider totally vanished. I don't know if I were more afraid of the Klansmen or the huge spider. I just know that I was scared stiff.

The "Hearse Man" rhetorically asked, "Can you imagine that, niggras and whites eating at the same lunch counter? I just don't know what this world is coming to. Have you heard about that Frinks boy in Edenton? They call him Golden. Yes, that's right! The coloreds call him Golden Frinks.

The Klansman asked, "Is that the boy who's been going all across North Carolina stirring up trouble for the niggras?"

The "Hearse Man" responded with, "Yes. That's the boy! He seems to have all the coloreds in the palms of his hands. A lot of the coloreds even refer to him as the Black Moses. Can you imagine that?

Then the "Hearse Man" said, "Wow! I would love to chat with you a little longer, but 'ole Luke' is decaying by the minute. I'd better get on to Manteo before he completely spoils back there. Here, take this twenty-dollar bill as a contribution to the cause. I know it takes money to keep the Klan strong!"

The Klansman happily accepted the twenty-dollar bill. He looked around, lifted his robe, and put it in his pocket. Then he looked a little perplexed and uneasy. It appeared that he became uneasy about the "Hearse Man."

After rubbing his nose, he inquisitively stated, "My nose doesn't lie to me. I can smell a niggra a mile away and my nose tells me that one is near."

The "Hearse Man" smiled and said, "You must be talking about 'Ole Ben' here. He's a good ole boy. If the rest of the niggras were like him, this country would be just perfect. He doesn't complain about anything!"

The Klansman slowly and cautiously walked around the hearse. Then he stuck his head inside and quickly jumped back. He hysterically said, "When I peeped in the back of this death mobile, a web covered my face and a big spider jumped on my nose. I can't stand spiders! I hate spiders as bad I do niggras"

The "Hearse Man" stoically stated, "When I get back to Columbia, I'll get 'Ole Ben' to vacuum and clean out the car. It's due a good cleaning anyway."

While rubbing his head, the Klansman stated, "Damn, it smells like a skunk is riding with you. I don't see how in hell you can do your job. It's rotten in there! Then he and asked, "Have you seen three niggras out here along the highway?"

The "Hearse Man" shook his head and said, "No, I haven't seen anyone at all. In fact, traffic has been rather slow tonight. I normally run into a lot of cars either leaving the beach, or going to the beach. But, traffic has been slow tonight."

The Klansman responded with, "I received word that three niggras tried to rob the "Snake Man" tonight. They tried to steal his truck and take his snakes, but he was able to trick them and escape. He had $3,000.00 worth of snakes in his truck and $462.00 in cash. Can you imagine that? Yea, you gotta watch the niggras because they'll steal grease right out of a biscuit."

The "Hearse Man" scratched his head and enthusiastically stated, "That's why we need decent white folks like you to protect our interest. This country is in an absolute mess. 'Ole Ben' here is a good boy; but I don't trust him but so much. I've watched him when he's around other coloreds. He's quite different!"

The Klansman responded with, "Yes! I know what you mean. Me and my boys have been keeping up with the *Black Power Movement.* I see the coloreds every night on television walking up and down highways yelling *Soul Power* and *Black Power.* Really, it's a damn shame!"

The Klansman looked at Ben Howard and asked, "Why is this niggra riding on the front seat? You know he should be sitting on the back seat, right"

The "Hearse Man" responded with, "Like I said, Ben is a good ole boy, but I don't really trust him. That's why he's sitting up here beside me; I need to keep an eye on him. He is my grave digger and he helps me pick up bodies from time to time. He may be a deaf mute. However, I don't ever take anything for granted! Some white folks take too many chances, I ain't one of them!"

The Klansman took his flashlight and pointed it to the rear of the hearse. Again, I clenched my switchblade tightly. He asked, "Looks like you got three bodies back there? Man, I couldn't do your job for all the money in the world. It gives me the creeps just to think about what you do for a living."

The "Hearse Man" responded with, "Yes. I bagged three and I am en route to Twiford Funeral Home in Manteo to embalm two of them before they completely spoil. 'Ole Luke' has probably spoiled already!"

The Klansman reaffirmed his position that the "Hearse Man" could have that job. He said he didn't want any part of work that dealt with dead people.

The "Hearse Man" asked, "Did you know that white folks turn as dark as niggras if they aren't embalmed and buried quickly? I discovered this while in the war. Some coloreds keep their bodies up for as long as a week. If we tried that, family members would sue us. Think about it, do you know any white folks who want to look like niggras?"

The Klansman pondered momentarily and stated, "No. Not really! Well, be safe and don't forget to watch out for the three koons. If we find those darkies, we are going to make an example out of them. They won't be eating any watermelon anytime soon!"

The "Hearse Man" slowly pulled off and Ben never said a word. After about three minutes, William Earl raised his head and asked, "Is it safe for us to get out of these bags now?"

The "Hearse Man" responded with, "It's safe now, but don't get completely out of the bags until we arrive in Manteo. These Klan boys can be tricky. Like I said, they swear they can smell a niggra a mile away."

Ben asked the "Hearse Man" if he could turn the heat back on. William Earl and I did not complain because we were cold as well. We arrived in Manteo in about twenty minutes. When we arrived, the "Hearse Man" told us that he would gladly give us a ride back to Hatton Junior's car and buy us something to eat, if we helped him get Old Luke out of the car. We all agreed to help because we were hungry and cold.

We stayed in the embalming room at Twiford Funeral Home while the "Hearse Man" went to the Manteo Motel and Restaurant to order us some food. He returned in about thirty minutes with ham steaks, rolls, green beans, applesauce, and tea. He even brought us huge hunks of homemade chocolate cake for dessert. We ate and smiled like hungry run-a-way slaves.

Mr. Twiford, owner of the funeral home, entered the area where we were eating and gave each of us a twenty-dollar bill. After eating, we helped the "Hearse Man" with Old Luke. He still smelled terrible; however, for some reason we had become somewhat immune to the stench. The two bodies that the "Hearse Man" had to take back to Columbia were fully dressed and in grey metal caskets. The caskets were seriously heavy and hard to maneuver inside the hearse. We all strained a little and carefully placed them on the rollers so they could easily slide inside the hearse. As we placed them in the car, Mr. Twiford walked to the hearse with a bright-red, metal five-gallon gas can, filled with gas. He said our plastic container had a small hole in it. He thanked us for helping the "Hearse Man" and told us to be extra careful as we travel through the woods back to Hyde County.

We got into the hearse and began our drive back to Hatton Junior's car. The hearse still had the smell of Old Luke in it; however, the smell was less pronounced. Regardless, the smell of a decaying dead body is indeed an unforgettable odor. The

"Hearse Man" played piano music on the way back and some of it actually sounded pretty decent. Nevertheless, William Earl couldn't stand the music and turned the radio station to a station in Virginia.

The "Hearse Man" said he really liked colored folk's music, especially the music by Wilson Pickett and Otis Redding. He said his favorite songs were *Sitting on the Dock of the Bay* and *Mustang Sally.* When we reached the area where the Klan meeting had taken place, everyone had departed. The only indicator of Klan activity was a semi-burnt charcoal black cross with a few embers still burning. As we slowly passed the site, a cold and eerie feeling consumed my body. No one said anything; there was absolute silence for about five minutes. The lighted embers on the charcoal-colored cross had all the makings of an electric billboard immersed with hatred. It sent chills throughout my body.

As a cold tear rolled down my face, the "Hearse Man" looked at us and said, "I want to thank you boys for the many lessons that I learned tonight. I realized that hate is an ugly monster and it is wrong to judge someone based on skin color. I also learned that people are people and we all have feelings and we should treat others as we would like to be treated."

Ben Howard responded by saying, "Man, you are cool with us. In fact, you probably saved our lives tonight. There are many twisted-minded people out there. We are simply glad that you are not one of them. We owe you man; we really do."

I was so tired that I fell asleep. When I awakened, we were in front of Hatton Junior's car. The "Hearse Man" used his headlights to provide lighting for him to put gas in the car. Truly, we were more concerned about snakes and bears than spilling a little gas. We all gave the "Hearse Man" a soul handshake and wished him well. We did not have enough gas to make it to Manteo; however, we did have enough to get back to Engelhard. After that night, Engelhard looked like Heaven to us.

# CHAPTER 27
# BEST FRIENDS

***Winter, spring, summer or fall, all you have to do is call, and I'll be there, you've got a friend.***

***—Carol King***

I essentially assumed the role of "Lone Ranger" after my sophomore year of high school. The guys with whom I believed to be my "best friends" betrayed my trust. Louis, David, Walter, Rudolph, and I were basically inseparable. We essentially hung together every single school day and on weekends. One Friday, we collectively decided to attend a dance at O.A. Peay, the rival high school in our county. We had laughed and joked all week about attending the dance and we were excited about the unknown. O.A. Peay was located about twenty-one miles west of our school, Davis High.

Each school was totally black; however, turf wars were real and not to be taken lightly. Resultantly, the guys of O.A. Peay couldn't stand the sight of the Davis High guys and the Davis High guys really could not stand the O.A. Peay guys. The rivalry was mean, fierce, and very real. My friends and I viewed the entire area of

Swan Quarter as enemy territory. We wouldn't dare go there alone and it wasn't safe for the Swan Quarter guys to frequent Engelhard solo. Truly, the rivalry and dislike for each other appeared to be torn straight from the pages of *The Outsiders.*

My friends and I thought the girls from O.A. Peay were much prettier than the girls at our school. We often talked about how fine and beautiful Neva, Brenda, Audrey, Dorene, Angela, and Nina were. The guys from O.A. Peay were extremely territorial and they often became highly irate and hostile when the guys from Davis High tried to talk to their girls. One Friday night, Louis, my cousin and good friend, decided to attend a dance at O.A. Peay. My friends and I tried to discourage him from going there without us. However, Louis was big and strong and was not easily intimidated by anyone. In fact, he was so self-assured that he would have readily challenged Mike Tyson or Joe Frazier without any semblance of fear.

Louis ended up going to the dance without us and inadvertently got into a violent altercation with Preston, a big, strong, and muscular guy at O.A. Peay. It took three guys to contain him and three guys to calm Preston. The rivalry between the two schools was intense and at times vicious. Preston, Dallas, Charles, Alonzo, Otto, and Floyd were the movers and shakers of O.A. Peay, and in the Swan Quarter community. To be honest, most of the Engelhard guys didn't like those guys and we gravitated to opportunities to challenge them. We really didn't know them very well at all; nevertheless, we simply couldn't stand their sight. The loss of a basketball or baseball game simply added fuel to the rivalry. Basketball games between Davis and Peay were comparable to a game between the Los Angeles Lakers and the Boston Celtics. The games were intense and the ownership of bragging rights appeared comparable to the Holy Grail.

It was through this intense rivalry that I got to learn who my true friends were. I considered Louis, David, Walter, and Rudolph my very best friends. We hung together all of the time; we were inseparable. None of us owned a car or possessed a driver's license; therefore, we hitchhiked wherever we desired to go. We honored an unspoken code of conduct, "All for one, and one for all." I really enjoyed hanging with my friends and I would have, without hesitation, given them the shirt off of my back. Truly, I would have protected them with my life, without any reservation or second thought. I simply loved my friends.

Friday finally arrived and my friends and I hitchhiked to O.A. Peay for the big dance. Once we got to the dance, we maintained close proximity with each other because we knew that we were in enemy territory. I watched Dallas and Preston from afar because I was truly afraid of them. We had fun that night laughing and talking with Patricia, Deborah, Barbara, Nina, and Annette.

I slow-danced with Patricia to Al Green's *For the Good Times* that night and truly felt an undeniable bond between us. As her face rested against mine, I experienced a woody that was difficult to conceal. Her skin was pillow-soft and the fragrance that she wore was amazingly sensual. I held her until the last syllable of *For the Good Times.* Al Green was right on point that night. I could have held her the entire night and would have enjoyed every second of it. At the end of the slow drag, I gently kissed her on her forehead. She simply smiled and said, "Alright now, I don't want any problems with any of these girls out here tonight! You know all eyes are on us!"

I was totally shocked because she didn't complain about the kiss. Patricia simply expressed concern about other young ladies who allegedly liked me. I responded with, "You are the one that I kissed! That should communicate a message to anyone else who may be watching. You are the rose of my choice!"

Patricia was a star-student at O.A. Peay and she carried herself in a classy and respectful manner. My buddy, Walter, liked her as well. However, I was the one brave enough to ask her for a dance that night and she politely said yes. David, Walter's brother, liked

Barbara and they were slow-dancing as well. It was really a fun-night and I enjoyed every second of the occasion. I felt as though I had fallen in love with Patricia after a single dance. The night was perfect. It was simply too brief!

The dance ended at 11:00 p.m. and then my best friends and I had to hitchhike back to Engelhard, a twenty-one mile trek. It was extremely cold and there were no streetlights to illuminate our walk. As we walked out of the gym, we continued our laughter with Patricia, Deborah, and Barbara. David escorted Barbara to her ride and I escorted Patricia to hers. Walter walked with Deborah and exchanged phone numbers. I was crazy about Patricia and I dreamed about her on numerous occasions. The mere fact that we attended rival schools made the relationship more exciting and embracing.

During the week before the dance, I would go in my bedroom and pretend-talk to her. Patricia was on my brain and I hadn't even kissed her. Tressia, one of Patricia's friends, lived right across the street from the school. After Patricia and Barbara left to go home, Tressia began to slowly walk home. I called to her and said, "Hold up! I'll walk you home. Even though you live right across the street, it's rather dark out there. Slow up, I'll walk with you."

I called to David and said, "Look, I'm going to walk Tressia home. It'll only take a few minutes and I'll catch up with you guys."

David responded with, "Sure Henry. Go on, we'll wait for you at the stop sign. Don't worry. Take your time. We'll wait for you."

I escorted Tressia to her door. She hugged me and thanked me for being a gentleman. Then I heard the slamming of car doors. Tressia shockingly looked at me and asked, "You don't think those guys left you, do you? I don't hear them laughing and talking anymore. Are you sure they didn't leave you?"

I smiled at Tressia and said, "No. They wouldn't leave me. They are just trying to scare me. My buddies are some real jokesters; they really are."

Tressia asked, "Are you really sure they didn't catch a ride?"

I responded with, "They're just teasing me. But, really, I better go because it's getting rather late and it's really cold out here. Hopefully, I'll talk with you soon. Good night!"

I briskly walked to the stop sign where my buddies said they would be waiting. My heart began to beat rapidly and an internal voice told me that my so-called buddies had indeed left me. I pleadingly called, "Louis, David, Walter, Rudolph, come on out! I know you are hiding; so come on out! Alright, you guys, this is not funny; so come on out!"

My "best friends" had actually left me alone; twenty-one miles from Engelhard. I felt like crying; I felt betrayed and deserted. It was difficult to really accept the fact that my so-called "best friends" would leave me alone in assumed enemy territory. I told my Mom about what happened that night and she looked at me and asked, "With friends like that, who needs enemies?"

After that night, I revisited my definition of friendship. I basically became the "Lone Ranger" and I never truly developed trusting relationships with anyone again. I constructed a massive wall to shield me from disappointment, pain, and pretense. That night presented me with a great epiphany. I learned that I should never depend on others to shield me from assumed enemies. Ralph Waldo Emerson's *Self-Reliance* had new meaning to me.

About six months after my so-called "best friends" deserted me, I received my driver's license and my dad bought me a beautiful red Mustang. I continued to respond to my so-called friends as if they were truly my friends; nevertheless, it was difficult to look at them and dismiss the fact that they had wronged me.

During my junior year of high school, I met Glen, Sandy, and Hardy. This was my school district's first year of court-ordered school desegregation and a time of relentless restlessness. Glen and Hardy were already best friends from their traditional black school, O.A. Peay. I didn't know them; however, they embraced me and the fact that I attended Davis High; their rival school, was a non-factor. Glen and Hardy redefined the term "friend" for me. As time progressed, we became inseparable. We traveled to basketball games, football games, played basketball, cards, shared money, and drank a little beer together.

One Friday night, we elected to travel to Pantego, North Carolina to attend a basketball game against our high school, Mattamuskeet. We had a very good team that year; Dick Tunnel, Caleb Holloway, Walter Farrow, Leroy, Spencer and Sam O'Neal ran the ball like the Los Angeles Lakers. Instead of each of us driving, we decided to ride with our friend, Alonza. He was nicknamed Toot. His uncle had bought him a blue Chevy Nova and we looked forward to riding to the basketball game with him in his new car. The coach of the Pantego team was a close friend of Toot's uncle, Mr. Philip Green. Mr. Green was a well-respected teacher and elementary school principal. Not only was he an educator, he was a community leader. We all respected him and responded to him as if he were our uncle as well. Additionally, he was a close friend of legendary Pantego basketball coach, Albert Baker. Coach Baker was an awesome coach who had won numerous conference championships. On the asphalt jungle of Pantego, Coach Baker was nothing less than a black version of Dean Smith, the legendary basketball coach at UNC-Chapel Hill. It was rumored that he had been courted by East Carolina University to become the institution's first black American head basketball coach. However, due to his personal commitment to his family, community, and high school basketball players, he declined the offer.

As we piled into the car at Toot's uncle's house, Mr. Green walked to the car and asked Toot to turn down the music. He looked at Toot and adamantly stated, "Toot, I want you guys to carry yourself like young gentlemen tonight. All of you guy are suppose to be smart. Prove this tonight and don't get caught up in something stupid, okay?"

We all nodded and said, "Yes, sir."

When we pulled off, Hardy sat still for a few minutes and inquisitively stated, "Gosh Toot, the backseat of this car is awfully hard. I feel like I'm sitting on a board."

I said, "That's the truth man. It fills like a board or baseball bat is hitting against my butt bone. These springs feel like iron."

Toot laughed and said, "Man those seats are fine. . . Just take your hand, follow along the back of the seat, and you'll see what's there."

Hardy looked at Sandy rather curiously and then followed his request. He took his fingers and followed along the separation of the backseat and pulled up the barrel of a twenty-two automatic rifle. Sandy followed suit and pulled up the rifle's stock. Hardy astonishingly asked, "Toot, you mean to tell me, we have sitting back here with our butts on a twenty-two rifle and you're just telling us about it? Man, that's dangerous!"

Toot laughed again and stated, "Man, don't worry; everything is cool. I sneaked it in the car while Uncle Philip's back was turned. Oh! You guys need to be a little careful because it is fully loaded and the trigger is very sensitive."

I frowned and asked, "You mean to tell me, we have been riding around with a fully-loaded rifle and you are just telling us about it?"

Glen laughed and said, "I am so glad that I hopped in front. Toot is always full of surprises. He just might have a couple hand grenades rolling around in the trunk. You know Linwood G. is his older brother and he just returned from Vietnam. There is no telling what Toot might have up in here."

Toot laughed again and said, "Oh Man, I was going to tell you, if it had gone off and shot one of you guys in the ass."

I responded with, "What? Man that's not funny. We could have been seriously injured. I respect guns. . . I really do!"

Toot noted that Hardy and I were serious. He quit joking and said, "Man, you guys are crazy if you think I am going to a basketball game in Pantego and not take some heat. Look, those fans are rowdy over there and it is not unusual for them to attack fans if they lose a game. Think about it, Mattamuskeet has had a good team this year. In fact, we are tied with them for the conference title. If someone comes at me, I am going to be well-prepared. Ain't nobody gonna give me a beatdown without a fight, okay? I simply brought a little heat as a security blanket."

Hardy and I did not respond to Toot's disposition. We eventually arrived at the Pantego gymnasium, popularly called the "Tin Can." We were excited about the game. The "Tin Can" was every bit as loud and intimidating as Cameron Indoor Stadium at Duke University. The fans could be dangerous and belligerent. We cautiously got out of the car and slowly walked to the gym. It was almost time for the varsity boys to play. There was a long line of patrons waiting to pay so they could enter the basketball court area.

Coach Cotton had told us to get there rather early because this was a big game and once it reached the capacity attendance limit, no one would be allowed to enter the gym. As we slowly walked up to the designated entry area, a female fan looked at us and said, "Here comes some of those funny-talking Hyde County hillbillies. They make me sick. We are going to kick their tails on the basketball court and then we are going to skin them alive after the game. We're going send them back to Hyde County in bandages. I just can't stand those funny- talking folks from Mattamuskeet."

# CHAPTER 28
# STICKS AND STONES

***Avenge not yourselves, but rather give place unto wrath: for it is written, Vengeance is mine; I will repay, saith the Lord.***

***—Romans 12:19***

Toot heard what she said and replied, "Look, you aren't going to do a damn thing to me. It's not like Pantego is some fancy city. It's not a metropolis; then again, based on the way you talk, you probably don't even know what a metropolis is. You all have just as many cornfields and ditches around here as we have in Hyde County. So, don't think you are better than we are, okay? After listening to you run your mouth, it is quite evident that you flunked every English class that you've taken. You are just as country as we are. You should look at yourself, with that nappy-ass fro. You have a real nerve to try to embarrass someone! You don't know me! I don't play that!"

The young lady became hostile and shouted, "That's okay, Smarty. Wait until the game is over. I got something for you."

Toot was determined to have the last word. He responded with, "Yes, I'm sure you have something for all five of us, if we wanted it. However, you can take it somewhere else; we aren't buying. Even if I were homeless and hadn't seen a female in ten years, you couldn't give me anything. Now get out of my face!"

Patrons standing around listening to the exchange began to laugh. Then a very tall dude walked to Toot and angrily stated, "Look, you can't talk to my cousin like that. She's family and you can't disrespect my cuz like that! We can get it on right now, okay? I really don't like you people either."

The young lady got between Toot and her cousin. Then she pleaded, "Come on cuz. We'll deal with these country-ass Negroes later, after the game. In fact, if you want to, you can bust a cap in him and then we can go on to the High Chaparral and get our party on."

The High Chaparral was a popular social club in Panteo where everyone gathered on Friday, Saturday, and Sunday nights. On Friday nights after a big game, the High Chaparral would be crowded elbow-to-elbow. Shootings and fist-fights occurred every weekend just like old school westerns. It wasn't the safest place to be, if Pantego High lost a basketball game. Their biggest rival was the Belhaven Bulldogs; they actually hated each other. However, Pantego High almost hated Mattamuskeet School (my high school) as much as they hated the Belhaven Bulldogs. Basketball supremacy was ultimate in eastern North Carolina. Toot had a low tolerance for being bullied.

When he got angry, it didn't matter who were watching. He wouldn't back down from a potential confrontation. As the verbal exchange with the young lady became more and more fierce, a big potbellied deputy sheriff walked over to us and adamantly stated, "Look, you people need to go on inside to the game or leave the school grounds right now. The decision is yours. You can't stand around here trying to start trouble!"

At that point, Coach Baker walked through the lobby and spoke to each of us. He turned to Toot and asked, "How's Philip? Tell him that I asked about him. In fact, I'll be in Swan Quarter on Sunday and I'll drop by for a few minutes."

The deputy sheriff looked toward Coach Baker and asked, "Coach, do you know these guys? I was about to escort them off the school grounds. I am so glad that you know them. I assume they are okay, right?

Coach Baker responded with, "These guys are cool. In fact, they can come on inside along with me. You don't have to worry about these guys. I've known these guys for several years. They're good boys!"

Toot looked at the deputy sheriff, rolled his eyes, and followed Coach Baker. I was so glad to enter the gymnasium. It was extremely crowded in there and extremely loud from fan cheering. The atmosphere appeared to be similar to that of a game between the Boston Celtics and the Los Angeles Lakers. The teams were warming up and the fans were ecstatic. I watched both teams warm-up and the players from Pantego were obviously taller and much faster than our team. One guy who was called Peartree almost slam dunked the ball during warm-up. The referees watched very closely because slam dunks were not allowed during the warm-up period in high school games. There were three guys on Pantego's team who could obviously slam dunk the ball with little effort. A fan sitting near me yelled, "Peartree, I want you to slam dunk at least four times tonight, okay? Come on now, I got a hundred placed on you!"

Peartree simply smiled at the fan and shouted, "No problem! Just don't blink your eyes, okay. I'm gonna put on a show tonight for these farm boys."

Another fan yelled, "Yo, Riddick, show me what you are made of tonight. Send these *Mosquito Lakers* back home crying like little babies."

Then I heard another Pantego fan yell, "Yo, Bruce, make your mama proud tonight. I know you can do it. Spank these *Mosquito Lakers*!"

During tipoff, Pantego easily controlled the ball. Pantego's guards were extremely fast and strategic. The basketball ended up in Riddick's hands and he immediately whirled the ball down court to Peartree. Peartree took three great strides and slam dunked the ball with both hands. The Pantego fans went wild and began to point fingers at the Mattamuskeet fans. Walter Farrow brought the ball down court for Mattamuskeet. He passed the ball to Sam O'Neal and he did a no-look pass to Dick Tunnel. Dick shot a 20-footer that was all-net. The Pantego fans began to boo and some even threw popcorn on the basketball court.

Coach Baker noted the unsportsmanlike conduct and requested a timeout. He reached for the microphone and pleadingly stated, "Fans let's be respectful and show our visitors that we are mature and intelligent young men and women. Please do not throw items on the basketball court. You really don't want anyone to get hurt over some unnecessary stupid act, right? Let's be courteous to our visitors, okay?"

The buzzer sounded and Pantego controlled the ball. Bruce attempted to pass the ball to Peartree; however, Sam stole the ball and passed it to Caleb Holloway and he shot a 10-footer that was all-net. It was a fast-paced game and the fans watched in anxious anticipation. Neither team took unnecessary chances nor did they showcase unnecessary fancy plays. The game was serious and well-coached and well-disciplined. It took Walter a few minutes to get acclimated to the intense noise and the fast pace of the game. He missed his first five field goals and was having difficulty finding open shots. When he did, he began to rain jump shots like Clyde "the Glide" Frazier. He cut, dashed, and passed the ball like Earl "the Pearl" Monroe. Then, with four minutes and 42 seconds remaining in the second quarter, Walter hit a 20-foot jumper. A minute later, he drove for an uncontested layup. Walter was in his zone!

Then Dick Tunnel got into a "can't miss zone." He hit a 27-footer and then drained two 20-footers and an 18-footer. Dick and Walter seemingly couldn't miss. However, Peartree stole the ball from Leroy and began to entertain the Pantego crowd with several medium-range bombs. He made two almost unbelievable running jumpers; a 15-footer and a 20-footer. He continued to rain jumpers until he misfired with 1:11 remaining in the second quarter. However, Dick and Walter were guarded so closely that they weren't able to score until the second half.

Dick Tunnel controlled the backboards and he was confident that Caleb Holloway would grab the rebounds that he missed. It was absolutely beautiful watching Dick and Caleb complement each other on the basketball court. They appeared to be synchronized and appeared know each other's moves. Watching them play basketball was similar to watching Tchaikovsky perform *The Nutcracker* in Carnegie Hall. It was a moving experience! Dick and Caleb seldom talked to each other while on the basketball court. Caleb was a young man of few words and Dick believed in action versus words.

Nevertheless, they appeared to know each other's thought process and were committed to team-play. Caleb customarily hovered above the rim like Chamberlain and Russell in old school basketball. He longed to pass the ball to guards or forwards and allow them to score points. Scoring wasn't his ultimate passion. Caleb's slow motion moves were nothing less than pure art. They looked as if they were professionally choreographed.

However, Dick was a consummate scoring machine. He was nothing less than Larry Bird at his finest. He wasn't one to showcase emotion or attempt to perform a fancy move to embarrass an opposing player. He allowed his playing to do the talking and played with poise, precision, and passion. Dick didn't appear to be intimidated by the "trees" of Pantego. His endeavor to give 100% of himself was his ultimate goal. At halftime, the game was tied and fans enthusiastically waited for the final buzzer.

Toot, Hardy, and I decided to go to the concession stand to get some popcorn and something to drink during halftime. Sandy and Glen did not follow us. They knew a few guys from Pantego and began to laugh and joke with them. While standing in line to make our purchases, three dudes from Pantego pushed us out of line and jumped ahead of us to make their order. Toot looked at Hardy and me and said, "No. Hell no! You just can't push us aside and jump ahead of us like that."

The three dudes were bigger than us and they appeared ready for a brawl. The tallest of the dudes walked to Toot and said, "Oh, I suppose you are the ringleader, right? Well, just watch your back. I got something for you, Mr. Tough Guy. I'll see you after the game. We'll see how tough you really are."

The same deputy sheriff who we had spoken with earlier walked over to us and said, "Look, I am about to get tired of you boys causing trouble. Go on, make your order and get out of here! I ain't in for no mess tonight, okay?"

No one responded to him. We made our order and went back into the gymnasium. The game was about to begin when all of a sudden, someone threw a cup of ice on Toot's head. We were sitting in the Pantego section and when Toot turned around, everyone looked innocent. I gave Toot my handkerchief and he wiped the ice off his head and neck. He was steaming angry and the Pantego patrons behind us were really laughing and grinning uncontrollably. Hardy and Glen eventually got Toot to calm down and enjoy the game. The game was really tight and an air of restlessness consumed the gymnasium. The leads fluctuated throughout the fourth quarter. Peartree did a thunderous slam dunk that gave Pantego a five-point lead.

Coach Cotton called for a timeout to minimize the slam dunk's effect. The adrenalin on the Pantego team was extraordinarily high and he appeared to sense a degree of bewilderment in his players. Leroy brought the ball down court and shot a bullet pass to Caleb. Caleb grabbed the ball with crab-like arms and passed it back to Leroy and he shot a short-jumper that was all-net. The score was cut to three points; nevertheless, Pantego still held the lead. The third quarter ended with Pantego ahead by three points.

Coach Cotton summoned the Mattamuskeet players together and gave them a brief motivational lecture. He emphatically stated, "You guys aren't giving it your all-in-all. Pantego is not relenting anything; however, you guys are looking like a bunch of old men. It looks to me that we are trying to *not lose,* while Pantego is *trying to win.* Now show me that you really want this game, okay?"

At the beginning to the fourth quarter, Peartree appeared to go up in the gym's rafters and snatched down passes. Then he dribbled the length of the court and thunderously slammed the ball with two hands. Dick Tunnel was playing with four fouls; therefore, he did not try to contest the shot. Coach Cotton had only one timeout left and he did not want to use it prematurely. After the two-hand slam dunk by Peartree, the Pantego fans went berserk. Someone threw some popcorn on me; however, I was too afraid to turn around to address the issue. Toot looked at me and said, "That's why I brought some heat. Some of these fans are ready for the nut-house and they don't even realize it. Man, you can take their junk if you want to. They're not going to disrespect me. That's for real man!"

Midway through the fourth quarter, Pantego had a seven-point lead. Then Sam O'Neal stole a pass and drove the length of the court for a lay-up and was intentionally fouled by Bruce. Not only did Sam make the lay-up, he made the free-throw as well. Bruce became irate and yelled at the referee, declaring that Sam flopped. There was sheer pandemonium in the "Tin Can" for a few minutes.

One of the referees threatened to call a technical foul on Bruce if he didn't calm down and be quiet.

Coach Baker recognized what could potentially happen and immediately called for a timeout. He looked at Peartree and Bruce and said, "I want you guys to play smart basketball. Mattamuskeet knows that you have four fouls on you. They're going to bring the ball to you whenever they have possession. Be prepared and above all, don't foul! We need each of you desperately in order to win this game. They're much stronger and smarter than I anticipated. Mattamuskeet is not backing off and neither are we. Now, let's go out there and play smart basketball. Let's play our game!"

Fans were on the edge of their seats in anxious anticipation. This was the game of the year and it solidified who were the better team. It was really noisy in the "Tin Can" and the Pantego fans were nervously angry. After Coach Baker's timeout, Bruce stole the ball from Leroy and dunked the ball over Walter Farrow. Walter flopped on the basketball court; however, a charging call was not made. The slam dunk was absolutely beautiful because Bruce was only 5-feet-11. He actually cuffed the ball as if he were 6-feet-11 and slammed it with amazing authority. I was actually speechless because I had never seen anyone that short slam the ball with such conviction.

Pantego had a six-point lead with three minutes remaining in the game. The Pantego fans were rejoicing and taunting the Mattamuskeet fans. They began to chant, "We're #1! We're #1! We're #1! Go home Lakers! Go home Lakers! Go home Lakers!"

Then all of a sudden, Caleb miraculously blocked Riddick's shot and Walter scooped up the ball and skirted down court for an uncontested layup. Pantego now had a four-point lead with less than two minutes remaining in regulation time.

Coach Baker elected to use his final timeout. He put his arms around Bruce and Peartree and adamantly stated, "Let's go into our four-corner offense and only shoot the ball if you are wide open. Let's rundown the clock and go to the basket only if it is a lay-up situation."

Coach Cotton gathered the Lakers together and said, "Look, we still have a chance at this game. However, we must play smart basketball. I want you to play tight defense; nevertheless, I don't want you to make any mental mistakes. Let them bring it to you, okay?"

Bruce and Peartree took control of the basketball and slowly brought the ball down court. They went into a zone and cautiously passed the ball to each other. The time-clock slowly ticked away and the Mattamuskeet fans became restless. However, Pantego had a four-point lead and they were determined to slow the pace of the game to potentially solidify a victory. Then Bruce sent a bullet pass to Riddick and it slipped out of his hands. The referee blew his whistle and the time-clock froze. Walter rushed to the sidelines to retrieve the ball. Coach Cotton didn't call for a timeout; he allowed Walter to guide the Lakers. Dick and Caleb positioned themselves in their respective forward positions and Walter lobbed the ball to Dick who quickly tapped the ball to Caleb. The tap couldn't have been more perfect!

Caleb extended his arms like a praying mantis. Then he jumped far above the rim and released the ball through the net like a mother bird feeding her young. The Laker crowd became delirious and optimistic that a victory over the powerful Pantego squad was within the realm of possibility. Mattamuskeet was now down by only two-points and Pantego had possession of the ball with forty seconds remaining in the game. They elected to return to a zone as everyone attentively watched the time-clock. The Mattamuskeet fans became so nervous that they began to stand and watch the time-clock as it slowly ticked away. It was nothing less than standing in the center of Times Square in New York City on New Year's Eve. To our amazement, the ball was thrown to Riddick again. However, he was looking up at the time-clock and the ball rolled out of bounds. Mattamuskket fans began to jump and shout with joy. Nevertheless, a sense of bewilderment consumed the Pantego patrons as they sat in disbelief. Walter rushed to take the ball out of bounds and then quickly passed the ball to Dick Tunnel, and he hit a 20-footer.

A referee immediately blew his whistle because Dick was intentionally fouled while in the act of shooting. As Dick went to the free-throw line, the "Tin Can" was totally silent. However, when the referee handed Dick the ball for the free-throw, the Pantego fans went ballistic and began to bang on the bleachers and throw popcorn. An extremely huge dark-skinned dude sitting near us yelled, "Yo, Ref, how much extra did Mattamuskeet pay you to call this game? Stevie Wonder could call a better game than you."

Someone threw a cup of Mountain Dew on Hardy. He simply looked at me without uttering a single word. I simply passed him my handkerchief and he wiped his neck and ignored the Pantego fans. Dick held the basketball in his hands momentarily before shooting the free-throw. Then he looked at the Pantego fans; smiled, and hit the free-throw all-net. Eight seconds remained in regulation time; however, Pantego wasn't swift enough to get the ball down court to score. The buzzer sounded and the game ended. The Mattamuskeet fans rushed on the court and jumped for joy. They shouted and screamed as reporters from the Washington Daily news snapped pictures. Coach Baker, being a consummate gentleman and sportsman, walked over to Coach Cotton and congratulated him. He smiled and said, "It was a great game. We'll see you during the conference tournament. Good luck."

Coach Baker's wife, Bertha, my cousin, wiped tears from her eyes and then gave him a passionate hug. I reluctantly walked to her; however, she saw my apprehension and said, "Come on over here cousin and give me a big hug. This was simply a basketball game. However, we will always be family. When you see your mom, tell her I said hello."

I hugged her and shook Coach Baker's hand. Glen, Hardy, Sandy, and Toot stood around talking with the cheerleaders as Coach Cotton talked with reporters. It was still very crowded in the "Tin Can" and it was quite obvious that the Pantego fans were seriously irate and disappointed. As we walked through the exit door en route to Toot's car, the young lady who Toot had a verbal confrontation with earlier, threw a cup of ice in his face. Then, three dudes who looked as though they qualified to play for the Chicago Bears, stepped between Toot and the young lady. The guys were so huge that Toot had to actually look up at them. He went totally ballistic and began to cry. He walked around his car crying. His face was soaking wet from tears of anger. Then he kicked a big oak tree and stopped momentarily. He angrily shouted, "No! Hell no! This just ain't right."

Hardy and Glen tried to contain Toot as he angrily cried and looked at the young lady who threw the ice in his face. Sandy looked at Toot and pleaded, "Come on man! Let's get out of here. I don't want to go to jail tonight."

Our parents had taught each of us to never hit a female; regardless of the situation. Nevertheless, this female was truly testing our upbringing. Toot had only one sister and he was very protective of her. He definitely didn't want any guys physically manhandling her. The young lady continued to taunt Toot. She boastfully said, "Yes, I threw the ice in your face. And what are you going to do about it, you big crybaby?"

Toot broke away from Glen and Hardy and ran to his car. He reached in the floor of the Nova and pulled out the twenty-two automatic rifle. He fired three shots at the three dudes protecting the young lady and they took off like scared deer. The young lady pleaded, "Please don't shoot me. I have a bad knee and it hurts to run. I was on the girl's basketball team until I fell and injured my knee. Please, please don't shoot me."

Hardy and Sandy pleaded with Toot to get in the car before the police arrived. The young lady pleadingly said, "I'm sorry. I was wrong. I simply got caught up in the moment. It was a simple basketball game and I overreacted."

Toot finally calmed down and got in the car. The young lady hobbled off and we headed back to Swan Quarter. As we sped away, I looked at the young lady and she stuck her tongue out at me and gave me the middle-finger. I simply ignored her and was overjoyed to get out of that predicament. There was total silence in the car for about ten minutes. Then all of a sudden, a police siren was heard. I turned around and a police cruiser with blue flashing lights was dead on our trail. Toot said, "Damn, that's the police. Look, take your coats and place it over the rifle. If he sees the rifle, we're all going to jail tonight."

We didn't argue with Toot; we immediately honored his request. The police officer slowly walked to the car with his hand on his firearm. As he got closer to the car, he popped lose the strap that held his pistol. The officer cautiously walked to Toot and asked, "What are you boys up to tonight?"

Toot responded with, "Sir, we came over here to the basketball game at Pantego. Mattamuskeet played Pantego tonight, that's all. We are on our way back to Hyde County."

The officer simply said, "Let me see your driver's license and registration."

Toot was a little nervous. He reached in his glove compartment and could not find the registration to the car. The officer became a little impatient and said, "Did you boys steal this car. It's awful nice for you young boys to be driving. I need to see a registration card or I'll have to take you to the sheriff's office."

Toot began to perspire profusely. Then he pulled out a small piece of paper that served as temporary registration documentation. Toot smiled and said, "Here's my registration, Sir. It's a temporary piece of paper to use until the official card comes in the mail."

The officer sternly said, "Look, boy, I know what this is. You just drove 53 mph in a 45 mph zone. I should give you a ticket; but, I feel generous tonight. Now, you boys get on back to Hyde County and if I catch you speeding around here again, I promise you; I won't be as generous."

Toot said, "Thank you, sir. Thank you so very much!"

After about two minutes, Toot looked in the rearview mirror and jokingly asked, "Do you think I should have asked the officer if he would like a doughnut or two?"

Hardy, Sandy and I sat in the backseat speechless because we were afraid that the officer was going to check the car and ask us to step outside. That Friday night was indeed "fright night" with all the amenities, including popcorn.

After meeting Toot, Glen, Sandy, and Hardy, we immediately became good friends I began to embrace them as unwavering friends. Sandy was a stocky and robust individual who weighed about 220 lbs. Nevertheless, he could move like someone who weighed about 140 lbs. Even though I was significantly taller than Sandy, he could out run me; out jump me, and beat me in basketball as well as tennis. I had never seen or met anyone with his size and agility. Sandy lifted weights religiously and he prided himself on his dexterity and his exceptional speed. He was a gentle giant without any semblance of selfishness. He was a serious jokester who possibly missed his calling as a professional comedian.

Cecil lived within close proximity of Glen. His father was a well-respected landowner and farmer. They lived a comfortable black middle-class lifestyle and appeared still in touch with the poor and disenfranchised. After meeting Cecil and crafting a trusting friendship, I deviated from calling him Cecil and began to call him "Farmer." He spoke with a very, very, slow southern dialect that was often frustrating at times. There were very few light-skinned guys in our neighborhoods; however, Cecil was member of this minority population. His sense of humor was phenomenal. However, due to his slow, extremely slow verbal articulation, it wasn't uncommon to lose the gist of his jokes. It was not uncommon for my friends and me to simply smile or nod as a friendly gesture because somewhere along the slow verbal articulation, we became lost.

Cecil worked well with his hands and he loved to race. His father bought him a beautiful white Camaro that was totally awesome. He modified the Camaro significantly and welcomed opportunities to race. Even though he was seriously mild-mannered, he loved the ladies and they appeared to love him. There were times when I actually wondered if it was because he was light-skinned or because of his beautiful Camaro.

In spite of the personal inquiry, Cecil was consistently a charitable and kindhearted individual. Like Sandy, Cecil was an individual who appeared to gain delight in helping others. He wasn't about bragging or demeaning the less fortunate. He was about treating others as you would like to be treated. Cecil and Sandy epitomized the concept of being neighborly. The new friendships that I crafted with Toot, Glen, Hardy, Cecil, and Sandy have proven to be genuine and lasting. Nevertheless, I am truly thankful for my earlier friendships with David, Walter, Louis, Rudolph, and Donald. There were many lessons learned and each friendship impacted my life significantly.

# CHAPTER 29
# ROAD TRIP

***The way to success is to never quit. That's it. But really be humble about it. . . You start out lowly and humble and you carefully try to learn an accretion of little things to help you get there.***

***—Alex Hailey***

About two years after the infamous trip to Manteo with Hatton Junior, I received my driver's license. This was a glorious day for me because I wasn't compelled to wait in vain for superficial friends who promised to give me a ride to popular high school functions, such as plays, basketball games and dances. I wasn't compelled to hitchhike everywhere I desired to go or subject myself to the humiliation of standing beside a dark and dreary highway and receive taunts and name-calling from white males as they happily sped by me. When I did not have a driver's license, I was disappointed by supposedly good friends far too often. However, when I received my license, the empowerment that came with this most significant rite of passage, changed my world significantly.

I was instantaneously cast into the superficial world of "Who's Who." My heart yearned for acceptance and recognition. However, the self-selected bourgeoisie of Davis School, excluded me from their so-called "A-List." Ralph Ellison's *Invisible Man* had true meaning to me because I had walked the demeaning and condescending journey of darkness and invisibility. Nevertheless, when I received my driver's license, I was no longer invisible and the pretty girls of Davis School reminded me of this metamorphosis each day. The transformation was far greater than I ever envisioned. And consequently, my voice was heard and my presence mattered. I hated being invisible with unprecedented passion.

David, Walter, Louis and I were truly inseparable during high school. We shared our money, sneakers, ties, and basketball socks on a weekly basis. We gave true meaning to the statement, "One for All and All for One." When we went out to our hotspots to have fun, we readily checked to see if we were all there. We did not have cell phones in the late sixties; therefore, it was impossible to simply text to get an immediate response. During my sophomore year in high school, I received my driver's license. The day that I received my driver's license was one of the happiest days of my entire life. Seemingly, I immediately transitioned from "Henry Nobody" to Michael Jordan. However, I was determined to maintain my "true friends," which were the guys who appeared to enjoy my presence, even though I was at best an outcast. I really wanted to be accepted by my peers; it meant a great deal to me.

I often watched from afar as Tony, Donnie, Tad Pole, Tink Link, Byron and Boogie drove around in their beautiful cars. I dreamed of becoming a member of that elite group. Their elite status was something that I longed for and I would visualize driving around in a beautiful fast car and watch the so-called pretty girls drool after me. The males who had driver's license and a car, instantaneously became Denzel Washington or Billie Dee Williams. It did not matter if they actually looked like Flavor-Flav; they possessed recognition and influence. For some unknown reason the ownership of a driver's license made aesthetically challenged dudes look movie-star ready. In open honesty, the donning of a driver's license and a car were the ultimate rite of passage.

When I finally received my driver's license, I felt more empowered, more confident, and I felt as though I was finally a member of "Who's Who." It was like looking into the mirror for the first time and recognizing all of one's positive attributes. However, females were not accorded this all-of-a-sudden transformation. It really did not matter to most guys whether their feminine pursuit had driver's license or not. Most guys preferred that their ladies did not have driver's license for fear being caught engaging their mischievous ways. I did not want my newly found popularity to compromise my morals or integrity. I vowed that I would keep my true friends, David, Walter, Louis, and Rudolph. Even though I was being invited to exclusive parties and the pretty girls were smiling at me from every direction, I vowed that I would remain loyal to my lifelong best friends. The decision to remain loyal to best friends was not even a remote challenge. At heart, I knew that I would gladly give these guys the shirt off my back.

David, Walter, and I were asked to serve as waiters for the junior and senior prom. We were sophomores at the time and were utterly shocked that we were selected to serve as waiters. The big question was, "How did this happen to us?" We were all invisible beings and we received amazing joy if any of the juniors or seniors of Davis High simply spoke to us. This was an honor; a big-time honor for each of my best friends. We smiled big smiles and acted as if we had just won a jackpot lottery. The honor meant that we were recognized as sophomores with clout and respect. It meant that someone recognized that we had promise and welcomed us into their world of "Who's Who."

We smiled for weeks after we received the honor. About two weeks before the prom, David, Walter, and I decided to take a trip to Washington, North Carolina to purchase new white shirts, black slacks, and black bowties for the joyful event. Louis was a grade ahead of us; as such, he was a junior in high school. I do not know if he played major a role in our selection as waiters or not. We were simply happy and thankful. We spoke with Louis at school and asked if he wanted to ride to Washington with us to do a little shopping. Louis responded with, "Yea man! I need to buy some new shoes and a dark jacket. This is great and I will give you some money for gas."

I had never driven any farther than Belhaven before, so I was a little nervous about driving in downTown Washington. Washington was seventy-five miles west of Engelhard and I was a little uneasy about the drive. My nervousness may have been centered on the fact that there were no traffic lights in Engelhard, only stop signs. Washington, Little Washington as we often referenced it, had one-way streets as well as several traffic lights. Nevertheless, I was excited about the excursion and it would be a thrill to hang-out with my best friends.

David, Louis, and Walter were relentless pranksters. Rudolph was very quiet and rather reserve; however, he would shed that persona occasionally. Saturday morning finally arrived and I got up very early because I wanted to wash my car. I walked through the kitchen and Mom was busy cooking bacon and eggs for Dad. He sat quietly at the table smoking a cigarette, sipping his coffee, and reading the News and Observer as I searched for the metal bucket to wash my car. Dad peeped up from the newspaper momentarily and vehemently stated, "Junior, you left the faucet running the last time you washed your car. I have to pay for the water now, since we don't have a pump any more. Don't let it happen again!"

I began to shake in my shoes because I knew that my Dad did not play when it came to spending money unnecessarily. Mom looked inquisitively at me and asked, "Junior, do you want bacon and eggs or you regular molasses and cornbread for breakfast? Jackie and Nessie said they wanted grape jelly, fried cornbread, and some streak-of-lean and streak-of-fat for breakfast. Tell me what you want because I don't plan to be in this hot kitchen all morning. Do you want me to cook a few pieces for you?"

I looked at Mom and told her that I was not hungry and headed out of the door to wash my car. After washing my car, I went in the bathroom, brushed my teeth and hit a few necessary spots and rushed out the backdoor to pick up Louis. As I approached Louis's house, I recognized him standing near their mailbox. Gary, his younger brother, was busy chopping wood. And Mary, his older sister, yelled, "Boy, wait a minute. Mama told me to give this to you to give Junior."

Mary was one of the most beautiful girls at Davis High. Not only was she beautiful, she was smart as well. She was built like she should have been the centerfold in *Jet.* Her pecan complexion and her curvy body made most of the guys at Davis High drool. I waited a few minutes for Louis to get to the car. He appeared to be eating something and a large white plastic cup rested against the base of the mailbox. As he reached for the door handle, a great smile graced his face. He did not know that his lips glistened with grease and yellow egg rested in the cracks of his teeth. After he sat down, he reached in his jacket and retrieved two cheese biscuits and one sausage biscuit. Then he said, "Holdup a minute. I forgot to tell Peaches something."

Louis called his younger brother, Gary, Peaches. He was much taller than Louis and he was muscle-bound as well. Then he yelled, "Peaches don't forget to feed the hogs and place some wood on the back porch. I'll bring you a surprise from Washington. We should get back before it gets dark."

He looked at me and said, "Here Henry, this is for you. Mama told me to share with you and to give you this ten-dollar bill. She said gas ain't cheap these days and this should help."

I had not eaten breakfast and the cheese on the cheese biscuit had melted like wax on a red Christmas candle. The aroma of the country sausage biscuit made my car smell like the entrance of a fancy diner in Charleston, South Carolina. Mom had raised us to believe that eating at other people's houses was taboo. However, this was Louis and he was family; therefore, I ate the cheese biscuit and sausage biscuit like buzzards eating road kill in mid-July. It was delectable and I enjoyed every single bite. I ate quickly because I didn't want to take the chance that I would have to share my food the Walter and David. By the time I reached David's house, I had eaten both biscuits. Walter and Rudolph had spent the night with David, so I did not have to drive to Slocum to pick up them. David had not closed the car door securely before he said, "Gosh! It smells like country ham or sausage in here. Did someone have some country ham or sausage and didn't save us any? Man, that's messed up. That's real messed up!"

Neither Louis nor I replied to David's inquiry. Louis looked at me and smiled; he still had yellow egg in the crevices teeth. My stomach was full and I was excited about the unknown. I was hanging with my best friends and I was in my own little world. We drove almost to Belhaven before anyone did any talking. The guys were still sleepy and I was sleepy as well. I could hardly keep my eyes open. I looked in my rearview mirror and noticed David and Walter leaning against each other with their mouths wide open snoring. Rudolph was leaning against the left rear window slobbering and snoring. His neck was drenching wet from the slobber. Louis was sitting in the front seat leaning against the passenger window sleeping like a big baby. Except for my radio playing and the snoring, the car was silent.

Seemingly, when I glanced at the guys sleeping, I became sleepier. My eyelids were so, so, heavy. I continued the drive and then all of a sudden, I lost my focus and tipped off the road. Rocks and oyster shells flew everywhere and a cloud of dust and dirt collapsed on my dad's beautiful white Chrysler Plymouth. Louis was the first to awaken. He hysterically awakened and yelled, "Henry, wake-up man! Damn, you are about to wreck. Wake-up man! Do you want me to drive?"

I immediately and frantically gained control of the car. Walter sat straight up and said, "Man that really scared me. I thought we were in a canal. That really scared me!"

Rudolph shook his head and vehemently stated, "That scared me too. In fact, I gotta pee now. I gotta pee right now. I cannot hold it much longer. I really gotta pee."

Louis wiped the sweat from his forehead and stated, "There's a gas station right around the next curb. Let's stop there. I need something to drink. I am super thirsty."

I drove to the gas station and Rudolph rushed to the counter to inquire about using the restroom. Three elderly white men sat at a small square table playing cards. They looked really startled as Rudolph virtually danced at the counter. The store owner didn't even acknowledge Rudolph's presence. He totally ignored him and appeared terribly angry. As a means to cope with his need to urinate, he placed one foot on top of the other and switched them from left to right and right to left. He appeared to be in total agony. Two white guys quietly stood in line ahead of Rudolph. They waited patiently to pay for gasoline that they had gotten and to purchase cigarettes. Then all of a sudden, a white female, wearing really tight pink shorts, entered the store and ran straight to the restroom. She stayed in there for about four minutes. After the two white guys paid for their purchases, Rudolph asked, "Sir, can I use your restroom? I really gotta go real badly."

The merchant shook his head and said in a real country dialect, "You boys must not be from 'round deez-here parts. We don't let coloreds use our inside toilets. Can I do anything else fer you?"

Louis looked at the merchant and asked, "Look, Jack really needs to use the restroom. How much will it cost to allow him to use the restroom?"

The old merchant looked at Louis and asked, "Where you boys from?"

Louis impatiently responded with, "We're from Hyde County. What does that have to do with anything?"

The old merchant reached under the counter and pulled out a beautiful double barreled shotgun and said in his redneck dialect, "I've heard how the coloreds in Hyde County's been marching up and down deez-here highways hollering *Soul Power* and *Black Power* trying to scare good law abiding white folks. I heard about that King feller and that Golden Franks. Well, I got news for you boys. You ain't bringing that mess to my store and you ain't gonna to use my in-door toilet. Do you understand me?"

Louis looked directly at the old merchant and angrily stated, "Look, his name is Dr. Martin Luther King, Jr. And his name is Golden Frinks, not Franks!"

The old merchant readily became irritated and intonated, "Look, I told you 'Jigs' that we don't allow coloreds to use our in-door toilets. Can't you understand that? It's not about money; it's about common decency. It just ain't right for white folks and coloreds to use the same toilet. You boys need to get on outta of here before I lose my temper. If you keep on driving on US-264, you'll see a big oak tree near an old tobacco barn. Most of our colored fieldworkers use that old oak or the side of the barn to release themselves. Now get on outta of here. I'm about to lose my patience."

Louis sarcastically and empathetically stated, "I really feel sorry for you."

The old merchant rapidly chewed his tobacco and then spit a huge spatter near Rudolph's right foot. Then he calmly said, "I'm not going to say it again. You young koons need to learn some manners. Now get on outta of here! I mean right now!"

We all rushed to the car as Rudolph held his zipper area and appeared to be in excruciating pain. He really needed to urinate terribly. After driving for about a half-mile, Walter spotted the old oak tree and the old tobacco barn. I pulled into the driveway and Rudolph quickly opened the car door and ran to the far right side of the barn. I had known Rudolph for many years; however, I never knew he could move so quickly. The far right side of the old barn gave him a degree of privacy. After about three minutes, he emerged from the barn looking down at his sneakers. The sneaker on his right foot had transitioned into an autumn brown. The sock on his right foot appeared to have transitioned into a dark shade of brown as well. In fact, it appeared that chocolate pudding was covering his entire right foot.

Rudolph had to urinate so badly that he did not watch where he was stepping. He had accidentally stepped into a huge lump of manure. He was at a loss as to what to do. Apparently, the field hands used the far right side of the barn to defecate and the old oak to urinate. The apparent problem rested on the fact that the old merchant did not make a distinction between the two. Rudolph's right sneaker appeared to be saturated in manure and he did not know what to do. Tears rolled down his face and he was afraid that I would not allow him get back in my car. I really did not know what to do; however, I knew I could not allow him to get in my car in his current condition. I had a date with JoAnn that night and I knew I could not allow her to enter my car after that terrible stench. As Rudolph slowly walked to the car, we began to smell him. The odor was terrible and it was difficult to avoid laughing. When the wind blew, the stench of a skunk appeared uncomfortably close.

David, the real comedian, could not wait to say something hilarious. We all tried to maintain a straight face but it was difficult to do. We stood around pondering about what to do. Then David said, "Henry, I know your dad is going to get real upset if Rudolph tracks that messy gunk into the car. The way I see it, Rudolph has two choices. He can get back on US-highway 264 and hitchhike a ride back to Engelhard, or he can take his shoes off and throw them over there in that canal."

Rudolph shook his head and cried, "Come on guys. I don't have any more sneakers and my Sunday shoes are too tight for my feet. These are the only shoes that I have. I can't throw away my only pair of sneakers. I will not be able to go to school until my dad sells his crop and that's three months from now. I don't need to flunk another grade."

We all felt sorry for Rudolph and we thoroughly empathized. As we pondered the predicament, we meandered near the old oak tree. The stench from endless urinations compelled us to move closer to US-highway 264. Rudolph sniffled as we brainstormed our next move. He continued to walk with us in his nasty-brown, smelly shoes. We kept a decent distance between him and us due to the unbearable stench.

Louis, the real problem-solver among us, scratched his head and asked, "Suppose we put our monies together and buy Rudolph a new pair of sneakers in Belhaven? He can take off those sneakers and leave them here."

I smiled and said, "Sure! I will pitch in and we will not have to worry about this mess. David and Walter agreed to contribute as well.

Louis said, "Great! The problem is solved. Now, I have to pee! I going over to the old oak and handle my business. I'll be right back."

Rudolph sat down on the steps of the old barn and began to slowly take off his sneakers. His right shoelace was clogged with residue from the manure. David, Walter, and I watched as he used a branch to untie his sneakers. Three of the first branches were rotten and broke in half. Walter broke a branch from a nearby pine tree and handed it to Rudolph. After several attempts, he was able to untie his right sneaker. However, the shoestring of the left sneaker was extremely tight. The left sneaker required a great deal of maneuvering and patience. After Louis finished handling his business near the old oak, he joined us near the steps of the old barn. Rudolph continued to struggle with removing the left sneaker. The knot that he tied was extremely secure.

David, again being the real comedian among us, suggested that we burn the sneaker off his foot. Then he asked, "What about Rudolph's socks. We aren't going to buy him socks as well, are we?"

Walter interrupted and said, "Man, this is May. He doesn't need any socks. I'll help out on the sneakers, but not on any socks. This ain't Christmas!"

Then all of a sudden, we heard police sirens. We rushed to US-highway 264 and noticed two highway patrol cruisers speeding, heading west on US-highway 264. We were traveling west on US-highway 264 as well. We simply did not make a connection; we never connected the dots. We had not done anything wrong; therefore, we had no dire concerns. We were simply handling our business. Then, the first cruiser began to slowdown and pulled right into the same driveway where my car was parked.

The patrol officer hopped out of his cruiser with his handgun pointed directly at us. Then within thirty seconds, the second cruiser arrived and that officer hopped out of his cruiser with his handgun pointed directly at us as well. Then a third cruiser arrived and parked on the same side of the highway where we parked. The first officer shouted, "Put your hands in the air! Put your hands in the air right now! I am not going to tell you a third time!"

I immediately complied with the officer and so did the rest of the guys. Louis asked, "What's wrong? Why are you pointing your pistols at us? What did we do?"

The first officer replied, "Don't let me have to tell you again. Keep those hands in the air. And, I'll ask the questions, okay?"

We looked like five escaped convicts with our hands raised in the air. The second officer asked, "Whose car is this?"

I politely responded with, "This is my car. Why are you asking?"

The first officer adamantly stated, "I'll ask the questions. You just keep your hands in the air. Don't force me to pop a cap into one of you boys!"

As he got closer and closer to us, the second officer said, "Damn, these boys stink! They smell like skunks! I need to hold my nostrils to simply interrogate them. Something weird is going on! This boy is wearing only one sneaker and he really, really, stinks. His toes are so black that they look like Brazil nuts. And he is wearing only one sock. Do you think these boys belong to some type cult?"

The entire ordeal was extremely scary. All five of us stood near each other with our hands held in the air as if we had just gotten caught robbing a bank. We were all sweating and trembling at the same time. When the officer asked who owned the car, I politely informed him that I was driving the car but my dad owned it. The officer sternly commanded, "Let me see your driver's license!"

I attempted to lower my arms to retrieve my driver's license when I heard a clicking sound. The second officer pulled the hammer on his handgun as he pointed it directly at me. When I heard the clicking sound, I almost urinated in my pants. I immediately shot my hands into the air. I shot my arms in the air so forcefully that I thought my shoulders were going to come out of socket. The first officer looked sternly at me and said, "Boy, you almost got your big black head blown off. Don't be making any deliberate moves around here. My partner doesn't particularly like your kind. You people make him kinda nervous. He hasn't spent much time around coloreds. He's from Arizona."

I politely said, "Officer Sir, I was only reaching in my back pocket to give you my driver's license. That's all I was doing."

He said, "Okay! But I got my eyes on you. Go on, get your license!

I showed the officer my driver's license. He took my driver's license, returned to his patrol cruiser, and got on his car phone. I heard the car phone ring just before he closed the door. We were all extremely tired from holding our hands in the air. My arms had become extremely heavy; they felt as if they had fifty-pound weights on them. I looked at Louis, David, Walter, and Rudolph. Rudolph had his eyes closed and appeared to be praying. He was sweating like an escaped prisoner trying to elude search dogs. We were extremely tired and terribly scared. When we momentarily lowered our arms from exhaustion, the second officer would shake his handgun recklessly at our heads. He appeared be more nervous and more afraid than we were. He was shaking so badly that he made Barney Fife look like a legitimate deputy. Resultantly, I was afraid that he was going to accidentally shoot one of us. Somehow, we gained additional strength to hold our hands up a little longer. I was tired and terribly scared. My arms ached terribly. We all perspired profusely.

After about six minutes, the officer who requested my driver's license returned and whispered in the other officer's ear. Then he walked to my car and inspected it thoroughly. The officers even looked inside my trunk and under my hood. My arms were extremely heavy and I was so tired that I felt as though I was going to collapse.

The officers looked at each of us from afar and then said, "You boys can put your arms down. I guess you are clean. I received a call from the Hyde County Sheriff's Department to be watchful for a white Buick traveling west on US-highway 264. The occupants, three colored males, took off without paying for gas at Speedee's grocer. You boys fit the profile. I apologize for inconveniencing you. Have a great day!"

Louis became extremely irate and courageously stated, "Have a great day! That's all you are going to say after pointing those pistols at us for the last thirty minutes. Man, this is not right! This is all the way messed up!"

The officer who appeared to be in charge, looked at Louis and angrily stated, "Look, we made a mistake. We all make mistakes. I cannot turn back the hands of time. I am sorry for any inconvenience that we created. Things happen!"

Louis was so angry that his bottom lip began to tremble. He looked directly at the officers and plainly asked, "Didn't you say that the black guys were driving a white Buick Electra 225? Well, this is a white Plymouth Fury I. The two cars aren't even remotely alike."

I glanced at Rudolph and noted that he was still praying and sweating profusely. My mom always told my sisters and me that prayer changes things. As such, I smiled at heart as Rudolph consistently prayed. His prayer appeared to be working.

David and Walter were sweating profusely and it was evident that they were angry and afraid. They were angry, very angry. Then the officer who held his pistol on us for over thirty minutes became brave enough to make a statement. He unapologetically stated, "Look, we carry a badge! You see this badge, I have the right to handcuff you and place you under arrest. The only thing I need is probable cause. Do you understand? We don't have to apologize to you for anything. I am not going to apologize to you or anyone else. My badge makes all of this legal. Now get on out of here before I really lose my temper!"

We slowly and exhaustively walked to the car. As I was about to pull off, the so-called 'nice officer' ran my car and asked, "Have you boys seen a pump or water faucet anywhere around here? I am so thirsty that I can hardly stand. Old man, Mr. Alligood, always took real good care of his fieldworkers. He always provided them with their own pump or water faucet. Have you seen one around here?"

Louis smiled and said, "Yes, I saw the pump. Rudolph, don't you remember that pump on the far right side of that old tobacco barn?"

Before Rudolph could respond, David said, "Yes! I saw it. Just run over there to the far right side of that old tobacco barn and you'll see it. The water is nice and cold. Boss, you have a real good day, okay!"

The officer enthusiastically ran toward the old barn. We laughed wholeheartedly because we felt as though justice was finally served. As I drove away, the guys watched attentively as the officer raised his hands into the air as he looked down at his manure saturated shoes.

# CHAPTER 30
# THE GAME

***Associate yourself with men of good quality if you esteem your own reputation, for 'tis better to be alone than be in bad company.***

***—George Washington***

After the traumatic experience near Belhaven, we continued our trek to Washington, North Carolina. The car was essentially quiet from Belhaven to Washington. As we entered downtown Washington, we were excited about unknown possibilities. Our first objective was to find Rudolph a new pair of sneakers. We went to Alligood's General Merchant to purchase the sneakers. The salesperson asked us where we were from and we readily said Hyde County. The owner of the store asked us if Hyde County had integrated its schools yet. Louis told the merchant that full integration of the schools would not begin until the fall of 1970. He shared with the merchant that he had visited Mattamuskeet School and he really liked what he saw.

The merchant enthusiastically asked, "Did you meet a gentleman by the name of Morgan Harris while visiting Mattamuskeet? Morgan is a Beaufort County native and he is the athletic director at Mattamuskeet School. He is a God-fearing and kind man and I love hearing his numerous fishing and hunting stories. Wow! He is a gifted artist as well. In fact, those two signs in the store's window were painted my Morgan. We tried to get him to come to Beaufort County Schools but he would not even consider the notion. He loves himself some Hyde County."

Louis smiled and said, "Yes. I met him. He was very nice and he said he looked forward to seeing me on the football field at Mattamuskeet School. Mr. Harris was real down-to-earth."

The owner of the store told the salesperson to give us 20% off all purchases. We thanked him and then went to work trying to find Rudolph a new pair of sneakers. After trying on several pairs of sneakers, Rudolph settled for the Pro Keds. I looked at him as he smiled from ear to ear. A new pair of sneakers could make any guy's day more perfect. We put our monies together and purchased the sneakers. The salesperson recognized that Rudolph did not have any socks, so he simply gave him two pairs without cost. After all the turmoil that we experienced en route to Washington, life appeared to be getting much better. It was amazing how God gave us immediate favor with the salesperson and storeowner. As I reflected on the early morning dynamics, I recognized that it is not wise to judge any one group of people based on one negative encounter. In essence, it is never wise to prejudge people. God works in mysterious ways.

After purchasing Rudolph a new pair of sneakers, we went to an eatery called the Chuck Wagon. I had heard David and Walter speak about the hamburgers and hotdogs at the eatery on many occasions. However, I had never eaten at there. I was extremely hungry, thirsty, and tired. We all rode in anxious anticipation. We could hardly wait to get to the Chuck Wagon. A big, juicy, hamburger, French fries, and hotdog would be a welcomed change from the norm. We were so hungry and so thirsty that we modeled the portrayal Native-Americans in western films. For a brief while, there was absolute silence as we ate our food with absolute delight. The chocolate milkshakes chilled our throats and rendered pain. Consequently, we smiled as the shakes slowly drained down our semi-frozen throats. The charcoal-grilled hamburgers and hotdogs were delicious and we could hardly hold the hot French fries; it was all good, real good. When one lived in Hyde County and an opportunity availed itself to purchase a charcoal-grilled hamburger and hotdog, it was a welcomed treat.

We ate our food and returned to downtown Washington to purchase white shirts and black ties for the prom. Since we were working as waiters for the junior and senior prom, were not required to wear black jackets. However, we wanted everything to be perfect. We decided to buy black vests so we would all look alike. The salesperson measured our necks and arm lengths to make sure the shirts fit perfectly. Louis' neck was so thick and muscular that the salesperson shook his head in utter disbelief. As we were about to exit the store, we coincidentally met five gorgeous young ladies. The ladies were so beautiful that we were all speechless. Rudolph held the door as they entered the store. As they slowly passed, each of them smiled and said, "Thank you very much."

The young ladies were so beautiful that we were too intimidated to try to initiate a conversation. We were truly mesmerized by their uncanny beauty. They looked as though they had just left an Ebony fashion show. We stood outside near the store and talked about their looks. I noticed an older black man sitting in a green four-door Fairlane Ford smoking a cigarette. A young boy, who appeared to be his son, sat happily near him. However, they never said a single word to each other. It was extremely hot and sweat rolled down their necks. The old man never replied when Louis said, "Hello Sir. How are you?"

After about twenty minutes of sitting in the hot car, the old man stepped out and retrieved a dingy white facecloth from the trunk. The facecloth appeared to be discolored dirt-brown from excessive use. Then he placed his pointer finger on his right nostril and blew his nose. After blowing his nose, he grabbed the dirty-brown facecloth again and wiped his nose and lips. A brown speckle of mucus remained on the upper-portion of his nose but I was too intimidated to tell him. I readily noticed a shotgun resting in the trunk of the Ford Fairlane. Two huge watermelons clung to each other like inseparable twins. In addition, I saw two heads of cabbage and a few cucumbers.

I concluded that the old man was either a farmer or a bank robber. He looked angry and appeared impatient as he periodically glanced at his watch. It was as if he had an appointment and was afraid he was going miss it. I watched the old man and wondered if he planned to rob the store, or the bank right down the street. Then all of a sudden, the five beautiful young ladies came out of the store and got into the car with the angry old man. I heard one of the young ladies say, "Daddy, we will have to go somewhere else. There wasn't anything in there that would fit us."

The old man shook his head, used an impatient voice, and said, "Look, it's too hot out here for you girls to be playing around. I will stop one more place and then I am taking you straight home. Your mama has some chores for you to do and Walter and I need to carry some vegetables to Blount's Creek. When it cools off, you need to water the garden and checkout the watermelon patch. I have things to do! I don't have all afternoon to waste waiting for y'all to make up your mind. I got things to do! In fact, I need to go to the bank right now to get enough money to pay the field workers."

After the carload of beautiful ladies disappeared in the hot sun, we decided to head back to Hyde County. Louis suggested that we do one last stop at the Chuck Wagon. That suggestion was fine with us. I loved their French fries, burgers, and hotdogs. As we approached the Chuck Wagon, David enthusiastically shouted, "Look over there! That's that carload of pretty girls."

"Louis responded with, I don't know about you guys, but I am going to talk to them. Those girls look like the sun has never shown on them."

Rudolph, the ever cautious among us, negatively shook his head and plainly stated, "I'm not going over there to talk to those girls. How do you know they don't have boyfriends? I have had enough drama for one day. As pretty as they are, they gotta have boyfriends. I have been humiliated today! In addition, I haven't gotten over looking down the barrels of those pistols. I've been praying for all of us all day. Man, this is one day that I will never, ever, forget!

David gave Louis a sigh of reluctance and pleaded, "Come on Louis, you know the girls' dad didn't look too friendly. I didn't come all the way to Washington to be shot by an old angry black man. You saw the shotgun in the trunk of his car. That man looked like he was ready to hurt someone. I really thought he was going shoot us this morning. Really, I have had my share of guns for one day. I have a new white shirt and a new tie. This is not a good day to die!"

Louis ignored David and meandered near the beautiful young ladies. The young ladies looked at him but never said a single word. Before he could initiate a conversation with them, two rather light-skinned guys walked up and began talking to the tallest sister. She blushed as the guy told her how pretty she looked. I watched as the shorter dark- skinned guy stared at Louis. The old man got out of his car and yelled, "Charlotte, bring Walter a few napkins before he gets ice cream all over these seats. He is so messy; I should have left him home with Gatsie. You girls leave those boys alone, go on now, and make your order. I need to get back to the farm to put some plugs in that old John Deere before tomorrow morning."

After the two guys beat Louis to the ladies, he simply ordered his food and returned to the car. We sat in the car and ate as if we had not had a meal all day. I stopped at an Esso station to get some gas and noticed the car on the right side of the gas pump contained three young ladies. They smiled at us and we reciprocated. They were not as pretty as the other young ladies; nevertheless, it really didn't really matter to us. Louis was the most assertive of us, so he initiated conversation with them. The young lady driving appeared to be the oldest. She said her name was Priscilla, but her friends call her Cookie. Then the young lady sitting in the front seat smiled and enthusiastically said, "Hi! My name is Amanda and this is my baby sister, Rosa. We live in Pantego. Do y'all live in Washington?"

Louis smiled from ear to ear and responded with, "No, we are from Hyde County. We came here to do some shopping for the prom. Tell me, do you know a guy by the name of Avron Oden? He is a good friend of ours and he lives in Pantego? His mother is named Rosa Oden and she teaches at Davis School. We really love her; she is an excellent teacher. I am a junior and my friends are sophomores."

Priscilla chuckled and said, "Yes, I know Avron and his mother. Avron is a real sweetheart and all the girls are crazy about him. He loves to play basketball and Coach Baker said if he continues to improve, he'll be a starter this year. You know; my mom use to tell us stories about how the people from Hyde County talk. She said black people in Hyde County talk like run-away slaves. Then she said they were real nice God-fearing people."

I went on in the store to pay for my gasoline. As I entered, I observed four blacks ahead of me, waiting to pay for their purchases. They appeared to be my age; however, they were purchasing beer, wine and cigarettes. The guys smelled as if they had worn the same clothes for weeks. It appeared that they had not washed their face, and their hands were filthy dirty. Apparently, the clerk knew one of the young brothers quite well. As he approached the counter, the clerk asked, "Do you want the regular today?"

The young brother reached in his right pocket and retrieved $5.89. The clerk shook his head and said, "You are sixteen cent short again today. Everything is going up, I just can't continue to loan you money. It seems as though here lately, you never have enough money. The *Bones Farm* (wine) has gone up since yesterday and of course, taxes must be added to the total cost. Uncle Sam has to get his part. I would lend you the sixteen cent, but you already owe me from the last time. I just can't continue to support your habit."

The young brother looked dejected as the clerk slid his money back to him. I readily noticed that the clerk used extreme care to avoid touching the young brother's hand. As the young brother disappointedly headed for the door, I tapped him on the shoulder and offered him a quarter. He smiled with a great smile and responded as if he had won the lottery. The young brother looked at me as if he knew me, and he appeared familiar to me as well. Then he said, "Henry Johnson is this you? Man, you are almost as big as I am."

I was startled as I looked closely at him. I asked, "Punkin, is this you man?"

He enthusiastically responded with, "Yea Man! How is Ms. Belle? How's the love of my life, your sister, Linda? Man, I miss her!"

A flurry of questions began to come at me instantaneously. It was great to see Punkin; I viewed him as a genuine friend. I really liked him and he did not pick on me like Bob Mackey and Nathaniel Gibbs. These guys were older and stronger than I and they gravitated to opportunities to make a hard fist and hit me on my shoulder with all their might. They said it was a means to make me tough. They said it was for my own good; they did not want me to be soft. Nevertheless, there were times when I was compelled to wipe tears from my eyes because they had seriously hurt me.

There were times when the guys would hit me so hard that I was unable to lift my right arm for days.

Punkin never picked on me with the regularity of Bob and Nathaniel. I believe he eased off on me because he liked my sister, Linda. His real name was Mature Benston, but we all knew him as Punkin. It had been years since I had seen him. After his grandmother, Mrs. Beatrice, died, he did not have much stability in his life. His grandmother was his Rock of Gibraltar and when she passed; his world became a place of endless turmoil. I hardly recognized him due to his tattered appearance. His teeth had decayed terribly and the once muscular physique that he customarily had had disappeared. It appeared that life's entrapments had consumed him and he was at best, a shadow of the brute that I remembered. I was really glad to see him and ironically, sad-hearted at the same time.

He enthusiastically asked again, "How is the love of my life, your sister, Linda? Man, I miss her. She is the only thing that I miss about Hyde County. Whenever, I feel down and out, I simply think about her and my clouds turn to sunshine. She's not married is she?"

I sadly responded with, "Punkin, Linda died last year. She was attending college at Beaufort Tech and met a guy from Grimesland that she hoped to marry. To make a long story short, she and her boyfriend died of carbon monoxide poisoning. She's been gone for almost a year. When she died, something inside of me died as well. I miss her every single day!"

Punkin almost collapsed with the news. He fell against one of the shelves in the store and almost overturned an aisle of groceries. His eyes began to water and he appeared too weak to walk. His response made my eyes water and my voice crack. I was still in the healing process with regard to Linda's death. Two giant tears rolled down my face as I reminisced momentarily about her unparalleled goodness. Punkin gathered himself and apologetically uttered, "I hate to do this, but I need something to drink. This is heavy, real heavy."

He took the quarter that I had given him and ordered a bottle of *Bones Farm* wine. His hands trembled terribly as he recounted his money. The clerked placed his change on the counter but Punkin did not even look at it. His eyes continued to water and he trembled incessantly. It appeared that his world had crumbled instantaneously and uncontrollably. He did not know how to deal with the death of his so-called, "love of his life."

It did not matter that she was in the process of marrying someone else. The word "dead" as applied to Linda seemed to rob Punkin of any purpose to live. I loved my sister tremendously and as a coping mechanism, I changed the subject immediately. The notion of death and Linda still resonated with excruciating pain.

I said, "Punkin, come on go to my car. He held on to the brown bag as if it were an oxygen canister. Then, he saw Louis, Jr. He said, "Boy, is that you? Oh, Man! It is great to see you. I'd better not try to tussle with you now. Y'all are about to make me homesick. Man! I am glad to see you guys."

Louis did not recognize Punkin immediately. Then he said, "Oh no! I know that is not my cousin, Punkin. Man, it is good to see you. I have been asking about you but no one knew where you were. I heard you had moved to New York with a cousin and you had gotten a real good job working as a security officer. It's really good to see you!"

As he showcased excitement, he gripped the brown paper bag like a baby dependent upon a milk bottle. It appeared that his ultimate delight rested in the content of the infamous wrinkled brown bag. He replied, "Yes. I was in New York for a while. Then I was robbed three times right after payday. After being robbed three times, I bought a pistol from this dude that I met on the subway. Then I was playing cards with some friends and drank a little too much. After playing cards until about 3:00 a.m., I started walking to my aunt's apartment when two black cops started harassing me for no reason at all. They said I looked like a criminal. Then they frisked me and found the pistol that I bought from the dude on the subway. They locked me up for three months and told me if I ever get in any more trouble that I would serve 7-10 years at Rikers Island, a federal prison. I knew I had to get out of New York quick, fast, and in a hurry. It was too busy for me and I really missed the country food and swamps of home. I couldn't take it any longer, so I moved to Washington with my aunt. The city just wasn't for me."

The ladies in the car listened and stared inquisitively as we talked. Then driver said, "Looks like we have a family reunion going on here. You guys go on, we understand. We need to get home anyway, before mom gets upset. She can be a real trip at times. If you are ever in the Pantego area, look us up. Just ask for the Peartree sisters or ask for me, Cookie. Everyone knows us. We have a large family. Take care!"

Punkin listened as Amanda spoke. He politely interjected with, "Look, y'all go on. Don't let me interrupt anything. I have three yards to mow and it is a perfect time right now to get started. It was too hot earlier, but I am ready now. Whenever you are in Washington again, come see me. I stay with my aunt on Fourth Street. It's the yellow house right beside the barber shop and Randolph Funeral Home. I keep the grass mowed at the funeral home. Y'all take care and keep your eyes open. This can be a dangerous Town for strangers. See ya!"

After Punkin left, I told Louis and the guys to wait a minute because I needed to buy some chewing gum. As I tried to re-enter the store, the old black man who was initially sitting on a tall stool, stood at the door looking directly me, dangling a set of keys. He possessed an air of arrogance about himself that depicted him as if he thought he were a super Negro. The smirk on his face conveyed the message that he didn't identify with black Americans and his ultimate goal was to maintain favor with his boss.

While standing at the door, he yelled to me, "Boss, don't allow more than five niggras in here at a time. You have to wait a few minutes until I let a couple out. It won't be long. Boss began to lose too much stuff. You know how we do! That's when he hired me as his security boy. He said that I would be his eyes and ears. No hard feelings, I'm just doing my job!"

I was truly astonished and could not believe what I just heard. The old man was from a different generation and he was stuck in that generation. He was devoid of self-respect and he had total disregard for brotherhood or sisterhood. I was so angry that I told the old man to forget about it. I refused to spend my money at a place where a black gatekeeper demeaned other blacks. I was angry, totally livid, and the more I looked at the old man, the more infuriated I became. The old black man appeared to have what many of friends call a "slave mentality." The slave mentality is centered on the belief that there are populations of black Americans who are so indoctrinated in appeasing white America that they lose any semblance of personal pride.

I angrily got in my car and headed to Hyde County. The guys knew I was angry, so there was total silence in the car. After driving for about fifteen minutes, David saw a sign that directed us to Bath, North Carolina. He suggested that we ride through Bath to go home. I thought it was a good idea and I could stop to visit my cousin, Buddy. His real name was Linvert, Jr., but everyone called him Buddy. Even though he was my cousin, I really didn't know him very well. He was one of those light-skinned brothers with very good hair.

Most ladies found him very charming and he appeared to enjoy his status on the playa's landscape. When he visited Aunt Alma, in Hyde County, most of my buddies couldn't believe that he was my cousin. It was without question, he was smooth and a major playa. His Shemar Moore and Smokey Robinson persona were quite captivating. He could dance and he could talk-the-talk without stuttering in any manner. Buddy's self-confidence was phenomenal.

When he visited Aunt Alma, and the local girls saw him, they would readily ask, "Henry, what happened to you? Your cousin is so, so, smooth!"

Judith responded with, "Gosh! Check out his eyes. Just his eyes alone will make me melt. When we play Bath in basketball, I'll be looking for him!"

Several of my friends who lived on the Ridge had met Millie Ann and Sharon, Buddy's sisters. They were by any measure very pretty with long thick hair. When they began wearing the afro, they were ready for any runway. Millie Ann, the older sister, could have passed for Whitney Houston's younger sister. However, she was a consummate lady and my friends soon learned that she was more a natural beauty, she had smarts.

Sharon, the younger sister, was a little shorter than Millie Ann. In addition, she was a little thicker and her dimples were simply beautiful. When my friends met them, they immediately wanted to get their phone numbers. However, most of my friends tried to be playas and I wouldn't even consider their requests. I was proud of my cousins and I wanted Louis, David, and Rudolph to meet them.

# CHAPTER 31
# THE AMAZON SISTERS

***If a man does not make new acquaintances as he advances through life, he will soon find himself left alone.***

***—Samuel Johnson***

As I drove to Bath, North Carolina, I recalled that I had introduced Walter and David to my cousins, Millie Ann and Sheryl. David declared they were fine enough for *Jet,* magazine. However, en route to visit my cousin, Buddy, David spotted three young ladies playing basketball on a makeshift basketball court. He declared they were gorgeous. I looked in my rear view mirror and noted Rudolph and Walter were asleep again. David was wide-awake and checking out the scenery. All of a sudden, he yelled, "HOLD UP! HOLD UP! Did you see that?"

Rudolph woke-up, rubbed his eyes, and asked, "Did Henry fall asleep again? Come on Henry, you're the only one with driver's license. We've had enough drama for one day."

Before I could respond, David said, "No! It was nothing like that. I saw three thick sistas playing basketball near an old tobacco barn. Man, they were stacked and thick like Bernice and Mary Lee. All three were wearing real tight short-shorts and real short tops."

Walter asked, "David, are you sure you didn't fall asleep again and have another one of your crazy, wild dreams?"

I was shocked that David would use the term "thick" as applied to Mary Lee. You see, Mary Lee was Louis' sister, and he was very protective of her. We would never look at her in a seductive manner due to our respect for him. There was an unwritten code of conduct that denounced us looking at our buddies' sisters. And it was truly taboo to include them in our so-called man-talk. Nevertheless, Mary Lee was indeed built like a centerfold in *Jet*. She was absolutely gorgeous and smart along with it. We could allude to Bernice because she wasn't the sister of anyone in our brotherhood.

David declared that he wasn't sleeping when he saw the three beautiful young ladies. Then he demanded, "Turn around, turn around, turn around right now, and you'll see. I am not lying! I was not dreaming!"

Walter looked at David and asked again, "Are you sure you weren't dreaming again? You know, you'll go to sleep in a heartbeat. And for real, I have had my share of disappointment for one day. If I don't ever see a tobacco barn again, I am cool with that."

I turned around and traveled about a half mile and then I saw three black females who were the closest to Amazon women that I had ever seen. As I slowly drove to the makeshift dirt basketball court, *Have You Seen Her* by the Chi-lites bellowed on the radio. The ladies smiled at us as I slowly rolled to a complete stop. Their teeth were ivory white and their smiles were compelling. Their arms were more muscular than mine but they still looked feminine in their skin-tight shorts. Their shorts were so tight that one could easily believe that they were painted on them. Two of the young ladies were almost as tall as Walter and Rudolph; however, they towered over David and Louis. I immediately noticed a huge German shepherd tied to a doghouse that was too small for the dog to enter. The dog simply stretched out near the house and appeared to rest. He never barked nor tried to approach us. However, he stood tall in a very protective stance as I slowly and cautiously stopped. His ears stood straight up and his eyes appeared to monitor our every move.

I kept my eyes on the German shepherd as I approached the ladies. When I finally stopped, the tallest one enthusiastically asked, "Do you guys play a little round ball? My sisters don't want to play anymore and I'm ready to play. They're soft and sissy-like at times. I can play basketball all day and never get tired."

As she talked to us, she lifted her top to wipe the perspiration from her face and neck. When she lifted her top, I saw fine, fuzzy, black hair circling her navel area. Her legs, ankles, hands, arms, and sneakers were terribly dirty, but it did not matter to us. Her sisters were equally as dirty; however, it really did not matter to us at all. I had never seen a female that hairy before in my entire life. I found it very, very, attractive. David whispered to Walter, "Did you see that fuzz around her navel?"

Walter didn't respond. He simply appeared hypnotized. I asked the young lady if she felt brave enough to play basketball with guys. She indicated that her family had just moved to Bath from Sumter, South Carolina and she and her sisters played against guys almost every day. Then she extended her right hand and looked directly at me and said, "Please excuse my manners. I am so excited about you guys stopping by that I forgot my manners. My name is Summer. This is my middle sister, Autumn; and this is my older sister, Winter. My baby sister, Spring, just went to the house to get some cold water and a towel. She'll be right back. She is so prissy that she refuses to drink water directly from the pump. We are all accustomed to playing *against* or *with* guys. It doesn't matter to us. Back in Sumter, the guys called us the Amazon Sisters."

Louis asked, "Are you sure you want to play *with* or *against* us. We play rather hard and we don't take any prisoners. We won't take it easy on you because you are females. We play aggressive basketball."

Summer responded with, "We understand and we would not have it any other way. Let's make it interesting and real fun. My sisters and I are very competitive and we love a real challenge. We really get excited about a real manly pick-up game".

Then she lifted her top one more time and wiped her stomach area. I watched as sweat slowly trickled down her stomach and navel area. Her stomach appeared as flat and as hard as a washboard. After wiping her stomach area, she inquisitively asked, "Suppose we play make-it-take-it by ones to ten. If we win, we'll get your pants, and if we lose, you'll get our tops. We'll exchange our clothes right here. I saw how you guys were staring at our chests. This will be fun! If you win the game, you'll get a much closer look at our chest areas. Who knows, we just might let you take our tops off, one-by-one, piece-by-piece? Doesn't this sound like fun?"

Louis immediately took off his shirt and adamantly and asked, "Why are we still standing around. I don't know about you guys, but I'm ready to play this game."

As we talked, my car was still running and Marvin Gaye's *What's Goin' On* began to scream out of my radio speakers. Summer began to move to the beat and her whole body appeared to gyrate to each beat. She had excellent rhythm. As she smiled and gyrated, I immediately envisioned her doing a lap-dance. She was terribly sexy, even though her hands, arms, feet, and ankles were filthy dirty.

Summer suggested that we shake hands as a means of agreement, an oath. After shaking hands, Rudolph said, "Well, it's only three of you and it's four of us. I don't mind sitting this one out. And besides, I don't want to get my new sneakers dirty."

April frowned and stated, "Wait a minute. I am sure our baby-sister, Spring, would like to play. I'll go get her."

She ran to the porch of the old house and called, "Spring, come on out. We got a game; a real fun game like we had in Sumter. Come on Sis, let's do this."

As April rushed to the porch, Michael Jackson's *Never Can Say Goodbye*, roared out of my radio speakers. Summer began to seductively move to the beat as David and Louis starred in a mesmerized state of being. They appeared to be in a trance and captivated by Summer's undeniable beauty. She had us in the palms of her hands and she knew that we were gullible and filled to the brink with testosterone.

Finally, Spring came out of the house. She was tall, slender, and absolutely gorgeous. Her chocolate brown complexion and long legs made her model-ready. She looked as if she could have been a star track athlete at some major University. The muscles in her arms and calves were profoundly noticeable. Her body appeared to be absolutely fat-free. When Louis saw her, he jokingly said, "Man all these sisters are super-fine. They're just kinda dirty and talk like they should be on the *Beverly Hillbillies.* They talk so backwoods that they make Elly May Clampett sound like a real genius. If we were to take a water hose and rinse them off a little bit, they would be ready for a runway. Man, if they look like this dirty, imagine what they would look like with a bath cloth and a little soap and water. At least, we'll get a chance to get a real good view of their chest-area today. Regardless, let's take it easy on these Amazon queen dirt-dobbers."

## CHAPTER 32

# TOPS AND BOTTOMS

***Don't fool yourself that you are going to have it all. You are not. Psychologically, having it all is not a valid concept. The marvelous thing about human beings is that we are perpetually reaching for the stars. The more we have, the more we want. And for this reason, we never have it all.***

***—Dr. Joyce Brothers***

After being mesmerized by Spring's compelling beauty, we were all energized and enthusiastic about the ensuing game. The rest of us took off our shirts and began to stretch. However, Rudolph, being the cautionary person that he personified each day was reluctant to play. Nevertheless, David, a consummate daredevil, was ready for the big showdown and encouraged Rudolph to let his guard down for a little while. Rudolph looked David in the eyes and said, "Man, I just got these new sneakers today. It's been two years since I had a pair of new sneakers. I really don't want to get them dirty playing out here on this hard dirt. You know exactly what I went through to get these sneakers. They have to last me until next summer."

Just as the game was about to begin, I noticed an old man sitting on a porcelain pee bucket in a cornfield across the road. He reached in his shirt pocket and retrieved his chewing tobacco and sat down to watch us as if he were watching the NBA playoffs. He saw me watching him and suddenly waved at me and beckoned me to come to him. I started across the road to see what he wanted when Louis yelled at me and said, "Come on Henry! I can't wait to tell Donnie and Byron about this day."

David looked at the sisters and said, "Being the gentlemen that we are, we'll let you have the first ball. Summer took the ball out of bounds and quickly passed it to Autumn.

Autumn took two dribbles and David stole the ball from her. She looked at her sisters and appeared totally bewildered. I could have sworn I saw a smile or smirk on her face. After stealing the ball, David looked to the right and shot a bullet pass Walter and he hit a wide-open jumper. There wasn't a net on the goal but the ball slid through the rim without touching it at all. Then I took the ball out of bounds and immediately passed it to Louis. Louis dribbled twice and hit a contested jumper. Summer was guarding him tightly; however, his jump shot was relentless on some days and this was one of those days. Walter and David knew that Louis could score from mostly anywhere when he was in his zone. Not only could he score, he would talk smack as he rained jumpers from left to right. After scoring a beautiful jumper, Louis took the ball out of bounds and immediately passed the ball to me. I had not scored and was waiting to assert myself with the Amazon sisters. I wanted to let them know that I could ball as well.

Instead of taking a shot, I passed the ball to David and he made a quick move to the basket for an uncontested layup. David was the type guy who would talk smack as well and he gravitated to competition. He was fast, very fast, and he could play football, basketball, and wrestle, and could be a star player in each sport. David was a consummate athlete. After scoring the layup, he took the ball out of bounds and immediately passed it to me. I caught the pass and went up for a jump shot. Summer appeared to be waiting for me to take a shot. As I elevated for my jump shot, Summer jumped up as well. She blocked my shot, rebounded the ball and shot a beautiful left-handed jumper that didn't even touch the rim. The ball entered the center of the rim beautifully and as she jumped with joy; she gave Autumn jubilant a high-five.

Louis looked at me and shook his head. Walter frowned and said, "Gosh Man! You let a girl block your shot. That's disgusting!"

After scoring, Summer took the ball out of bounds. There score was 3-1 and we had the lead. I was the sole reason that the Amazon sisters had even gotten on the scoreboard. I felt bad about the whole ordeal but I could not change what had occurred. Summer passed the ball to Autumn and then ran near the goal for a quick pass. Walter intercepted the pass and tapped the ball in the rim for a quick score. The score was now 4-1 and we felt rather confident about winning the game. I had not scored and Rudolph had not scored a single point either. Walter took the ball out of bounds and immediately passed it to Rudolph. He noticed that I was wide-open and quickly passed the ball to me. I caught the ball and drove to the basketball for a layup. En route to the basket, I tripped over Summer's leg and fell to the ground. Autumn scooped up the ball and shot a beautiful jumper. She missed the shot and Rudolph snatched down the rebound and passed the ball to Louis for a fifteen-footer. The score was now 5-1 and I still had not scored. Even though the score was now 5-1, the Amazon sisters didn't appear to be concerned.

Louis began to talk smack to them; however, they simply smiled and didn't appear to be overly concerned. Louis jokingly asked, "Do you girls want to get your mama to come out here to help you win this game?"

Just as Louis made the statement, a blue Ford, Pinto, stopped on the side of the road where we were playing. A semi-tall, slender, beautiful light-skinned lady climbed out of the backseat of the car. She resembled my cousin, Shirley, who lived in Bronx, New York. I got a glimpse of her muscular legs and healthy thighs as she scrambled to get out of the car. As with my cousin, Shirley, her skin was flawless and her smile was compelling. It appeared that the burning sun of the summer months and the frigid cold of the winter months had escaped her. She was gorgeous, absolutely beautiful. Rudolph and Walter appeared mesmerized by her beauty as she struggled to get out of the Ford Pinto. She tightly gripped two huge brown bags of groceries as she worked earnestly to get out of the tiny car. As she maneuvered her body, she briefly exposed her red panties. Louis responded with, "Damn! Did you see that?"

Then the lady's pocketbook fell to the ground. She frustratingly yelled, "Summer, you and Autumn, get on over here and help me with these groceries! You are the laziest bunch of girls I've ever seen!"

They stopped playing instantaneously and ran over to the car to get the groceries. We watched as their buttocks bounced, and jiggled, and bounced, and their chest areas flopped like clothes hanging on a clothesline in mid-July. Apparently, the Amazon girls' mother had hired the driver to take her to Little Washington to purchase some groceries.

After struggling to get out of the Ford Pinto, she reached in her bra area and gave the old man a five-dollar bill. It was about 2:15 p.m. and extremely hot. The five-dollar bill appeared to be wet from being snuggly placed in her bosom area. Then, she proceeded to the house to store her groceries. As she approached us, she stopped momentarily and asked, "Why didn't you boys come over to help me with my groceries? You could see that I was struggling to get out of that little car. By the way, who are you boys anyway? I don't recall seeing you boys around here before. Forget the question! Autumn, you are in trouble! I've told you on numerous occasions about inviting boys to the house when I am not at home! Will you ever learn?

I stood in absolute shock when I concluded that the lady was the Amazon girls' mother. She was gorgeous and was equally as stacked as her daughters. Her legs were thick and muscles protruded in the middle of her calves. As she quickly walked, I noticed a slight bow in her legs. The Amazon sisters' mother was "hot" real hot and my testosterone level was more than sufficient.

The short red skirt that she wore made her the apple of everyone's eye. She was indeed the center of attention. The skirt was tight, very tight and revealed every curve imaginable. When the Amazon sisters' mother passed the two bags of groceries to Summer and Autumn, her pocketbook fell to the ground again.

The old man who dropped her off at the house appeared to have about five good teeth in his mouth. And when she bent down to retrieve her pocketbook; a robust grin governed his face. In fact, he actually took off his sunglasses. He shook his head and drove away smiling from ear-to-ear.

Consequently, when she bent over to pick up her pocketbook, we saw her red panties again. Rudolph was not one to use many cuss words, but he unconsciously said "Damn!"

This lady was old enough to be our mom; but, it really did not matter to us. We were extremely hormonal and our organs were extremely alive and active. She was absolutely gorgeous and we were all at the innocent and energetic ages of sixteen and seventeen. Our hormones were jumping around like popcorn in a hot frying pan and we were relentlessly seeking the unspoken rite of passage. In open honesty, we were all virgins just waiting for the opportune time to cross the hot sands of manhood.

It was difficult to determine who was more sexually appealing, the girls, or their mom. The girls were beautiful, simply insanely dirty and they talked as if they had flunked every English class that they had ever taken. They made a pure mess of the English language but it didn't really matter to us because they were superfine. The Amazon sisters' buttocks and chest areas made their sub-standard English mainstream-ready. At this point, we didn't care if they couldn't spell their names. Their sculptured anatomies made up for their intellectual deficits.

After becoming momentarily mesmerized, Louis introduced us and apologized for failing to come to the car to help with the groceries. He told her that we were from Engelhard but had gone to Little Washington to order tuxedos for the prom. The lady smiled, extended her right hand and said, "My name is Ruth but most of my daughters' friends call me Ms. Ruth."

Then she asked, "Oh! You are from Engelhard, right? Do you know a big guy from there who goes to Elizabeth City Teacher's College? He's a real big guy with huge hands and big feet. I believe he plays basketball at that college. I think his name is Claudie Jones or Claudie James, something like that. Well, my cousin, Shirley, from Belhaven really liked him and he went away to college and she hasn't heard from him at all. Well, she did read about him in the newspaper a few times. There were several articles in the paper about him playing basketball at that teacher's college. If you see him, tell him that Ms. Ruth, Shirley's cousin, asked about him. You might want to tell him Shirley's brothers are looking for him. He'd better be careful because her brothers are really crazy. Those Belhaven folks will hurt you in a heartbeat."

I smiled and stated, "Mrs. Ruth, you really resemble my cousin, Shirley. She lives in New York and you two could pass for sisters, or twins. I told my buddies the very same thing and they laughed at me and declared that there is no way in the world that I could have a cousin as light skinned and as pretty as you."

She smiled and said, "Well, thank you! I believe you just complimented me! You are so kind!"

Louis interjected, "Yes. Of course we know Claudie James, not Jones. He's one of our heroes and he has mad skills on the basketball court. We know his brother, Erskine, and his cousin, Floyd, as well. They are all real cool. Claudie has moves like "Earl, The Pearl Monroe," he can really ball.

David exclaimed, "I don't think those Belhaven guys want to challenge Claudie James and Erskine. Those guys are as strong as grizzlies. They can handle themselves quite well."

Then Louis interrupted with, "Claudie's fingers are the size of baseball gloves. Really, I don't think Claudie James has to worry about Shirley's brothers bothering him. Erskine, Claudie's older brother, doesn't take any mess either, at all. He carries a loaded pistol and a switchblade every day of the week. Now his cousin, Floyd, is real quiet and real clean. He is often described as a quiet storm. Believe me, the 'Mackey Boys' don't back down."

After the brief chat and helping the Amazon girls place the groceries on shelves, we headed back to the makeshift basketball court. Summer had to fold a few clothes before she could resume playing. As she folded the clothes, we loosened up a bit by practicing our jump shots and dribbling on the uneven surface. Summer eventually came out of the house and then Autumn had to leave abruptly. She unapologetically announced to everyone that she had to pee. Again, the girls were fine; but they didn't have any semblance etiquette at all. However, their lack of etiquette really didn't matter to us. David said he believed they were raised by the very same family that raised Tarzan, the king of the jungle. We all chuckled in total agreement.

As we waited for Autumn to return to the makeshift basketball court, a green Chevy pulled over on the left side of the road. The German shepherd that was lying near the "too-small dog house" jumped up immediately and began to wiggle its tail and run from side to side. The dog appeared to be happy and very excited. A tall black dude hurried and got out of the car and ran to the German shepherd. He reached in his back pockets and retrieved a bag of bones. The German shepherd appeared to jump about five feet high with excitement. The guy smiled from ear to ear as he wrestled the dog to the ground. The German shepherd licked him on his face, neck, and chin.

I looked in utter disgust as the dog slobbered and licked him as if he were a human chocolate bar. The dog's saliva was terribly nasty-looking and the black guy didn't appear to matter at all. Louis looked at me, frowned, and said, "Man, that's nasty. That's big time nasty!"

We were ready to begin the basketball game; however, we were interrupted so many times that we were about to become frustrated. The sun appeared to focus on our every move. It was hot, very hot. After about four minutes of playing with the German shepherd, the black dude stood up, brushed dirt off his neatly pressed slacks, and inquisitively glanced at us. He sported a neatly trimmed afro and thick gold chains decorated his neck. I assumed that he was from up North and he must have been related to the Amazon sisters. He smiled relentlessly as he retrieved a small mirror from his back pants pocket. Then he ran to his car and retrieved a huge afro pick.

He stood on the side of the road and picked his mid-sized afro for about ten minutes. As he picked his hair, he meticulously removed brown fur, grass, and brown straw. Then, he went to the trunk of his car and changed into a beautiful short-sleeved white silk shirt. After that, he switched his shoes to a pair of brown 'gators. The brotha was clean, real clean.

David looked at us and jokingly asked, "Who does he think he is? If he didn't want to get dirty, he shouldn't have wrestled with that old dirty dog."

Louis responded with, "Check him out! He is trying to walk like Linc. You know; the black dude on *Mod Squad* with the big afro. Check out that jewelry bouncing around his neck, and that fancy watch. That brother must be from New York or Hollywood."

The brotha was smooth, real smooth. And I was so glad that he didn't live in Engelhard. I knew the pretty girls would just drool over him. If he lived in Engelhard, I knew for a fact that the current playas would hate on him to the max. His afro was thick, like that of the Rev. Jesse Jackson, and he knew how to dress. The slow-talking brothas of Engelhard would not stand a chance against the "Don King" of Pantego.

# CHAPTER 33
# BOO JACK

***A person interested in success has to learn to view failure as a healthy, inevitable part of the process of getting to the top.***

***—Dr. Joyce Brothers***

The tall dude eventually came over to us and extended his hand to introduce himself. We all reciprocated and continued to loosen up by shooting jump shots. The guy said his name was Walter, but his friends call him Boo Jack. Then all of a sudden, Autumn returned to the makeshift basketball court yelling, "Boo Jack, Boo Jack, where have you been? We missed you! Did you bring us anything this time?"

Boo Jack smiled from ear to ear as he jingled the coins within his pockets. Then he politely replied, "I got a little something for you. It's in the trunk of the car. I just got in from New York visiting my mom. I made a few dollars up there and decided that the South is a much safer place to live. I was robbed two times within three weeks while staying with my cousin in Brooklyn. Then I went to the Bronx and the same thing happened to me and my friends. I have several stories to share with you all and a few gifts as well. In fact, I got a little something for everyone, even your mom. She's really going to like what I have for her. I can see her in it already. You know she loves to dress and what I have for her is going make her look real Hollywood. Look, you all go on and finish your game. I'll sit over here like a spectator. Don't embarrass them too badly, ok!"

Louis had begun to get a little impatient and sarcastically asked, "Look, are we going to listen to stories about New York or are we going to finish this game?"

Boo Jack looked at Autumn and told her to go on and dust us off. He appeared to be confident that we would lose the game. He didn't know that we had a 5-1 lead and Louis was in his zone. I hadn't scored but I felt confident that we would school the girls real quickly and then get ready for our peep show. Autumn took the ball out of bounds and immediately passed it to Summer. Summer dribbled the ball twice and went up for a jump shot. I blocked the shot, grabbed the ball, and finger-rolled it through the rim. I smiled from ear to ear and Louis said, "Good move, Prez! Let's go on and teach these ladies how to play this game."

The score was now 6-1 and we only needed to score four more baskets and we would be ready for the much anticipated peep show. After scoring the last basket, Boo Jack called Louis to the side and asked, "Would you boys like to place a small wager on this game? I have eighty dollars and I would like to place it on the girls versus you guys?"

Louis smiled and said, "Man, I don't want to take your money like that. We already lead these girls 6-1 and we even have Henry scoring now. I don't want to take your money; but, if you want to throw it away, I'll take it."

Louis summoned all of us together and stated, "Look, that fast-talking dude sitting over there said he had eighty dollars to put on the Amazon girls versus us. Look, it's four of us and that's twenty dollars apiece. Jack said, "I don't know. This is my last twenty dollars and I need to stretch it until the end of the month."

David interrupted and vehemently stated, "Man, this is a sure thing. That dude is a city slicker. Let's teach him a real country lesson."

Jack shook his head and said, "I don't feel good about this at all. But I'll put in my last twenty dollars. Something deep down inside tells me that this is the same thing as gambling. Gambling is a serious sin!"

Just as we collected the eighty dollars, Ms. Ruth walked to the mailbox to get the mail. She saw Boo Jack and ran to him and gave him a big hug and a kiss on his forehead. She was wearing a pair of cut-off jeans that were extremely short and very, very, tight. Rudolph was staring at her as if she were a runway model. We had to catch ourselves because she was indeed old enough to be our mom. I watched attentively as Boo Jack and Ms. Ruth spoke lightly and almost whispered as they periodically glanced at us. Then the conversation terminated as Ms. Ruth cautiously returned to the house. Louis collected the eighty dollars from us and called Boo Jack over to finalize the wager. After watching Ms. Ruth and Boo Jack whisper and glance at us periodically, I became a little uneasy. Nevertheless, the score was now 6-1 and we possessed the ball. Louis was in his zone and I had scored, the odds were unanimously in my favor. David had become a little uneasy as well. As such, he asked Boo Jack, "Who's going to hold on to the money while we finish the game?"

Boo Jack vehemently stated, "Since I am not playing, I'll hold on to the money." None of the guys felt comfortable with Boo Jack holding the money. After much pondering, Louis suggested that Ms. Ruth hold the money until the game ended. Summer called Ms. Ruth and she rushed to the front door and asked, "Summer, what on earth do you want? I'm trying to fix dinner. I don't have time for your mess. Since Boo Jack is back in Town, I thought we would have fried chicken and cabbage for dinner. However, if you keep bothering me, you just might have mayonnaise sandwiches and cold water."

Summer pleadingly asked, "Mom, will you hold on to this money while we finish the game? These guys made a wager with Boo Jack against us, but they don't want him to hold on to the money. They don't really trust him; but they trust you. Will you hold on to this money until after the game?"

Ms. Ruth shook her head and matter-of-factly stated, "This looks and smells too much like gambling to me. I'm a Christian-woman and I don't fancy to gambling or betting of any kind. Gambling is sinful and I am trying to live a Godly life. However, since Boo Jack brought you girls a few gifts and brought me a beautiful Sunday dress, how can I say no?"

Boo Jack didn't like the fact that we didn't trust him. His whole demeanor changed and the great smile that graced his face disappeared. He was angry, very angry. Even with his angst, he was able to mutter, "So, what are you going to do, stand here and talk or play ball? I don't have all day long to stand around with you country boys. Either you accept this wager or not. I have my money."

Louis began to sweat on his nose. All of the guys knew when Louis perspired on his nose that he was angry, very angry. He handed Ms. Ruth $80.00 and watched attentively as Boo Jack counted out $80.00 to Ms. Ruth. He presented her with four $20.00 bills and appeared to have at least $275.00 still in his possession. We all wanted to make sure that he had $80.00. Ms. Ruth immediately pulled down her tightly-fitted top and placed the money somewhere in her bra area. She smiled, patted her voluptuous breasts, and asked, "Is this safe enough for you boys?"

Boo Jack sarcastically asked, "Are you farm boys ready now? You'd better hurry up before it gets dark and you won't be able to milk the cows." No one responded to Boo Jack, we simply ignored his snide remark. Louis was steaming hot at this point. He didn't even respond. It was all business and all about the money. It wasn't good when Louis got angry, because when he got angry, his game would be off significantly. In fact, when he got angry, he didn't talk smack at all. He simply played the game with very little to no conversation. To this end, Louis took the ball out of bounds and passed it immediately to Rudolph. Rudolph took one dribble and passed the ball to David. David drove to the basket and made a beautiful bank-shot. Louis still did not smile or say anything. He was all business! The score was now 7-1 and we needed to score only three more baskets.

I took the ball out of bounds and immediately passed it to Louis. Louis was wide open. He missed the shot but Walter snatched down the rebound. It was obvious that Louis was angry because he would customarily make that shot even with his eyes closed. Walter rebounded the ball and passed it to Rudolph. Rudolph fumbled the ball a bit and then threw the ball through the goal. It was almost unbelievable because Rudolph hardly ever played basketball. His shot was awkward, very awkward. He was tall but not much of an athlete. The score was now 8-1. However, the money factor robbed the game of its initial joy. Louis was not talking smack and everyone appeared to be on edge. We were no longer giving the high-five and laughing and joking. The fun element of the game had disappeared at the onset of the $80.00 wager. I immediately thought about what I had heard in church. Rev. Gathan Harris would vehemently state, "The love of money is the route to all evil."

We only needed to score two more baskets and each of us would get an extra twenty dollar bill and a peep at the Amazon girls' chest area. Louis still didn't smile; he was all business. As I rushed to take the ball out of bounds, I noticed a big, muscle bound, dark-skinned guy clumsily trying to make his way through a cornfield. A big dark-brown German shepherd appeared to drag him between the cornstalks. This guy's muscle looked as if he had eaten a chocolate caramel apple for lunch and it had settled in the middle of his biceps. He had all the makings of a country version of Issac Hayes. As he approached us, the other dog attached to the too-small dog house began to jump around crazily and bark ferociously. Then all of a sudden, Summer called, "Hercules, come over here. You can have the next game. This game is almost over."

Hercules asked, "What's the score? It's too hot to be out here bouncing a basketball. I came by to pay mom the twenty dollars that I owe her. You know how mom is about money."

Again, I thought about Rev. Harris' statement in church, "The love of money is the root of all evil."

The statement had new meaning to me. For the first time in my life, I was acknowledging the absolute truths of the Bible. Its actualization was being manifested to me on a makeshift basketball court in a lust induced setting.

Louis became impatient and asked, "Can't you do your family reunion later? We're playing a big game right now. Every time we get a roll going, there's some type of interruption. Are you going to play ball or talk to this dude?"

The guy became annoyed with Louis and sarcastically repeated, "This dude!" Look man when I am talking to my sister, you need to be quiet. This is my sister! I don't need to ask for permission to talk to her. Look, I just got out of the joint; I don't mind going back. Don't you ever interrupt me when I'm talking to my sisters! Do you understand me? I don't play! I don't play at all! Do you understand me! I don't know you and you don't know me. Don't you ever try to belittle me in front of my sisters again?"

The German shepherd growled, barked, and jumped around insanely as Hercules vented his frustration with Louis. The dog in the too-small dog house barked viciously and dragged the dog house about five feet trying to get to Louis. Boo Jack smiled relentlessly as Hercules angrily explained his position. We were all momentarily frozen as we kept our eyes on the vicious dogs and this muscle-bound stranger talking smack to Louis.

David grabbed Louis and convinced him to calm down. He whispered to him that we simply needed to score only two more baskets and we would be on our merry way back to Engelhard. He told Louis to leave the convict alone and finish the game so we could get back on the road.

Mrs. Ruth heard the commotion and rushed to the makeshift basketball court. She had changed clothes again and was now wearing a pair of Daisy Duke jean shorts with a red halter top. Her navel area was exposed and her stomach was as flat as a washing board. Summer yelled, "Mom, please come get Hercules. He is about to break his parole."

Rudolph looked at Walter and Walter looked at David. We had no idea that a simple basketball game would lead to such chaos. I watched as the veins in Hercules' neck palpitated in angst. Louis did not back down even though the huge German shepherd was simply waiting to introduce him to his big, needle sharp teeth.

Mrs. Ruth walked rapidly to the basketball court and yelled, "Hercules, come here! Come here right now! I know you don't want to go back to the joint over a stupid basketball game! You are much too smart for that!"

Hercules held his mother in high esteem. He calmly said, "Mom, that dude disrespected me right in front of my sisters. That's wrong mom; that's big time wrong!"

Boo Jack rushed over to Mrs. Ruth and Hercules. He whispered something in Hercules' ear and then shook his hand. A semi-smile graced his face as Boo Jack looked at us and continued to whisper. I wondered what he was saying that caused Hercules to calm down. Mrs. Ruth was able to convince Hercules to come to the house with her. As he reluctantly meandered to the house, he gave Louis a serious stare-down. Mrs. Ruth became impatient and decided to grab Hercules' right arm and pulled him toward the house. Hatred appeared to consume him as he sat on the porch and watched attentively. It was a very eerie feeling. Hercules was nothing less than a pit bull terrier and he was terribly angry. The game resumed after about thirty minutes of interruption. I took the ball out of bounds and passed it directly to Walter. There was a hump on the ground and Walter lost his balance and collapsed to the ground. David immediately scooped up the ball and shot a three-footer that went swiftly through the rim.

Then, all of a sudden, Summer called for timeout. She beckoned her sisters to come together as she whispered something into their ears. As she whispered, all of the sisters looked directly at us. Then Summer clapped her hands and said, "We are ready. Let's play ball!"

We needed to score only one more basket and then we would get back on the road. It didn't matter to us anymore about getting a peep at the Amazon sisters' chest area. After all the chaos that we had experienced, the sisters didn't look good to us anymore. Now, our ultimate focus was retrieving our $20.00 bills and going back to Engelhard.

I took the ball out of bounds and passed it to Walter; he passed it back to me; and I immediately passed it to Louis. Louis was still angry and his game was off terribly. He went up for a jump shot; however, Summer blocked it. After blocking the jump shot, she passed the ball to Autumn and she scored a beautiful fifteen-footer. The score was now 9-2 and we still needed to score only one basket. Autumn took the ball out of bounds and immediately passed the ball to Spring. Spring dribbled twice and then yelled, "Chopping block!" After yelling "Chopping block", she shot a five-footer that slid through the center of the goal.

The score was now 9-3 and the Amazon sisters still had possession of the ball. Spring took the ball out of bounds and then passed it to Winter. After receiving the pass, Summer yelled, "Clothes line" and Winter passed the ball to her. Summer didn't even look at the goal and scored a perfect five-footer. The score was now 9-4 and our lead was slowly slipping away. Boo Jack smiled a mischievous smile as the game continued. His smile made me feel very uneasy. Summer took the ball out of bounds and immediately passed it to Winter.

Winter didn't even dribble, she simply yelled "Oak Tree" and shot the ball and it sank swiftly through the goal. The score was now 9-5 and we were doing our very best to score our last basket. Summer took the ball out of bounds and passed it to Autumn. Autumn ran to the right side of an old tobacco barn and yelled "Barn" and Summer passed her the ball. Autumn didn't even look at the goal and scored an almost unbelievable fifteen-foot jump shot. The score was now 9-6 and we couldn't even get our hands on the ball to score.

Louis was still angry; therefore, he wasn't talking smack. He was serious; very serious. He called for a timeout and Summer said, "Sure, no problem! Take as much time as you need."

A car passed by as we huddled together. It was rather strange; however, Al Green's *Let's Stay Together* bellowed out of the car's speakers. Louis looked at each of us and sternly said, "Look, we need only one basket. Let's go on and win this game and get our money. I think Boo Jack has something up his sleeves. I just don't trust that dude. Come on now! Let's go on and get this money!"

While we were huddling, the Amazon girls' brother came out of the house. He immediately went to Boo Jack and began to whisper. Their whispering made me feel very uncomfortable. As I watched them from afar, I noticed an old oak tree. Some of its branches appeared to be rotten and withered but the very center of the old oak appeared to take the shape of a cross. I wondered if this was a signal from God to tell me that I know that it is wrong to gamble. Our fun game of basketball had instantaneously transitioned into a gambling undertaking and each touch of the basketball was totally serious.

After about a three minute break to strategize and refocus to win the game, Boo Jack yelled, "Are you farm boys ready to play this game or are you going to pray and sing one those old Negro hymns while you are huddling together? I have things to do; I can't wait here all day for you farm boys to figure out this game." Then the Amazon sisters' brother interjected with, "Yea, that's right, we got things to do. We have a life to live. Are you going to play ball or are you going to whisper to each other like little sissies all day?"

We ignored all the smack-talk and told the girls that we were ready. As the game resumed, for some reason, I could not keep my eyes off the old oak tree and the sign of the cross. I wondered if God was trying to communicate a message to me. Nevertheless, I ignored any potential signs and symbols and continued my path into the unknown. The old man who sat on the bucket and watched us had all of a sudden disappeared.

Summer took the ball out of bounds and Winter yelled, "Barn." She threw her a bullet pass and Winter hit a fifteen-footer that didn't even touch the rim. The score was now 9-7 and the Amazon girls still had possession of the ball. Boo Jack and the Amazon sisters' brother gave each other a high-five. They laughed and gave high-fives about three times. Louis became angrier and angrier each time the guys made snide remarks. Then all of a sudden, he reached his boiling point. He stormed off the makeshift basketball court and stepped to Boo Jack. The Amazon sisters' brother stepped in front of Boo Jack as if he were going to handle the situation. When David saw what was about to happen, he stepped to the guy and said, "I have had enough of you guys acting like you are superior to us. Look, both of you guys aren't going to jump Louis. Now, are we going to play ball or we are going to brawl? I am not afraid of you guys and I am sick and tired of you acting like you are smarter than us."

Summer saw what was about to happen and pleaded that we forget about our differences and finish the game. Ms. Ruth must have been watching the entire scenario. I heard the front door slam and she stormed to the makeshift basketball court and grabbed her son by his "wife-beater t-shirt" and dragged him to the porch. The Amazon sisters' brother had so much love and respect for his mother that he simply complied with her request. Boo Jack must have gotten angry as well. For the very first time, he wasn't smiling and acting as if he knew something that we did not. His stoic demeanor was unsettling.

Winter apologized for her brother's behavior and asked, "Can we go on and finish the game? I just love playing basketball; I don't care about the money."

# CHAPTER 34
# READING THE TEA LEAVES

***A man isn't poor if he can still laugh.***

***—Raymond Hitchcock***

We all agreed to finish the game. Winter took the ball out of bounds and passed it to Spring. Then all of a sudden, Summer yelled "Chopping block!"

Summer honestly didn't even look at the goal. She dribbled the ball twice and took a hook-shot. The ball rolled around the rim three times before falling through the rim. We all stood in sheer amazement as the ball spun around on the rim. Walter had positioned himself into an advantageous stance to snatch down the rebound. However, the ball miraculously fell through the rim.

I looked on the porch and watched as the Amazon sisters' brother danced in jubilation after his sister's shot. He was doing a combination of the *Twist, the Jerk*, and *the Running Man* on the rotten planks of the porch. At heart, I was hoping he would fall through so we could get a great laugh. He was trying to be a menace to us, even though he couldn't even leave the front porch. I could hear Marvin Gaye's *Let's Get It On* playing on the family stereo. He had been locked up so long that he didn't even know the latest dances and I wasn't about to school him at all. Truly, I didn't know how to do them, either. My friends always teased me that I danced like a white boy. I would customarily respond to them with, "I might not be able to dance well; however, I do know my multiplication tables."

The score was now 9-8 and the Amazon sisters still had possession of the ball. David looked at me and shook his head. We were concerned, very concerned. It would be very embarrassing to be beaten by a group of girls. Our pride and our honor were at stake and we just didn't know what to do. I looked to the right where the chopping block rested and noticed that Boo Jack was smiling again. He went in his right front pocket and began to count his cash as he glanced at us in a very mischievous manner. The smile that graced his face made me angry, very angry. I did my very best to not let him know that I was at my boiling point. Then all of a sudden, Boo Jack yelled and asked, "Ms. Ruth, would you mind coming over here to help me count this money? It's burning a hole in my pocket."

Summer smiled and said, "Ignore him and let's play ball."

Autumn took the basketball out of bounds and yelled, "Tree trunk!" Winter ran near the tree trunk that I had not even noticed and shot the basketball. The basketball went *swish* through the rim without touching the rim at all. It was another amazing shot and Winter didn't even look at the goal. The score was now 9-9 apiece and the next basket would determine the winner. When Winter scored the basket, the Amazon sisters jumped around and gave jubilant high-fives. Boo Jack smiled and began doing *The Twist.* The dance was old but he was doing it as if he were dancing for money. His dance routine had had all the makings of *Mr. Bojangles.* He was teasing us and we were so dirty and distraught that we truly looked like field Negros in *Gone with the Wind.* I stood still momentarily and reflected on Sunday school lessons thematically-centered on the sins and ills of gambling. As such, I felt like I was committing a terrible sin for a few dollars. My conscience was beating me up terribly.

While the girls and Boo Jack briefly danced around in merriment, Louis called us together to brainstorm how we were going to score the last shot to win the game and go home with our money and pride intact. David whispered, "I noticed that the Amazon sisters know this basketball court in-and-out. They don't even look at the goal at all. I feel as though Boo Jack and the Amazon sisters have been playing us all along. They suckered us into this game to win our money. We have been suckered, big-time!

After extreme jubilation, Winter smilingly said, "Well this is the game-winning-point. Are you guys ready? I hope you guys won't have any hard feelings."

For some reason, the Amazon sisters weren't appealing to us anymore. We felt as though we had been hoodwinked throughout the whole ordeal. Boo Jack continued to smile a conniving smile and the more he smiled, the angrier we became. However, this was the game- point and we couldn't afford to lose our money. Louis called another quick timeout. He whispered, "I tell you what, let's watch the Amazon sisters' eyes. If we can read their eyes, we can get our hands on the ball again, and win the game. We can do this! We should stop looking at their bodacious chests and big buttocks, and start reading their eyes. I believe their eyes tell the real story."

Boo Jack became impatient and yelled, "Hey, you farm boys better go on and take this whipping so you can get home in time to feed the hogs. Oh! And don't forget, you need to go to the well to fetch some clean water to take a bath. You boys look like you got a starring role in *Roots*. I'm tired waiting; let's finish this game. I need to count my money!"

David and I ignored Boo Jack; however, he had gotten on our last nerve. Louis didn't seem to be as angry as he had been early on in the game. He appeared to have regained his composure and a sense of urgency was at hand. We were all focused on winning the game and everything else was irrelevant. The Amazon sisters, as fine as they were, didn't mean anything to us anymore. The basketball was the "money ball" and we were on a serious mission. It was do or die and we did not care to die!

Rudolph threw the basketball to Winter and she took the ball out of bounds to resume the game. We appeared to have the eye of the tiger and a relentless urgency to win this game. As Louis had eloquently stated, "Look in their eyes. Their eyes told the real story."

Winter passed the ball to Autumn. She dribbled the basketball six times. Then she innocently looked at Summer and attempted to pass the ball to her. However, Louis read her eyes and intercepted the basketball. After intercepting the ball, he called for an immediate timeout. David and Rudolph smiled great smiles and gave each other high-fives. I looked at Boo Jack as he leaned against the old tobacco barn in utter shock. A wasp nest buzzed above his head and he didn't even see it. I started to tell him about the wasp nest; but, he had been such a menace throughout the game that I felt a good sting would teach him a good lesson. Boo Jack paced back and forth continuously under the wasp nest. I just knew that he was going to upset the wasps. Then all of a sudden, he began to perspire heavily and talk to himself.

During the brief timeout, Louis told us to maintain a clear focus and to only take a high percentage shot. He encouraged us to allow the game to come to us and above all, don't rush anything. Louis called time-in and took the ball out of bounds for the last shot. The Amazon sisters weren't smiling anymore; they were serious, very serious. Louis shot a bullet pass to David and he immediately passed the ball to Walter. Walter was wide open with no one really guarding him. He went in the air and released a perfect jump shot. The ball slid perfectly through the rim and the game was over.

After jumping around in jubilation for about three minutes, we ran to the porch to get our money from Ms. Ruth. Boo Jack wasn't smiling anymore and he appeared to be totally devastated. Rudolph, the most religious of us, fell upon his knees and thanked God for the miraculous win. The win for us was comparable to an NBA finals game between the Boston Celtics and the Los Angeles Lakers. We were so happy to get the win that we forgot all about getting a peep at the Amazon sisters' chest area.

Ms. Ruth disappointingly came out of the house and reached in her bodacious bosom and retrieved $200.00. We watched as she placed her soft and gentle hands into her buoyant breast area. It appeared that she had $100.00 dollars hidden on each breast. Our hormones raged like an inmate who had been incarcerated for ten long years. Nevertheless, we weren't going to say, "That's okay Ms. Ruth, you can keep the money. She passed each of us forty dollars and suggested that we go on home because the girls had some chores to do. I was the last to receive my $40.00.

After collecting and counting our money, a Beaufort County Sheriff's Department cruiser drove up. Two deputies rushed into the yard and demanded that we raise our hands. The deputies appeared angry and deadly serious. I was aghast and totally at a loss for words. However, Boo Jack had disappeared almost instantaneously. It appeared that he indeed had the last laugh. Rudolph began to pray, "Lord, please don't allow me to die in Bath, North Carolina."

# CHAPTER 35
# KLAN ENCOUNTER

***A man does what he must in spite of obstacles and dangers and pressures—and that is the basis of all morality.***

***—John F. Kennedy***

As the Black Power Movement became a national focus, Blacks in Hyde County began to use extra care when they needed to travel at night. Fear of the Klan kidnapping someone and making an example of him or her was relentless. Hate-mail began to be distributed within select black communities like weekly newspapers. The distribution of hate-mail became so ordinary that black people began to make jokes about its delivery. Daddy and I were riding to Engelhard one Saturday morning when he decided to stop at Robert's Grocery (The Ridge Store) to purchase some gas.

Mr. Robert looked at daddy and jokingly said, "Vanderbilt, it looks like them Klan boys didn't ride last night. If they did, they forgot to drop off me a flier. I was looking forward for a news update, flier, newspaper, or something. They didn't leave me a damn thing. How am I suppose to keep up with what's happening, when you can't even depend on them to show up on a regular basis? I sat in the store until 3:00 a.m. with my shotgun and pistols loaded, waiting for those boys. I had a real surprise for them and they didn't even show up. You can't depend on anyone these days, not even the Klan."

Daddy smiled at Mr. Robert and replied, "The Klan is just trying to bully black people and it's not really working. If I ever catch them trying to throw anything in my yard, you will probably have to go to Swan Quarter to get me out of jail. I am like you about the Klan; they're not going to intimidate me, nor my family. As we drove to Engelhard, Daddy slowed down rather slowly as we approached Captain Harry's house. He turned toward me and said, "That's where Capt. Harry lives. I hate it that your mom works for him; but it is her choice. Uncle Sam pays me enough money each month that your mother doesn't have to get up at 2:00 a.m. each day to come down here to that cold and wet crab house. But she wants to be independent and she loves having her own money. You know Captain Harry is believed to be the local leader of the KKK. He treats all his workers like he can't stand them, even though they make him wealthier and wealthier each day. Your mother is a good woman and she doesn't bother anyone. If he ever attempts to mistreat her, I'll be in jail because like I said, Belle doesn't bother anyone."

I responded to Dad by asking, "Why is he called Captain Harry? Was he an officer in the military like you?"

Dad shook his head and said, "No. Definitely not! He wouldn't even know how to hold a weapon correctly. You see, there was a time in history when large plantation owners demanded to be held in high regard by their slaves and overseers. To maintain their high status, all slaves and overseers were required to call them "captain" as a sign of respect and prestige. It had nothing to do with having earned valor on the battlefield or having earned military rank. Captain Harry is called Captain Harry because the poor people of Hyde County, black and white, feared him so much that they felt the need to call him 'Captain Harry. Well, to quite honest, he was a fisherman and he had his own boat, there are those who call him 'Captain Harry' for that reason. You see, Son, there is a difference between fear and respect. For the most part, the poor blacks of Hyde County feared 'Captain Harry' because they needed their jobs and he provided a paycheck for them. Think about it; there are very few employment options in Hyde County and people have to have a roof over their heads and they need to put food on their tables. These are serious basic needs and when you are poor with very few options, you work extra hard to avoid knocking over the apple cart. I hope you understand what I am saying. Son, it's more about survival and less about fear. I really believe that there are very few blacks or poor whites that are actually afraid of 'Captain Harry.' They aren't afraid of him; they are afraid of losing their jobs. You will understand what I mean one day; believe me. As you grow older and experience life's lessons . . . the bulb will come on. You will remember this conversation; believe me"

It was not uncommon for dad to talk to me rhetorically. I never responded to dad's comments, I simply listened attentively. After arriving in Engelhard, daddy went directly to Elwood's service station to purchase a quart of oil and to check his transmission fluid. Mr. Midgette came out of the store immediately and asked, "Vanderbilt, how are you? What can I do for you today?"

Daddy responded with, "Oh, I am fine. How about checking my transmission fluid and I want a quart of oil for my lawn mower?"

Mr. Midgette, listened and said, "No problem; I can handle that. I'm running a special on tires this week. Looks like you could use two on the front."

Before daddy could respond, Capt. Harry drove up to the next gas tank. He was a big man and he was smoking a cigar and sipping a cold Budweiser. As soon as Mr. Midgette saw Capt. Harry, he seemingly forgot about my dad and began to respond to Capt. Harry as if he were President Kennedy. Capt. Harry was one of the wealthiest men in Hyde County and he acted like he had a very low tolerance for black people and poor whites. He slowly got out of his car puffing a cigar and holding his Budweiser. He looked at daddy and then at me. I, like daddy, did not speak to him. Most black people viewed Capt. Harry as a racist and a local Klan leader. I knew that daddy didn't really like him even though my mom worked for him. Dad basically ignored his presence and so did I.

Capt. Harry responded to daddy and me as if we were invisible. Nevertheless, Mr. Midgette greeted him with an emphatic hello and good morning. Capt. Harry reciprocated with a cold and indifferent posture. Mr. Midgette continued to shower Capt. Harry with pleasantries and niceties; however, Capt. Harry maintained his stoic demeanor and posture of superiority.

Daddy readily noticed that Mr. Midgette completely ignored him after Capt. Harry's arrival. It was almost as if daddy's dollar suddenly became insignificant. Daddy became impatient and somewhat irate with Mr. Midgette. He impatiently went to Mr. Midgette and stated, "Elwood, I was here first. Why are you ignoring me and treating him (pointing at Capt. Harry) like he is a king or president? What about my quart of oil and the checking of my transmission?"

Mr. Midgette never had an opportunity to respond before Capt. Harry intervened and said, "Look boy! Do you know who I am? I can buy you and that little skinny bucktooth boy of yours. Around here, they call me Capt. Harry and I command and demand respect. I was right; I said to myself that you looked like one of those uppity niggras. We don't need your kind around here. I can make you disappear overnight. Do you understand?"

Daddy angrily looked at Capt. Harry and said, "First of all, I don't give a damn who you are. Secondly, I am nobody's niggra. I simply want to be treated with respect. I came here to purchase a quart of oil and have my transmission fluid checked. Then you showed up and Elwood completely forgot about what I needed. I don't give a damn about other people calling you 'Capt. Harry.' To me, you are simply a fat-ass old white man about to get his ass kicked."

Mr. Midgette interjected and responded with, "Vanderbilt, don't get upset, okay! I haven't forgotten you. Here's your quart of oil and Tommy is checking your transmission fluid right now. Since you had to wait so long, the oil is free of charge."

Daddy responded with, "Elwood, I didn't come here today trying to get something free. I simply wanted you to check my transmission fluid and to purchase a quart of oil for my lawn mower? Everything was going fine until you ignored me and started treating that fat-ass like he's somebody special."

Capt. Harry shook his head and started walking toward Daddy. Dad rolled up his sleeves and said, "Son, get in the car. Don't worry; you won't have to wait long. When I finish with him, he's gonna look like the Pillsbury Dough Boy."

Just as Capt. Harry and Daddy were about to hook-up, when Mr. Fred drove up driving his beautiful '65 burgundy Pontiac Catalina. He had just gotten off from work at Georgia Timberland and noticed that he needed to put some air in his back tires. The car was shining from every angle possible and its beautiful burgundy interior appeared brand new and devoid of human interaction.

Mr. Fred looked at Daddy and noticed that he was upset. He appeared puzzled and asked, "Johnson, what's going on?"

Capt. Harry didn't give Daddy an opportunity to respond. He immediately said, "I see we have another fancy niggra driving up like he owns the world. I got something for all you fancy niggras.

In fact, I have a rope for both you boys and that little monkey sitting in the car."

Fred smiled at Daddy and said, "I know he didn't say what I think he said. Look, I don't know what's going on here. I simply came here to put some air in my tires. Why do you feel the need to disrespect me? I am not anybody's fancy "niggra." I work for a living. In fact, I work real hard and I am not going to allow you or anyone else to disrespect me. I don't play that niggra stuff, okay?"

Mr. Midgette rushed out of the service station and said, "Johnson, you're taken care of and don't forget to come back and look at some tires. Since you had to wait, the quart of oil is free and your transmission fluid is on level. Come back and see me real soon, okay?"

Capt. Harry rolled his eyes at Mr. Midgette and adamantly stated, "Elwood, you treat these people too nicely. In fact, you treat them like they're white and that is not right. That's the problem with these people; they don't know their rightful place because of meek white folks like you. Gosh! You make your own race look bad. As I look at you, you make me want to puke. You don't have to worry about me coming here again. In the future, I'll take all of my business to Bill Harvey."

Capt. Harry slowly walked to his car and sped off kicking up dirt and rocks. In fact, he actually kicked dirt and rocks on Daddy's car and Mr. Fred's car. Mr. Midgette saw what happened and told Tommy to give Daddy and Mr. Fred a free carwash and a free vacuuming. Tommy looked at both cars; shook his head and grabbed the water hose. Mr. Midgette worked hard to gain and maintain a healthy and harmonious line of communication between blacks and whites. He was a savvy businessman and he didn't care to lose the patronage of black Americans. As the potential skirmish was about to unfold, I witnessed a host of dynamics. I saw black Americans who responded as if the "Capt. Harry vs. Vanderbilt Johnson" was a personal matter and not a matter that showcased truisms about the landscape of black Americans *versus* white Americans in Hyde County. I saw white Americans who viewed the potential skirmish as a tug of war between the "haves and the have-nots". I saw black Americans who viewed my dad and Mr. Fred as "comfortable blacks" who forgot that they were black and needed a reminder. Finally, I saw a host of black Americans who were so socially conditioned that they had no sense of right or wrong, and others who were absolutely indifferent about equity matters.

After that early morning confrontation, I went out that night over to Fred's Playground. I didn't have driver's license; so I stood at the end of my road and hitchhiked to Slocum. I stood at the end of my road for about forty-five minutes before anyone would stop to give me a ride. Finally, Willie Gibbs came by driving about eighty miles per hour and eventually stopped. He was going so fast that he had to stop and back up for about a half mile to give me a ride. He was driving a white '61 Chevy that he and his mother shared. Willie kept the little Chevy in the wind and it was always fun riding with him. Seemingly, when one is rather young, the fear factor is non-existent. Mom would often say to me, "Junior, God always protects babies, old folks, and fools."

I often thought about mom's proclamation and concluded that I fell in the "fool" category far too often. When I finally arrived in Slocum, many of my friends were standing around laughing and joking. Fred had a dee-jay that night and cars were parked on both sides of the highway. Willie Gibbs dropped me off right in front of the main entrance of the nightspot. He took off squealing tires and people scurried to get out of his way. It was not uncommon for patrons to stop right in front of the nightspot; rush their engines, depress their accelerators in such manner that their mufflers roared and then hold their brakes to build up rpm's and then peel rubber. It was a cool and macho thing to do.

The guys with fast cars gravitated to the right time and place to showcase their muscle cars. I loved every second of it even though

I didn't own a car or have driver's license. Fred's nightspot was the place to be on Saturday night and my friends Joseph, Raymond, Richard, Larry, Byron, and Ben were always trying to be in the mix. Seemingly, anybody who was somebody was at Fred's nightspot, "The Playground". Our parents didn't mind us going to "The Playground" because they felt confident that Fred maintained a safe and orderly place of business. They were absolutely correct, Mr. Fred was a business man who demanded and commanded respect. He had a very quiet demeanor; however, everyone knew that he didn't tolerate a great deal of foolishness.

Mr. Fred saw me when I entered the nightspot. He waved for me to come to him and when I got to him, he asked, "Were you a little afraid this morning? I thought we might have to jack Capt. Harry up this morning. When you see your dad, tell him that I have a twenty-two pistol for him that would fit perfectly in his glove compartment. With the Klan and people like Capt. Harry walking around like they own the world, it's not safe for black people. Look, go on and have some fun. If anyone bothers you, just let Donnie, Melvin, or Fred, Jr. know and I'll handle it, okay?"

I really had a wonderful time at "The Playground" that night. After the music slowed down and patrons began to leave, I had to worry about getting back home. Hitchhiking was common practice for my buddies and me. As I came out of "The Playground", Joseph yelled at me and said, "Prez, Meat Ball said he would give us a ride home if we didn't mind sitting in the back of his truck. I know it's freezing cold; but it's better than walking all the way home. I told him that you needed a ride also. He said he would stop and let you off before he drops us off on the Ridge."

I crawled on the back of the truck and Meat Ball took off squealing tires. During the changing of gears, the mufflers of the old pickup backfired repeatedly. It was so cold on the back of the pickup that I was actually trembling uncontrollably and my teeth were clattering. Meat Ball drove his old pickup like a race driver on the Indianapolis Five Hundred. As he encountered curves, we rolled from the right to the left and from the left to the right. We were too cold to be scared; so, we stretched out on the bed of the pickup to avoid the freezing wind chill. I was so cold that my fingers felt like tootsie rolls and my toes felt like brown marbles. My legs and arms appeared to stiffen like the onset of rigor mortis. Then all of a sudden, I felt and heard Meat Ball slowing down. Someone from the inside of the truck yelled, "Henry, we're at your road. Take care and don't let the Klan get you."

I happily climbed off the back of the pickup. My vision was blurred from the cold and wind velocity. I stood up and stepped down thinking that Meat Ball had actually stopped and learned that he was actually gearing down to come to a complete stop. When I stepped down, the ground appeared to be moving so fast that when I hit the highway I rolled over and over for about three times. The impact of the fall left a big hole in the right knee of my pants and the left elbow of my shirt. Then I felt the excruciating pain of my right knee; however, I could not admit that I was hurt. My knee was burning like someone had placed a match to it. The entire skin over my right knee was missing and the cap of my knee had transitioned from bright pink to bloody red. Joseph saw me when I stepped off the pickup before it came to a complete stop. He called to me, "Yo, Prez, are you okay?"

I hopped up and yelled back with tears in my eyes, "Jid, I'm fine. See you tomorrow. Thanks."

I hobbled up my newly paved road as blood oozed down my right leg and my elbow appeared to stiffen to the extent that I could not bend it. I was in pain, serious pain. Then I heard some loud singing and the sound of boots stomping the pavement in cadence. I said to myself, "Damn, that's the Klan. What should I do? I hurt too badly to run and I don't care to be another Klan statistic."

The sound of boots pounding the asphalt became more and more pronounced as I got closer and closer to them. I glanced at my watch and it was 2:45 a.m. The sound of boots pounding the asphalt grew louder and louder. I had to do something; however, I really didn't know what to do. Then I remembered that a big ditch was used a boundary line to separate different properties. Mr. Harvey Mann told me that bears had been eating his corn and destroying his pea fields. He hired me to set bear traps near the ditch because deer and bears would often go to the ditch to quench their thirst after a hefty meal of peas and corn. I knew where I had placed the bear traps and I knew the ill-effects of getting caught in one of them. Cornfields governed the road on the right and pea fields governed the road on the left. I elected to navigate through the tall cornfields and hide on the edge of the ditch midway between two huge bear traps. I was so cold that the pain in my right knee and elbow was nonexistent. The cadence of the boots stomping the asphalt suddenly ceased. My heart began to pound and as cold as it was; I was now sweating. Everything got extremely quiet and then the leader of the Klan began to sing, *I wish I was in Dixie* in a proud and mighty roar.

Then there was silence again, and the leader said, "My nose doesn't fool me. I know I smell a niggra. In fact, I know I smell a dirty, nasty, stinking, and scared niggra. Brothers, that's the most dangerous kind of niggra. A scared niggra is more dangerous than a wounded wild bear. You see, sometimes niggras can think. A thinking niggra is mighty dangerous. Then he yelled, "Boy, I tell you what. If you come on out and don't cause me to get my boots dirty, I promise you that you will see another sunset. Now bring your black ass on out of that cornfield, okay? You really don't want to make us mad. If you come on out, I promise you that you will be able to make it to your fried chicken Sunday dinner. I know you don't want to miss some finger-licking southern fried chicken. Now do you, boy? Now, you come on out, you hear!"

Another Klansman jokingly said, "I tell you what Your Honor, suppose we go get a basketball and bounce it about four times. I guarantee you; he'll bring his black ass out faster than a hungry fox chasing a rabbit. You know the niggras love some basketball. In fact, if you give them a couple chicken wings and a basketball, they'll sell their own mammy."

I remained motionless between the two huge bear traps. It was freezing cold and I had gotten wet as I navigated through the cornfield to the edge of the ditch. The Klan leader became very impatient and angrily said, "Boy, I'm gonna to count to ten and if you don't bring your black ass out, we're gonna go in after you. I promise you, you'll be sorry if we mess up our boots trying to find your black ass."

I ignored everything the Klan leader said. Then one of the Klan members said, "Let's go to the truck and let Rufus flush him out. Then we won't have to get our boots dirty."

I continued to lie on the edge of the ditch motionlessly. Then about three minutes later, I heard the sound of a huge dog barking. I said to myself, "Damn, Rufus must be a dog."

The leader of the Klan yelled, "Bring Rufus over here. Let's send him on a niggra-finding expedition. Rufus, go make your master proud."

Then a different voice said, "Here boy, go find me that scared, nasty, niggra. It's getting late and we have to go to Sunday school."

Apparently, he had given Rufus a treat and he took off through the cornfield on my trail. I was scared stiff and I could not move, even if I wanted to move. About two minutes later, I heard the dog whimper and moan as if in great pain. I slowly raised my head and I could see that the dog, which appeared to be a German shepherd, had stumbled into one of the bear traps. I felt sorry for the dog; however, I felt as though my life was at stake. After the dog bellowed in pain, three huge Klansmen rushed to his rescue. Then I heard the clasping of three metals and the excruciating cry of three men in great pain. The three Klansmen who rushed to the aid of Rufus had gotten caught in three of the traps along edge of the ditch where I was lying. They were caught within twenty feet of where I was lying. The dog was sadly crying and moaning and the three men were moaning as well. The apparent owner of the dog completely ignored his Klan brothers and elected to help Rufus. I heard constant murmuring and then I heard someone say, "Damn, his leg looks a mess. It almost cut slam through his leg. I just don't know what to do!"

Apparently, the bear trap had cut deeply into Rufus' left leg. The Klansman took his huge hunting knife and pried open the trap. Rufus continued his crying and moaning. The Klansman yelled to his brothers, "Look, Rufus is my kid's dog. I have to take him to Washington to the veterinarian. If he dies, my wife will kill me. I'll talk with you guys later."

All three of the men rolled around on the ground holding their lower legs. I felt sorry for them but I couldn't afford to take the risk of helping them. I sensed that once they were released from the bear traps that they would physically harm me. The bear trap was heavy and cumbersome to handle. It was virtually impossible for them to free themselves without the assistance of someone else. In an act of frustration and excruciating pain, they immediately took off their headgear and grabbed their ankles. Their white robes were no longer white and their head-gear rested on the ground saturated in mud and dirt. They cried and moaned that their ankles and legs were broken. I raised my head up again to see if I could identify any of the Klansmen. They must not have been from Hyde County because I had never seen any of them before. They spoke with a real deep southern dialect. I concluded that they were from South Carolina or Georgia. As I hid on the cold and wet ground, I wondered if Capt. Harry was one of the covered Klansmen. I listened carefully, but, I never heard his voice.

The leader of the Klansmen rushed to the aid of his brothers and then I heard the clasping of irons again. Then I heard the resounding scream of a grown man saying, "Help! Help! Somebody, please help me! Please help me! I believe my whole foot is broken!"

There were six Klansmen left and they were moving around very slowly. They acted as if they were stepping on a mine field and each step could be their last. They tiptoed as if they were afraid they were going to accidentally step on an IED (Improvised Explosive Device). Each step appeared to be carefully calculated for fear of the unknown. It was rather funny watching the men tiptoe around like they were afraid of being blown up. The four guys in the bear traps were crying like little sissies. Their sense of pride had escaped them and they were in so much pain that their tears didn't matter. In fact, as they knelt to try to open the traps, they cried like little kids who were being forced to learn to tie their own shoes. They did not know that it was almost impossible for them to open the traps with their bare hands. Finally, one of the four remaining Klansmen decided to use the flat end of a lug wrench to open the traps. The four Klansmen walked slowly from trap to trap to avoid any unwanted surprises. When they got to the first entrapped Klansman, the flat end of the lug wrench slipped and the trap clasped back on the Klansman's leg. The Klansman screamed and cried like a young baby. His foot had swollen so badly that he could not walk to his pickup. Another Klansmen cradled him like a small child and carried him to the truck. The scene was comparable to saving a wounded soldier on the battlefield. The Klansman cried and moaned from excruciating pain.

The second entrapped Klansman sat on the wet ground and rubbed his leg and foot passionately. Another Klansman took the flat end of the lug wrench and inserted it between the jaws of the bear trap. The flat end of the lug wrench slipped and closed powerfully against the ankle and lower leg of the Klansman. He cried out like a prisoner of war being tortured for information. He was rather large, so, it took two guys to help him to his truck. The third entrapped guy didn't incur any difficulty in being released from the bear trap. However, the fourth guy, the Klan leader, encountered the most pain. The flat end of the lug wrench slipped twice against his lower leg and he cried out like a hog being slaughtered. His fellow Klansmen encouraged him to calm down because they feared that he was on the verge of hyperventilating. His right foot and leg swelled so large that the other Klansmen felt the need to rush him to emergency care at Beaufort County Hospital. They feared the potential onset of gangrene. It required two Klansmen to take him to his truck. One of them said, "Sir, Your Honor, you were right . . . a thinking niggra is a dangerous animal."

I waited about ten minutes and then I got up and hobbled home. I was so cold that my feet and hands appeared to be numb. As I navigated through the cornfield, I stepped over six Klan robes, three pairs of apparently new black boots and six black books that appeared to be a book on Klan rituals. I decided to keep one pair of the black boots and I gave a pair to Joseph and a pair to Richard. They put spit-shines on their boots and wore them to school. After noting the attention that Joseph and Richard received with their boots, I began to wear my boots as well. In fact, we actually began a fad and all the so-called cool guys at Davis High began to wear black boots on a daily basis. I gave three of the six pairs of black books to Martin and he gave one to Michael and they shared selective information with the Kool Kolored Kidz. After that night, I never met the Klan marching up my road again. I often wondered about ole Rufus. Whenever I saw a big brown German shepherd, I thought about ole Rufus. The Kool Kolored Kidz became a formidable nonviolent pro-equal rights clan. We worked diligently to bridge the line of communication between the black community and the white community. Klan activity in Hyde County became less and less pronounced and a sense of community appeared to incubate in the black as well as the white community.

I hitchhiked back to Slocum the very next weekend. It was a very cold Saturday night and I stood at the end of my road for about an hour before anyone came along to offer me a ride. Fred Junior eventually came along driving his dad's '65 Pontiac Catalina.

He had gone to Engelhard to see Carolyn, his girlfriend. Fred Junior was a very clean-cut guy. He had all the attributes of an absolute nerd and he stuttered relentlessly. When he stopped to give me a ride, he looked at me and stuttered, "*You been-been out-out there a long-long time?*"

I said, "Yes and I thought I was going to freeze standing out there. I am so glad that you came along and stopped. I was about to give up and walk back home."

Fred Junior took off squealing tires. He had the pedal to the metal and I enjoyed every second of the ride. When we got to the Lake Landing Bridge, he was going so fast that he had to keep going because he was driving too fast to make the left turn to go to Slocum. He turned around in the middle of the highway and took off squealing tires again. He took the steep curves to Slocum so fast that I was leaning from the right to the left and then from the left to the right. And again, I enjoyed every second of the ride. As we approached "The Playground", Fred Junior turned toward me and said, "Look, don't tell Donnie and Melvin about my driving okay? I don't want to get grounded."

I said, "No Problem. I won't say a word. I promise you. In fact, I really like driving fast. Gosh! This Pontiac will fly."

Patrons were lined up on both sides of the highway again near the juke joint. I couldn't wait to enter the nightspot. As usual, the place was filled with cigarette smoke, the smell of beer, loud talking, and laughter. The fine ladies from Fairfield kept the floor bouncing that night. Gerald Lee had gone to Fairfield and returned with a car full of young ladies. The first person I saw to get out of the car was Janice, then Dianne, then Flora Jane, and lastly Catherine Ann and Dollie. Catherine Ann, Dollie, and

Flora Jane were sisters and they looked as if they were undiscovered *Jet* centerfolds. They were cocoa brown with big boobs, small waists, and just-right buttocks. Catherine Ann and Dollie were my schoolmates; however, they gravitated to the attention of older, adult men. Older men had the finances to make Catherine Ann and Dollie smile from ear to ear. There were times when I would say, "Gosh! I would give the world to be Meat Ball and Laurence for just one night."

Meat Ball and Laurence were older guys who epitomized the term "playa". They had ladies in every corner of Hyde County and they carried themselves as if they were consummate Casanovas. It was rather strange, most of the young ladies who were curvaceous and physically endowed gravitated to older guys who were not academically inclined. It appeared that supposedly smart guys were absolute Geeks and they received little to no attention. However, guys who were loud, boisterous, cursed most of the time, drank beer, and smoked cigarettes were the guys of choice. I was deemed a Geek; therefore, Catherine Ann, Janice, Dollie, Flora Jane, and Dianne would not give me a five- minute conversation. Then again, if they had, I wouldn't have known what to say to them. My hormones were raging uncontrollably and I had not experienced the pleasure of sex. Nevertheless, my many nights of wet dreams conveyed to me that I was anxious and excited about crossing the hot sands to sexual ecstasy.

Many of my older schoolmates like Van, Thad, and Charlie would tease me about my virgin status. I simply didn't want to be Johnny Appleseed and have babies by several different women. My vision for me did not include having to send money in two and three different directions for child support. Several of my buddies became fathers during high school and I really didn't want that to happen to me. I really had my mind set on college and I didn't want to jeopardize my dream by becoming a father before I legitimately became a man.

My so-called friends would tease me that I was going to explode because my sexual energy had built up so much power. They would often blow up balloons to the max and then burst them and jokingly say that I was going to pop just like the balloons. The joking was often embarrassing because they would do it in the presence of young ladies. Peer pressure to engage sexual activity was real and quite powerful. For some dumb reason, these so-called friends viewed sexual activity as a rite of passage into *Who's Who* on the popularity chart.

There were guys my own age who were having sex like the older guys, Meat Ball and Laurence. Tony and Thurman were two of the most popular guys at my school. They were never in line to receive academic awards on Awards Day. Nevertheless, all of the pretty girls appeared to adore them. They were always *GQ* clean and they were confident and assertive. Tony and Thurman knew how to make beautiful young ladies smile and laugh and feel good about themselves. When it was time to be serious, they knew how to showcase their sensitivity side and maintain their manhood. As for me, in retrospect, I apparently appeared too serious and probably too nerdy to be embraced by the ladies of *Who's Who.*

I didn't become an official member of *Who's Who* until I got my driver's license. Seemingly, the possession of a driver's license was the ticket to admission to the right parties and the right connections. I didn't get my driver's license until the age of eighteen. I couldn't wait to get my driver's license because my dad had two cars and he was going to give me his work car. It did not matter to me that my dad's work car was ugly. I simply wanted my driver's license and a car so I could get around without having to hitchhike everywhere. Many of my friends had become fathers twice by the innocent age of eighteen. Not me, I had never had sex even though the act crossed my mind day and night. I had a serious phobia for getting someone pregnant that I really didn't care to marry. Several of my friends had gotten caught in this entrapment and I didn't want to add to the statistic. Then again, I didn't have a steady girlfriend, nor, did I have my driver's license. Seemingly, there was a serious correlation between sexual activity and car ownership. Guys without driver's license and without access to transportation were reduced to nobodies. They were essentially invisible. I hated being invisible with a passion.

It was absolutely amazing how I transitioned from Pee Wee Herman to Michael Jordan overnight after I got my driver's license. My dad bought me a beautiful red Mustang during my sophomore year of high school. When he unexpectedly bought me the Mustang, I almost instantaneously became Denzel Washington." The pretty girls who would not give me a five-minute conversation were now smiling at me and trying to get my attention. I felt like a celebrity and I really did not know how to handle all of the newly found attention. I was smart enough to know that my newly found notoriety was anchored on materialism. To this end, I vowed to myself to maintain and embrace all of the people who befriended me before I got my driver's license and a car. I could sense and feel the superficiality centered on the "new Henry." I endeavored to stay true to my old and dependable friends. Then, I thought, even before I got my driver's license and a car, my so-called friends often treated me like an outcast.

My driver's license and my beautiful red Mustang gave me a renewed sense of self. I became more assertive and more confident. If a pretty girl "dissed" me, I didn't allow it to destroy my self-esteem. I developed a Teflon coating that kept me secure and free of negative energy. If someone tried to steal my joy, I would readily remove myself from that environment and seek a positive and more wholesome setting. The "old Henry" would have wallowed in self-pity and relegated himself into a state of serious doldrums.

As I reflect on those days of endless trials, I recognize that God subjected me to those experiences to equip me for the challenges that lay ahead. Numerous lessons were learned and many of the challenges that I experienced; I would have avoided if I were so empowered. I learned that life is filled with endless twists and turns. It's how we respond to those twists and turns that determine our quality of life. I embrace each day with a renewed sense of urgency and enthusiasm. This is based on the premise that life is terribly short, and we pass this way but once.

40177311R00195

Made in the USA
Middletown, DE
05 February 2017